LIGHT
for our
PATH
2005

Bible readings with short notes

International
Bible Reading
Association

Cover photograph – Sister Paula Fairlie OSB

Editor – Kate Hughes

Published by:
The International Bible Reading Association
1020 Bristol Road
Selly Oak
Birmingham B29 6LB
Great Britain

ISBN 1–904024–49–1
ISSN 0140–8267

Typeset by Christian Education Publications

Printed and bound in Great Britain by Biddles

CONTENTS

FOREWORD

Dear friends

Welcome to this year's *Light for our Path*. The readings are grouped into fourteen themes, which are numbered and named in the Contents list on pages 3 and 4. Some of the themes concentrate on one book of the Bible, and the names of the books are also mentioned in the Contents list. Some readers value the continuous reading of a biblical book, others particularly value the insights provided by the wider themes which draw on both the Old and New Testaments; I hope that the group which prepares the readings has got the balance between the two types of theme about right this year.

This year we welcome new writers from Romania, Croatia, Malaysia and the Caribbean, as well as established contributors from many different countries and a wide range of churches. I love writing as well as editing, and usually write one or two weeks of notes myself. I have just finished writing notes on the theme of 'Symbolic actions: Signs of hope'. So much of the Bible speaks about hope – hope for the future, but also the hope that God gives us here and now. As you study these notes day by day, may they renew your own hope and so enable you to share God's gift of hope with a world which needs it so desperately.

Kate

Kate Hughes (Editor)

Bible readings online!
IBRA's Bible readings scheme is available via our website. You can view the current month's scheme on screen, or download a card with the full year's readings in either English or Spanish. See www.christianeducation.org.uk/ibra.htm

Reading LIGHT FOR OUR PATH

● Before reading, be quiet and remember that God is with you. Ask for God's Holy Spirit to guide your reading.

● If you do not have a Bible with you, you can work solely from *Light for our Path* by referring to the short Bible passage printed in bold type. (Only the editions printed in English have this.)

● You can begin by reading just the short extract from the daily Bible passage which appears in the notes. Or you may prefer to read the full text of the day's passage from your Bible. The notes use a variety of different Bible translations, which are named at the beginning of each week. You may like to see how the extract in bold type compares with the same passage in your own Bible. And if your Bible mentions parallel passages in other places, comparing these passages can widen your thinking.

● At the beginning of each week's notes there is a text for the week, which can be used as a focus for worship or reflection throughout the week.

● When you finish each day's reading, spend a little time reflecting on it. What does it say to you about God? About yourself? About others? About the world in which we live? Has it changed your thinking? Does it suggest something that you should do? Then use the final prayer (marked with a cross), or any prayer of your own you need to make.

● At the end of each week's notes, there are questions and suggestions for group discussion or personal thought. These are only suggestions – your own reading and prayer may have drawn your attention to other aspects which you would like to explore further. The important thing is that you should let God speak to you through God's Word, so that as you read steadily through the year you will be able to look back and see that you have got to know God better and have grown spiritually.

ABBREVIATIONS AND ACKNOWLEDGEMENTS

We are grateful for permission to quote from the following Bible versions:

GNB *Good News Bible*, 4th edition, published by The Bible Societies/HarperCollins, © American Bible Society, 1976.

NEB *New English Bible*, © Oxford and Cambridge University Presses, 1970.

NIV *The Holy Bible, New International Version*, Hodder & Stoughton, © International Bible Society, 1980.

NJB *The New Jerusalem Bible*, published by Darton, Longman & Todd, © Darton, Longman & Todd Ltd and Doubleday & Company, Inc., 1985.

NKJV *New King James Version*, © Thomas Nelson & Sons. Used by permission.

NRSV *New Revised Standard Version Bible*, published by HarperCollins, © Division of Christian Education of the National Council of the Churches of Christ in the United States of America, 1989.

REB *Revised English Bible*, © Oxford and Cambridge University Presses, 1989.

RSV *The Holy Bible, Revised Standard Version*, published by Thomas Nelson & Sons, © Division of Christian Education of the National Council of the Churches of Christ in the United States of America, 1952.

IBRA INTERNATIONAL APPEAL

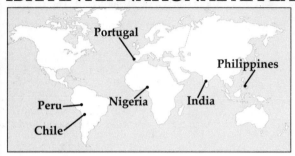

In five continents you will find Christians using IBRA material.

Some will be using books and Bible reading cards translated into their local language, whilst others use English books. Some of the books are printed in the UK, but more and more countries are printing the books and cards themselves. The IBRA International Fund works through churches, Christian groups and Christian publishing houses overseas to make these publications available.

Each year we receive more requests for help from the IBRA International Fund, with greater emphasis on helping our overseas friends to produce their own version of IBRA material.

The only money we have to send is the money you give, so please help us again by giving generously.

Place your gift in the envelope provided and give it to your IBRA representative, or send it direct to:

The IBRA International Appeal

1020 Bristol Road, Selly Oak,
Birmingham B29 6LB, Great Britain

Thank you for your help.

WISDOM 1
God's gift of wisdom

Notes by Jules Gomes

based on the New Revised Standard Version

Jules Gomes teaches Old Testament at the United Theological College, Bangalore. He has recently spent time in Britain, completing a doctorate at the University of Cambridge, but has now returned to India. Before coming into the ministry he pursued a career as a journalist in one of the world's most populated cities.

'It was the best of times, it was the worst of times; it was the age of wisdom, it was the age of foolishness; it was the epoch of belief, it was the epoch of incredulity; it was the season of light, it was the season of darkness; it was the spring of hope, it was the winter of despair; we had everything before us, we had nothing before us; we were all going direct to Heaven, we were all going direct the other way', wrote Charles Dickens in the prologue to his famous novel *A Tale of Two Cities*. He was describing the period just before the French Revolution erupted in 1789. Whizzing through over 200 years brings us to the year 2005! We are staring two postmodern revolutions in the face: the Digital Revolution and the Genetic Revolution. Information is available at the click of a mouse. Humans are poised to clone and create designer babies. These are indeed the best of times. But these are also the worst of times. Information and knowledge is one thing. Wisdom is something else. This week's readings and reflections navigate the reader through the enigmatic route of biblical wisdom. For wisdom alone will carry us through the surprises that the new year may spring on us.

Text for the week: Job 28:28

Saturday January 1   Job 28:12–28

THE JEWEL IN THE CROWN Knowledge, information or data are often communicated through insipid prose; the vehicle of wisdom is sublimely lyrical poetry. Like poetry, wisdom is elusive: 'Where shall wisdom be found?' asks Job (*verse 12*). He is expressing humankind's ultimate quest, humanity's ultimate question. Does the answer lie in unravelling the human genome? Or in penetrating the limits of outer space? A grand cascade of poetic parallelisms strung together like pearls on a necklace (*verses 13–22*) tease and tantalise the seeker, only to disclose the disappointing answer: '[Wisdom] is hidden from the eyes of all living' (*verse 21*). Wisdom, says the poem, cannot be found among mortals (*verse 13*). Neither can wisdom be found in the mythological cosmic order. The Hebrew words for 'deep' and 'sea' (*verse 14*) and 'Abaddon' and 'Death' (*verse 22*) play on the names of Ancient Near Eastern mythological deities. Neither can wisdom be bought with precious metals and jewels – the currency of the ancient market (*verses 15–19*). The negative particle appears seven times in the Hebrew, suggesting that wisdom eludes those who seek it in mortals, myths or metals. But as the seeker's fingers go down each bead, he suddenly discovers the answer. Knowledge and information can be found in creation, but wisdom can be found only in the creator. And then comes the pearl of great price which explains what wisdom is all about:

'Truly, the fear of the Lord, that is wisdom;
and to depart from evil is understanding.'   (part of verse 28)

† *Creator God, who art the source of all wisdom and in whose Son Jesus Christ all things were created; grant that we might be recipients of his wisdom and be recreated in him, for he is our wisdom, sanctification and righteousness, Jesus Christ our Lord. Amen*

Sunday January 2   **1 Kings 3:5–14**

I'D RATHER HAVE WISDOM THAN SILVER OR GOLD
Solomon is not given a clean bill of health by his biographer. His very first royal act is a political and marital alliance with Egypt (*verse 1*). Egypt was the antithesis of all Israel stood for. It was the archetype of a system that had oppressed God's people for 400 years. Solomon claims to 'love' Yahweh, but he sacrifices at the high places (*verse 3*). These were later condemned as centres where people were led away from the worship of the true God. Worse still, the king offers extravagant sacrifices at Gibeon (*verse 4*). It was at Gibeon that Joshua's invading army was tricked into a peace treaty (*Joshua 9:3 – 10:15*). Solomon clearly falls short of the glory of God – a prelude to his later more grievous misdemeanours. But a gracious God is not easily spurned. He appears to Solomon, and the king asks him for the supreme gift of wisdom. It is this that really pleases Yahweh. Solomon has his heart in the right place

and his priorities right, at least for now. Here wisdom is understood as the ability to exercise moral judgement:

> 'Give your servant therefore an understanding mind to govern your people, able to discern between good and evil.' (part of verse 9)

Solomon's prayer is answered in a much greater way than all that he has asked or desired. God's faithfulness triumphs over Solomon's fickleness. The story ends with his return to Jerusalem where he again offers sacrifices – this time at the place authorised by God. We are asked to make the same choice for the wisdom of God, who is Jesus.

✝ *I would rather have Jesus than silver or gold, riches, houses or lands; I would rather be led by the crucified one, which the world regards as foolishness but is the true wisdom of God. Amen*

Monday January 3   **1 Kings 4:29–34**

THE WORKS OF GOD AND THE WORD OF GOD Solomon should be nominated for Nobel prizes in literature, music and science! His prodigious output of proverbs and songs and his knowledge of plant and animal life are a consequence of being gifted by God:

> **God gave Solomon very great wisdom, discernment, and breadth of understanding as vast as the sand on the seashore.** (verse 29)

Solomon's legendary wisdom becomes a means of communicating the glory of Israel's God to other nations – Israel's traditional rival, Egypt, is singled out for mention. The chronicler makes this explicit when he says, 'all the kings of the earth sought the presence of Solomon to hear his wisdom, *which God had put into his mind*' (*2 Chronicles 9:23*, our italics). The eminent scientist Isaac Newton, who was also a committed Christian, was convinced that the 'works of God' in nature and the 'word of God' in scripture both revealed the glory of God. Newton's faith became the basis for his scientific studies. The correlation between wisdom and creation theology is reflected in scripture, most succinctly in the words of the psalmist: 'O Lord, how manifold are your works! In wisdom you have made them all; the earth is full of your creatures' (*Psalm 104:24*). At the beginning of a new year, let us seek this wisdom that it may result in excellence in our professional lives and become a witness to the world around us.

✝ *Heavenly Father, with whom are hidden the treasures of wisdom, and who has permitted men and women of our day to learn things kept secret from the foundation of the world: help us to set forth by all means your most worthy praise, that the arts and sciences of humankind may echo the glory of God, through him who is the pioneer and perfecter of all things, even Jesus Christ our Lord. Amen*

Tuesday January 4   Proverbs 1:1–7

WISDOM IS A MANY-SPLENDOURED THING It is left to the wisest man, Solomon, to share his wisdom with others so that they too may learn to cope with life. The first seven verses are a prologue to this vast compendium of wisdom garnered from the tradition of the elders (*Proverbs 4:1–4*). In a world where yesterday's technology lies on today's scrap heap, where stock markets rise and fall like tidal waves, and where the words of the hymn, 'change and decay in all around I see', are sung by many a Christian, it is the biblical wisdom that the cloud of witnesses has left for us that keeps us firmly anchored in the harbour of hope. This wisdom is hardly elitist – it is for the simple and the young, as well as for the wise and discerning (*verses 4–5*). Wisdom is a many-splendoured thing. It encompasses a variety of gifts – from skill in technical matters (*Exodus 28:3; 1 Kings 7:14*) to moral discernment; from judicial astuteness to artistic, literary and poetic dexterity (*1 Kings 4:29ff*); and from piety (*Psalm 90:12*) to

**gaining instruction in wise dealing,
   righteousness, justice and equity.**   **(verse 3)**

But these are merely the spokes of the wheel. The hub of wisdom, its origin and fulcrum, is the 'fear of the Lord', also translated as 'reverence for the Lord'. When the centre no longer holds, things fall apart.

✝ *O Loving Wisdom of our God
   When all was sin and shame
   A second Adam to the fight
   And to the rescue came.*   (John Henry Newman)

Wednesday January 5   Proverbs 2:1–15

OUR UTMOST FOR HIS HIGHEST Instruction was often communicated through poetry. For it not only sparked off alternative ideas in the listeners' imaginations, but also helped them to memorise and retain what was being taught. Proverbs 2:1–22 is a carefully fashioned poem of 22 lines; it corresponds to the number of letters in the Hebrew alphabet and constitutes one continuous sentence. Like a palette on which many colours are splattered, the poet uses a number of synonyms for wisdom. It also functions like the trailer of a movie, quickly introducing themes that will be spelt out in detail later in the book. It urges the listener to push the limits to the utmost in his or her quest for wisdom. On the other hand it paradoxically reiterates the community's belief that wisdom is a gift whose source is Yahweh and no other (*verse 6*) and so to seek wisdom is to seek its source. But it also elaborates the happy results of obedience and searching. Wisdom guards its recipients from the way of evil men and loose women (*verses 9–19*), and guides them in the way of the good (*verses 20–22*). The prize is worth the toil. Through all the changing scenes of life, in trouble and in joy, it is wisdom that will carry us through the new year.

✝ *O God, you taught the hearts of your faithful people by sending them the wisdom of your Holy Spirit. Make us, by the same Spirit, wise unto salvation and wise unto all things that pertain to life, through Christ our Lord. Amen*

Thursday January 6   **Exodus 35:30–35**

AD MAJOREM DEI GLORIAM: ALL TO THE GREATER GLORY OF GOD How wonderful it is when all the work of our hands and the labour of our lives tend to the greater glory of God. *Ad majorem Dei gloriam!* No wonder the greatest composer of all, Johann Sebastian Bach, always began his compositions with the abbreviation J.J. (*Jesu Juva* – Jesus help me) at the top of the page and ended with the tribute S.D.G. (*Soli Deo Gloria* – Solely to the glory of God). God's gift of wisdom enables human creativity to reach the pinnacle of perfection it was intended for. Kings do not have any monopoly on God's gift of wisdom. It is not only Solomon who is endowed with wisdom, but Bezalel, too, is

> **called by name ... to devise artistic designs, to work in gold, silver, and bronze.   (part of verse 30, and verse 32)**

This is the vocation that he is called to live out. It is God who supplies the skills required. This is yet another aspect of the gift of wisdom. God calls us to bear fruit in our daily work – fruit that will endure and bring fulfilment to the worker and blessing to the community. While much work may seem monotonous rather than creative, as the hymn says, 'If done to obey Thy laws, Even servile labours shine. Hallowed is toil, if this the cause, The meanest work divine.' Today, as we celebrate the Feast of the Epiphany, we remember that the wise men sought wisdom in one who would soon be the carpenter of Nazareth. No wonder they brought their best gifts to worship him with.

✝ *God of creation and creativity, by whose word the heavens and the earth were created, and by whose wisdom beauty and art were established, accept the works of our hands, the words of our lips, the wonders of our minds, the weaving of our communities and the wealth of our cultures. For the glory of your name and for the good of every tribe, tongue and nation. Amen*

Friday January 7   **Daniel 2:20–30**

WISDOM IN THE LION'S DEN   How does one subtly, yet subversively, negotiate difficulties when living under an arbitrary and tyrannical imperial power? The book of Daniel is a manual of practical wisdom cryptically written in apocalyptic and narrative code against the imperial hegemony of the Babylonian, Persian and Hellenistic empires. Imperialism often demands the impossible and irrational. How can anybody read the king's mind and explain his dream as well as its interpretation? The wisest men of the empire throw up their hands in despair and defeat. Only 'the gods, whose dwelling is not with mortals' have access to the king's secret dreams (*verse 11*). But are these foreign gods and their wisdom accessible to ordinary mortals? The wisdom of Daniel's god and his relationship with his worshippers is different. 'Wisdom and power are his,' undoubtedly, but he also

> **'gives wisdom to the wise**
> **and knowledge to those who have understanding.**
> **He reveals deep and hidden things.' (parts of verses 21–22)**

Daniel seeks this gift of divine wisdom in the community of believers – the trio of his friends – and in prayer. He seeks, he finds and he acknowledges that God has revealed to him the wisdom he needed (*verse 23*). Ultimately the king, too, acknowledges Daniel's god as the 'god of gods'. The empire stands for any system that demands totalitarian allegiance and brooks no alternative – be it the new world order or the monotheism of the free market. We are called to beard the imperial lion in his own den. Dare we pray for wisdom to do so?

† *Almighty God, who gives wisdom to the wise and understanding to the discerning, grant unto the rulers of this world and their councillors very great wisdom, discernment and breadth of understanding, that from them just governance might flow, that the peoples of this earth may enjoy peace and prosperity, and that you might be acknowledged as the God of gods, who lives and reigns for ever and ever. Amen*

Saturday January 8   Acts 6:1–10

VENI CREATOR SPIRITUS – COME HOLY SPIRIT! There is an administrative problem that is further complicated because it involves two ethnic and linguistic groups within the church – the Greek-speaking versus the Aramaic-speaking Christians. The apostles recognise that the problem of distributing food to the widows has to be solved wisely. And so a search committee is appointed to

> **'select from among yourselves seven men of good standing, full of the Spirit and of wisdom' ... and they chose Stephen, a man full of faith and the Holy Spirit**
> **(parts of verses 3 and 5)**

to carry out this task. Note the parallelism between the 'Spirit' and 'wisdom'. Wisdom is one of the gifts of the Holy Spirit. The Holy Spirit is the Spirit of wisdom. Isaiah had prophesied that the Messiah would be filled with the Spirit of the Lord, who is 'the spirit of wisdom and understanding, the spirit of counsel and might, the spirit of knowledge and the fear of the Lord' (*Isaiah 11:2*) – a verse which gloriously sums up the range of the biblical wisdom tradition we have been studying through this week. Let us daily endeavour to fear the Lord and to seek the infilling of the Holy Spirit and so to be filled with all wisdom and godliness.

† *Come, Holy Ghost, our souls inspire,*
And lighten with celestial fire;
Thou the anointing Spirit art,
Who dost thy sevenfold gifts impart. Amen

For group discussion and personal thought

● What is true wisdom for this day and age? How can you grow in this wisdom?

WISDOM 2
Wisdom, the guide of life

Notes by Peter Ibison

based on the New International Version

Married, with two children, Peter is a member of the Anglican Church in Buckinghamshire where he serves on the PCC, plays guitar in a worship band and is a member of a prayer ministry team. He is studying with the Open Theological College and has worked for the past seventeen years in various roles in the Telecommunications industry.

Over the next few days we shall see Wisdom personified as a woman offering advice on how to live life. Jesus himself talks of Wisdom in this way and on a number of occasions draws from the book of Proverbs. Wisdom is concerned with coping with life's practical difficulties and living in such a way that our lives, as God's people, are 'distinctive'. Wisdom does not offer us a new set of commandments, but teaches us how to live the old ones.

Text for the week: Proverbs 9:10

Sunday January 9   **Proverbs 1:20–33**

WISDOM'S CALL   In our passage today, Wisdom does not come to us in a place of quiet contemplation. Instead, she offers her insight where we need it most – amidst the hubbub of daily life.

> **Wisdom calls aloud in the street, she raises her voice in the public squares.**   **(verse 20)**

Wisdom calls to us at the top of the street and at the gateways of the city – in places where daily choices are to be made; in schools, courts and places of work. Life presents us with many choices; some are straightforward, others are more difficult because it is not only Wisdom that speaks. We find around us a clamour for our attention and a variety of enticements from the world. Here, Wisdom does not call in a gentle persuasive way; instead she raises her voice, she shouts, pleads and urges. Like a town crier or public speaker, she calls aloud in the noisy streets and busy market-places so that we can hear her invitation more clearly. Some people plainly ignore her words and are even hostile to them; their fate is sealed. If, on the other hand, we choose to listen to the lessons of Wisdom – her advice and even her rebuke – then she promises peace. What is our response to Wisdom's call? Do we welcome her advice?

† *Help me, Lord, to hear Wisdom's call and to apply wisdom to all the practical details of the day.*

Monday January 10   Proverbs 3:13–26

WISDOM'S BENEFITS   Wisdom is not discovered by accident, she has to be found. She is infinitely more precious than all that the world can offer. The world will offer silver, gold and rubies: its money, its status symbols and whatever else is valued by human beings. Wisdom, however, is more precious than all of these and yields a better reward.

> **She is more profitable than silver and yields better returns than gold.**   **(verse 14)**

Wisdom offers length of days. This is more than an offer to extend our 'three score years and ten'; it says as much about the quality of life as the length of it. Wisdom also offers riches and honour – but these are held in the left hand, the less used side for most people. There is no guarantee of money and riches and in fact Jesus warns of the foolishness of a life given to hoarding wealth. However, we can observe that life is 'better off' for doing what is wise, and 'poorer' for doing what is foolish. The Lord applied wisdom in creating the world, the sea, the sky and clouds. We do not outgrow Wisdom, nor should we neglect it as we try to imitate the Lord of wisdom. Wisdom urges us to demonstrate sound judgement and discernment – not merely to meditate on the truth (laudable though this is) but to apply the wisdom of God's Word to our daily lives and in practical ways.

† *Lord, thank you for the benefits that wisdom can bring to life. May I seek wisdom and cherish its contribution to my life.*

Tuesday January 11   Proverbs 8:1–21

WISDOM'S CHOICE   From a biblical perspective, the opposite of wisdom is folly. If we do not choose 'wisdom', we do not choose 'nothing'; we choose 'folly'. This may be a hard truth to accept, for in today's passage Wisdom offers a critical choice.

> **Choose my instruction instead of silver,**
> **knowledge rather than choice gold,**
> **for wisdom is more precious than rubies,**
> **and nothing you desire can compare with her.   (verses 10–11)**

Wisdom's tone is softer and beckons men to listen to her words. What benefits does she bring? Firstly she offers truth ('my mouth speaks what is true') – and the discerning will recognise the value of this. Accepting the truth can be painful and inflict wounds if it is carelessly applied. Wisdom, however, promises benefits to those who hear the truth, and although her truth may not be an easy option, its value is indisputable. Secondly, Wisdom offers sound judgement. Here she does not seek status; she offers her advice not just to rulers and royalty but also to all who seek her. Wisdom is not restricted to an élite few, the clever or learned. She offers her advice in equal measure to all who love her. Finally, she offers prudence and discretion. Do we seek advice about forming a relationship, managing our money, buying a property? Wisdom brings prudence to those who call on her. Is there a difficult relationship or delicate matter to be resolved? Wisdom brings discretion.

† *Lord, guide me and give me wisdom and discernment in the decisions I face today. Help me to see truth from falsehood, good from evil, right from wrong.*

Wednesday January 12   Proverbs 8:22–36

WISDOM'S CREDENTIALS   Having called out in the streets and public squares, Wisdom now presents her credentials. In what reads like a poem, she is described as being at God's right hand, working as a craftsman in creation. Wisdom therefore is not 'new', a passing fad or fancy:

> **I was appointed from eternity,**
> **from the beginning, before the world began.   (verse 23)**

She has endured for a long time and no situation we may face today is beyond Wisdom's scope or experience. Wisdom was the midwife present at our birth, observing all who have lived since the dawn of time. If Wisdom was the basis of Creation, then we know that it is better to live life in accordance with Wisdom's design. Our first response, then, to Wisdom's credentials is to be confident, for Wisdom preceded all creation.

Our second response is to listen. Three times the writer urges us to 'listen' to Wisdom and be attentive to her instruction, waiting at her doors. We listen like Moses at the door of the Tent of Meeting, waiting on the Lord. We listen like a beggar waiting at the door to receive alms and food.

✝ *Lord, I praise you for your wisdom. Teach me a little about wisdom today and create within me a hunger for Wisdom's teaching.*

Thursday January 13   **Proverbs 9:1–12**

WISDOM'S INVITATION   Once again, Wisdom calls out to us, like a hostess inviting all humankind to a meal. This is a meal where the meat and good wine of God's Word are served. At this feast we do not bring our own refreshments or prepare our own food – our own insight or understanding; we eat and drink what is prepared for us. The challenge for us is to listen to what Wisdom says. The cynics and the mockers are not interested in her teachings, but some people have a teachable spirit; they listen and thereby add to their wisdom and learning. These are the ones for whom

> **The fear of the LORD is the beginning of wisdom,**
> **and knowledge of the Holy One is understanding.   (verse 10)**

Today's passage teaches us that as we fear God, we enjoy Wisdom's reward: a long and fruitful life. This is no vain promise, for a wise man enjoys the spiritual, physical and psychological benefits of Wisdom – striving less, working honestly, resting well, managing finances carefully ... the list could go on.

✝ *Grant me, Lord, a listening ear so that I can hear your teaching and apply the lessons of Wisdom to my life.*

Friday January 14   **Ecclesiastes 7:1–13**

WISDOM'S DEPTH   Solomon was the wisest of Israel's kings and in his writings he tries to look at wisdom's practical application and advises us to 'look below the surface'.

> **The heart of the wise is in the house of mourning,**
> **but the heart of fools is in the house of pleasure.   (verse 4)**

Solomon does not suggest that feasting, merriment and laughter are bad. Rather, if we are searching for signposts for living, then wisdom is more likely to come when we look below the surface than if we fill our lives with food, drink and laughter. This 'looking below the surface' will involve sorrow (*verse 3*), mourning (*verse 4*) and even rebuke (*verse 5*) but it does offer increased wisdom. Solomon does not want his readers to be gloomy as they consider life's realities, but to recognise that true Wisdom has depth and if we want her benefits we shall need to dig deep, rather than focus our lives on what is superficial.

† *Lord, give me courage to face life's realities and the lessons of wisdom they can bring.*

Saturday January 15   **Ecclesiastes 9:13 – 10:4**

WISDOM'S POWER   Our final passage on wisdom presents us with two warnings. The first is that wisdom will not always be recognised. Our passage tells the story of a poor but wise man who saved a city by his wisdom. Wisdom can have great influence: all Egypt was saved from the effects of famine through the wisdom given to one man, Joseph. All the wise men of Babylon were saved through the wisdom given to one man, Daniel. But influence is not always recognised. The poor but wise man's good deeds were quickly forgotten:

he saved the city by his wisdom. But nobody remembered that poor man.   **(part of verse 15)**

This serves as a warning to us in our pursuit of wisdom. Even if others benefit, we cannot expect great applause: other people may neither recognise nor acknowledge wisdom. This does not, however, detract from wisdom's value; despite people's response to wisdom, its benefits remain. The second warning is to be on our guard against wisdom's opponent: folly. Wisdom may guide us to a correct course of action but it can be outweighed by a little folly. Wisdom may give a good plan but its benefits will only be realised if that plan is wisely put into action.

† *Lord, thank you for the wisdom you give and for the power of wisdom to change circumstances for the better.*

For group discussion and personal thought

● For what purpose is wisdom given – to benefit us, to benefit other people, or for something else?
● What obstacles hinder us from gaining wisdom and how can these be avoided?
● Why do you think that wisdom's value is not universally acknowledged in the world?

WISDOM 3
True wisdom and false

Notes by Lesley G Anderson

based on the New Revised Standard Version

Lesley G Anderson is the Senior Methodist Ministerial Tutor and Warden at the United Theological College of the West Indies in Jamaica.

The idea of wisdom runs throughout the Bible. People like Solomon are respected for their wisdom. It is a gift of God which gives people the ability to live and work well. The yearning for wisdom is wisdom itself. The Greek philosophers, such as Socrates, Plato and Aristotle, were highly regarded as lovers of wisdom. They searched for and claimed to teach wisdom. Jewish teachers looked for wisdom in the scriptures. Paul recognised wisdom as coming in Christ and given to people whom the world sees as simple. This is the true wisdom. In this week's readings, notice how James describes the difference between God-given and earthly wisdom. In Colossians 1:24 – 2:5 Paul presents true wisdom which is found only in Christ. Psalm 104:24ff and Romans 11:33 describe the fullness of wisdom which is found only in God, whose wisdom made the world.

Text for the week: 1 Corinthians 1:20–21

Sunday January 16   **1 Corinthians 1:18–30**

GOD'S SAVING POWER AND WISDOM   Human wisdom (in Greek, *sophia*) and clever rhetoric are nothing compared with divine wisdom.

> **For it is written,**
> **'I will destroy the wisdom of the wise,**
> **and the discernment of the discerning I will thwart.' (verse 19)**

Was Christ crucified, as the crucified Messiah, a stumbling-block? This feeling may have stemmed from the interpretation given to the Suffering Servant of Isaiah 53. If not, then most certainly it relates to Galatians 3:13: 'Cursed is every one who hangs on a tree.' That Jesus should die for the sins of the world on a wooden cross is foolishness to the world, but to us, God's adopted children, it is God's saving power and wisdom. God continues to choose the 'foolishness' of the gospel through which to reveal himself to people of all nations, cultures and races. Unfortunately, some people rely on signs and human wisdom rather than steadfast faith in Christ. I have travelled to Africa, Central, North and South America, Asia, the Caribbean, Europe and the Pacific, and have met men and women, boys and girls of great intellect and wisdom. The world, however, needs a Saviour, the incarnate Christ, wisdom himself.

† *O Lord our God, teach us how to humble ourselves and cling to your Son, Jesus, the Christ. Amen*

Monday January 17   1 Corinthians 2:1–13

GOD'S WISDOM IS THE TRUEST WISDOM   Paul was on his way to continue his persecution of the Christian church when he was converted by the living Christ himself on the road to Damascus. This first-hand experience of the power of the cross laid hold on his mind and heart. He did not claim to have wisdom. Those who did had no first-hand experience of Christ; they only knew him second-hand. His apparent failure in Athens (*Acts 17:32*) convinced him of two things: firstly, if he had been successful in Athens by his persuasive oratory, it would have been to his credit and not through God's power or his ability to save. Secondly, the proclamation of the cross in God's divine plan of salvation is above and beyond human wisdom, because

we speak God's wisdom, secret and hidden, which God decreed before the ages for our glory.   (verse 7)

This secret and hidden wisdom of God is the truest wisdom. It recognises Jesus as Lord and enables us to put our trust in him. It leads us to seek him always and keep confidence in him.

† *O God, bless us in all our work and help us to truly follow Jesus, our truest wisdom. Amen*

Tuesday January 18   Romans 1:18–25

WISDOM, THE GUIDE OF LIFE   Wisdom was and still is a highly prized gift in society. During my high school days living on the Canal Zone in the Republic of Panama, the ideal was to seek after it. To be regarded as possessing wisdom was a great honour, for it was to become a Solomon. I knew of such people and they lived up to the expectations of their peers and the community as a whole. They lived wisely, a life of godliness. Others who claimed to be wise did not.

Claiming to be wise, they became fools. **(verse 22)**

Their involvement in 'fornication, impurity, licentiousness, idolatry, sorcery, enmity, strife, jealousy, anger, quarrels, dissension, factions, envy, drunkenness, carousing, and things like these' (*Galatians 5:19–21*) contradicted their claim to be 'wise'. They failed to remember that Solomon became wise because he did not presume to be wise. Their conduct revealed the measure of their wisdom. In this context, I can still hear my grandparents, Allan and Beatrice Dale, telling their children, 'In all of life be wise and use your common sense! Stay away from human unrighteousness. Seek God's righteousness and his power, and ever remain faithful to him.'

† *You are the wisest, O Lord. Lead me and guide my footsteps along the way of life. Amen*

Wednesday January 19 — James 3:13–17

GENTLENESS BORN OF WISDOM

Who is wise and understanding among you? Show by your good life that your works are done with gentleness born of wisdom. **(verse 13)**

Under the wise and able leadership of Tom Curtis, healings, renovations and building projects took place in Latin America, the Caribbean, Europe and Africa. For many years he led the United Methodist Volunteers in Mission (UMVIM), breaking down barriers between different races, while building formidable bridges of friendship between them. He was always a gentleman, exemplifying gentleness of spirit and the power of love to bring people together. All that he stood for is still demonstrated in the life and work of UMVIM, a commitment to causes greater than one's self. Tom taught that pious words were of no help to people in need, unless they were accompanied by a sacrificial depth of genuine Christian love and practical relief.

† *Lord Jesus, give me the spirit of gentleness and let me never forget that in serving others, I serve you. Amen*

THE GOSPEL OF ALL WISDOM AND KNOWLEDGE   Christ is the focus of the whole gospel and the whole gospel is Christ:

Christ himself, in whom are hidden all the treasures of wisdom and knowledge.   **(chapter 2, verse 3)**

The whole gospel is all our wisdom and knowledge, proclaimed and offered to all. What is offered is God's hidden secret, the mystery (in Greek, *mysterion*) – the indwelling Christ in us. In him we have the gift of our salvation and the guarantee of our hope. He alone deserves our love, faith and trust. In his wisdom and knowledge of all our situations and conditions of life, he gives us comfort in our times of sadness, strength in our weakness, joy in our sorrow, light in our darkness and life in our death. So we glory in the cross of Christ, the instrument of our redemption. We put our trust in him, who is the rock of our salvation. In him we are saved and safe.

✝ *Lord, you are my refuge and strength, the only rock of my salvation. Amen*

GOD'S CREATIVE WISDOM   Have you given any thought to God's creative wisdom and how this has impacted on your life? I have taken time to give this question some thought and have come to the reaffirmation that we are all dependent on God for our existence. Without the Spirit (or breath) of God, we have no life-giving support (*Genesis 1:2*). In God's wisdom, salvation (everlasting life) in and through Jesus Christ is offered to all who believe. The sinful, the voiceless, the hopeless, the homeless, the powerless – in short, everyone is invited to come and share in God's love. The powerful are not preferred over the weak, nor the rich over the poor, nor the popular over the marginalised. Whoever wants to come can come!

O LORD, how manifold are your works!
In wisdom you have made them all;
the earth is full of your creatures.   **(verse 24)**

Through Jesus Christ, we all have access to the unlimited resources of God's love and the riches of his grace.

✝ *Lord, may my daily life be a constant witness that I am your child. Amen*

Saturday January 22   **Romans 11:33–36**

THE WISDOM AND KNOWLEDGE OF GOD   Wisdom is the art of living and knowledge is the foundation of life because, together, they seek the truth of God. The truth of God is the gospel and the gospel is God's wisdom and knowledge. There is no greater wisdom and knowledge.

O the depth of the riches and wisdom and knowledge of God! How unsearchable are his judgements and how inscrutable his ways! (verse 33)

When I reflect on the riches of the wisdom and knowledge of God, there is only room for admiration, adoration, wonder and awe. The book of Proverbs (quoted in the New Testament by the writer of the letter to the Hebrews) tells us that 'wisdom is better than jewels' (*Proverbs 8:11*) and 'the fear of the Lord is the beginning of knowledge' (*Proverbs 1:7*). The person who confesses Jesus as Lord is truly wise. Knowledge of our Lord and reverence for him are the foundation for building further knowledge. This will inspire us to love our Lord and serve him faithfully.

† *Lord Jesus, I acknowledge you as my Saviour and Friend. You are far greater than any wisdom or knowledge I possess. Let your mind be visible in my mind, that I may always seek to live a holy life. Amen*

For group discussion and personal thought

● Christians have to make critical decisions and judgements all the time. What words of wisdom or guidance can you give to others who have lost their way, perhaps through stealing, drugs or alcohol? What kinds of decisions and/or judgements will you have to make regarding people suffering from HIV/AIDS? How can you help them?
● Apart from God, our wisdom and knowledge together are not very great. What are some practical ways in which you can use both your wisdom and knowledge to share Christ with others? How can you help people to know that having both wisdom and knowledge can enrich one's life?
● What difficulties are you likely to encounter when you try to discern between true and false wisdom? Give concrete examples.

READINGS IN MATTHEW 1
Baptism, temptation and calling disciples

Notes by Estela Lamas

based on the New Revised Standard Version

Estela Lamas has had the opportunity of going back to Africa. She is living in the Cape Verde Islands where she was given the task of starting and leading a new university. Being born in Mozambique and having lived there for three decades, she received this opportunity as a blessing from God. Along with her job of lecturing at the university, she has been developing studies in feminist theology, particularly on pastoral work with women; though not progressing as fast as she would like, these studies are providing new insights through the experience of meeting Cape Verde women.

This is the first week of our 'Readings in Matthew' theme, which will recur in 2-week blocks throughout the year. This week we focus on how Matthew records God's offer to us of the possibility of being loved and of entering the heavenly kingdom. He sent Jesus to redeem us, to call us to be his disciples. Without God we are powerless; without us, God cannot help our sinful world. We are called to accomplish the mission he commits to each one of us.

Text for the week: Mathew 4:18–20

Sunday January 23   **Matthew 1:1–17**

THE SON OF DAVID, THE SON OF ABRAHAM The genealogy of Jesus the Messiah calls our attention to the fact that Jesus' life is linked to the history of Israel.

> **So all the generations from Abraham to David are fourteen generations; and from David to the deportation to Babylon, fourteen generations; and from the deportation to Babylon to the Messiah, fourteen generations.** (verse 17)

Matthew leads us, generation after generation, through the history of Israel, to let us know how everything that happens to the people is reflected in Jesus' life. The links are strengthened by the repetition of the words 'was the father of', as if each generation was handing over the testimony received from the preceding generation. However, when we get to Jesus this repetition is broken and we find a different phrase, 'of whom Jesus was born', an expression which seems to emphasise that the history has come to an end – the target has been reached!

† *O Lord, you have been with my family throughout the years. May I not be so worried and distracted by the daily tasks that I forget your presence in the history of my family. May I, like my mother and my father, pass on to my children the certainty of being loved by you. Please show me how I can tell them how important it is to seek your face day after day.*

Monday January 24   **Matthew 3:1–12**

HISTORY REPEATS THE FACTS History calls our attention to God's message. The prophets announced to the people the happenings related to Christ's life. John the Baptist remembers the great moments of Israel's history; he repeats the prophet's words as if he wanted the people following him to receive God's message proclaimed throughout history.

> **This is the one of whom the prophet Isaiah spoke when
>   he said,
> 'The voice of one crying out in the wilderness:
> "Prepare the way of the Lord,
> make his paths straight."'**   **(verse 3)**

Today, around the world, things happen which call our attention to God's word. People raise their voices, just as John the Baptist did, calling our attention to God's will. Jesus touches some human beings' lives in such a way that they testify to his love for humanity. Those lives are valuable not for themselves, but for the testimony they give of Christ. Just as John said, they tell us 'but one who is more powerful than I is coming after me' (*verse 11*).

† *May we open our eyes to the signs God shows us all over the world, day after day; may we open our hearts to God's message; may we let God work in our lives through his Holy Spirit; may we be aware of his coming to us and let him work in our lives.*

Tuesday January 25   **Matthew 3:13–17**

ARE WE CHOSEN BY GOD? God came to meet John as foretold by the scriptures. John was not only surprised, he also considered himself unworthy to be sought by the Messiah. However, Jesus reminded him that they had to fulfil what was written in the scriptures and immediately John submitted himself to Jesus' word. How do we react when we are told Jesus' will, when Jesus calls us to act in a certain situation?

> **But Jesus answered him, 'Let it be so now; for it is proper for us in this way to fulfil all righteousness.' Then he consented.** (verse 15)

Sometimes we fight against God's will as if we could change God's plans. When we sit passively, without a purpose, without something to do or think about, we usually get sleepy and are no longer aware of what is happening around us. We must move, seek God, seek the face of the God of our ancestors, the God our mother and our father loved and praised.

† *Help me, O God, to seek you, and be before your face. May I lift up my heart so that you may come into my life. Help me, O God, not to cut the ties that bind me to you, but on the contrary to look for new ties which will strengthen my spiritual life.*

Wednesday January 26   **Matthew 4:1–11**

THE LIVING WORD   The written word, the living word, nourishes our souls. Do we listen to God's word as John the Baptist did? Do we listen when someone cries out and reminds us, as John the Baptist did? How often do we turn our backs on God's word?

> **But he answered, 'It is written,**
> **"One does not live by bread alone,**
> **but by every word that comes from the mouth of God."'**
> (verse 4)

† *Help me, O God, so that I may act according to your will; help me, so that I may do what is right and so be invited to abide with you, to be called your daughter, your son. Through baptism, may we become your children; through the action of the Holy Spirit may we enter your kingdom.*

Thursday January 27   **Matthew 4:12–17**

CHANGING OUR VIEW OF THE WORLD   How difficult it is to recognise our errors and sins! However, when we do recognise them, it is as if the world around us changes completely. Light changes the view we have of what surrounds us; we see the world with different eyes.

'[T]he people who sat in darkness
have seen a great light,
and for those who sat in the region and shadow of death
light has dawned.'
From that time Jesus began to proclaim, 'Repent, for the
kingdom of heaven has come near.'   (verses 16–17)

Unfortunately, the twenty-first century has been marked by
wars, tragedies, crimes – our world sits in darkness. Following
the action of Jesus, we are called by our heavenly Father to
proclaim the kingdom of heaven. If we want, our lives can be
used by God to change this terrible world we live in.

† *Father, give us the discernment to recognise your presence in our
lives, to recognise the blessings we receive each day. May we be
aware of your offer to us – the kingdom of heaven!*

Friday January 28   Matthew 4:18–22

ANSWERING THE CALL How can anyone ignore the calling
of a special voice? How can anyone run the risk of not
responding to the call of the person we are expecting? Jesus is
calling disciples. It is important for us to know what it is to be a
disciple. According to the dictionary, to be a disciple implies a
special condition: the readiness to learn from someone else (the
master, the teacher), following his or her advice, guidance,
teachings and example without hesitation. The master is
usually accepted as a model, someone who knows everything,
someone who has the power (perhaps even the magic) to pass
on knowledge, understanding, life experience.

And he said to them, 'Follow me, and I will make you fish
for people.' Immediately they left their nets and followed
him.   (verses 19–20)

Is it possible for us to put restrictions on the relationship we
establish with God? To be a disciple of Christ implies our total
dedication to Jesus' cause; it implies that we must be willing to
undergo an inner change. Jesus calls us as he called Peter and
Andrew, James and John. They left their nets, their way of
living, and followed him. How do we react to Jesus' call, we
who are his people in the twenty-first century?

† *We want to be ready for your call, to answer your voice – give us,
loving God, the promptness you want us to show. We want to be awake
when you come to us – O God, give us the strength to walk on the way
you have opened for us and dedicate every minute of our lives to you.*

JESUS' FAME SPREADS BEYOND ISRAEL Jesus fulfilled the scriptures in coming to his people. He did not sit waiting for people to come to him. He went throughout Galilee, throughout all Syria... He talked to the people, he approached them and touched them. They felt his presence and were touched inside themselves. Having experienced the loving presence of the Lord in their lives, they followed him:

> **Jesus went throughout Galilee, teaching in their synagogues and proclaiming the good news of the kingdom ... So his fame spread throughout all Syria ... And great crowds followed him from Galilee, the Decapolis, Jerusalem, Judea, and from beyond the Jordan.**   **(parts of verses 23 and 24 and verse 25)**

What about us, people living in Africa, Asia, Europe, all over the world? Don't we also, in this troubled century, experience the loving presence of our Lord in our lives? If we experience his presence, even if it is only once, we cannot imagine what it would be like without him beside us! Try to remember a special time in your life when you felt God's presence very strongly; are you still constantly aware of this presence? What must we do in order to be revisited by God from time to time? We must follow him and dedicate our lives to his cause. Let us be his disciples. Let us seek God each day of our lives and open our hearts to him and allow him to command our lives. Let us pray in the words of Saint Patrick:

✝ *Christ be with me, Christ within me, Christ behind me, Christ before me,*
  Christ beside me, Christ to win me, Christ to comfort and restore me;
  Christ beneath me, Christ above me, Christ in quiet, Christ in danger,
  Christ in hearts of all that love me, Christ in mouth of friend and stranger.

For group discussion and personal thought

- Do we act today, in our own countries, as John the Baptist did, calling our neighbours' attention to God's will?
- How often do you seek God during the day, to talk to him, to listen to his voice, to keep silence in order to open your heart and your life to him? What could you do to increase these moments in your life?
- What does it mean for you, today, in the twenty-first century, in your country, to be God's disciple(s)?
- Are you ready to follow Jesus unconditionally? What are you willing – and unwilling – to leave behind in order to follow him?

MATTHEW 2
Teaching on prayer, fasting and faith

Notes by Sister Paula Fairlie OSB

based on the New Jerusalem Bible

Paula Fairlie has lived the enclosed Benedictine monastic life for thirty-three years. Her life is balanced between prayer, spiritual reading and manual work in and on behalf of her community. She finds the daily praying of the Psalms the supreme means of remaining intimately connected with the needs of suffering and rejoicing humanity – including her own.

Some of us can only climb the mountains of memory or imagination, while others – like Moses – are called up a high mountain which has all the attributes of an exploding volcano. Moses met the transcendent God, who gave him the ten basic stepping-stones of the Law which are the foundation of three monotheistic religions. This transcendent God is also the supreme realist: he begins by giving his chosen people instructions which have a practical effect upon their daily, ordinary lives. From practical restraints and positive injunctions about how we are to treat our fellow human beings, the contemplative insight of the prophets shows the need for a heart-felt response which goes beyond externals.

Text for the week: Matthew 7:12

Sunday January 30   **Matthew 5:1–12**

THE SPIRIT OF THE KINGDOM OF GOD

> **Seeing the crowds, he went onto the mountain. And when he was seated his disciples came to him. Then he began to speak.**   **(verses 1–2a)**

This is the formal preparation for a serious discourse: the Master sits while the disciples stand. Moses encountered God on the shuddering heights of Sinai; Jesus meets us in the serene calm of the Galilean hills and teaches us what sort of person is receptive to the spirit of the kingdom of God. Although he has come to fulfil the Law and the teaching of the prophets, he tells us where our true identity lies – in our spirit and heart. Too often we are concerned with externals and forget that a loving and contrite heart is more acceptable to God. The phrases beginning 'How blessed' have been gathered together to form a composite picture of the spirit within those who are 'upright'. We all aspire to this, and need time to attend peacefully and lovingly to God. When we were children, we still had clear vision and, if our parents were loving, we could recognise their concern for us. However, if our childhood was wretched, we were never certain of their love. In the same way, a childlike loving dependence on God is not possible in a state of wretchedness. Jesus calls us 'beloved children', and on the mountain of memory speaks to our hearts.

† *May the blessedness described in the Beatitudes be ours.*

Monday January 31   Matthew 5:13–20

SALT AND LIGHT: FOR GOODNESS' SAKE!   When it is used effectively, salt is invisible. It seasons food, cleanses wounds and preserves meat and fish. We are to be salt in society, preserving what is good, healing what is wounded, and adding flavour. We may not be able to evangelise through words: we can proclaim the spirit of the kingdom through our lives. Jesus shares one of his titles with us: we are light for the world. Light is also invisible, but its rays reveal the world around. The light of Christ is to radiate forth through our loving acts. We are the hands of God, bringing help to the needy. If we do not act on his behalf, we fail to preserve and enlighten life.

'If your uprightness does not surpass that of the scribes and Pharisees, you will never get into the kingdom of Heaven.'   **(verse 20)**

Merely obeying the Law is not enough: the spirit within us must flow from God. Jesus came to fulfil the Law and the teaching of the prophets, and added to them the loving heart of the Beatitudes. Here we have the outside and inside of goodness, with the severe warning that corruption will distance us from God and from each other. We were created for life, and nothing will prevent the fulfilment of God's purpose, except our wilful refusal.

† *Thy kingdom come, thy will be done on earth as it is in heaven.*

Tuesday February 1 Matthew 5:21–48

INSIDE OUT OR THREE STEPS DOWN Matthew gathered sayings together and then edited them according to contemporary need. The first Christians weren't always sure whether they were to follow the Law or not. Jesus made it quite clear that each commandment required a heart as well as a decision, and that the passion of unruly instincts was the cause of social disruption. It was popular at one time to say that seven cardinal sins were the means by which the devil clasped us in his hands: covetousness, lust, anger, sloth, pride, envy and drunkenness. The sayings of Jesus in this section confirm this, as anger can take us three steps down from litigation to a local court case, trial by the Sanhedrin and being cast into hell fire. This is a severe statement to demonstrate how important it is not only to forgive our enemies but also to love them. The commandments highlighted by Jesus are murder, adultery, divorce, oaths and vows. Vengeance and hatred of enemies are to be completely changed into non-resistance.

> **'You have heard how it was said, You will love your neighbour, and hate your enemy. But I say this to you, love your enemies and pray for those who persecute you; so that you may be children of your Father in heaven, for he causes his sun to rise on the bad as well as the good.'**
>
> **(verses 43, 44 and part of 45)**

From the Beatitudes onwards we are being led to the prayer which will sum up the whole of Jesus' teaching.

† *Our Father ... forgive us as we forgive.*

Wednesday February 2 Matthew 6:1–18

YOUR FATHER KNOWS... Salt and light work unobtrusively but powerfully; so do the three religious duties prescribed for all observant Jews: almsgiving, prayer and fasting. These duties make a person 'upright' or 'righteous', worthy of reward from God the Father. We all like to parade our virtue from time to time, and in so doing we lose all merit. Our almsgiving in money or goods or kind acts must be discreet, and forgotten by us as soon as possible. Neither must our personal prayer be ostentatious or wordy, but simple. It would be enough just to pray the Lord's Prayer. It contains all the seeds of a loving relationship between God and human beings, with concern also for ourselves. The words indicate communion with others, either present or in spirit. We will be treated by God as we treat others, which is a great incentive towards goodness!

'If you forgive others their failings, your heavenly Father will forgive you yours; but if you do not forgive others, your Father will not forgive your failings either.' **(verses 14–15)**

Religious fasting is an act of contrition or atonement. We are not to display our feelings when we fast voluntarily. God knows all we do.

✝ *May we be filled with the Spirit of the kingdom, and learn to live and love as children of God.*

Thursday February 3   Matthew 6:19–34

BLESSED ARE THOSE WHO HUNGER AND THIRST FOR UPRIGHTNESS   Are the following verses a commentary on this Beatitude (*Matthew 5:6a*)? What is the treasure we can store up for ourselves in heaven? What do we truly love? To be 'upright' is to be acceptable to God. If this is indeed our desire, then that is our treasure, our heart's desire. If our spiritual eye is blind, we shall fail to understand any of this and will make choices for earthly security rather than trusting in God. To whom are these words addressed? To the disciples of Jesus: they have the mission to go out and spread the news of the Kingdom of God.

'I am telling you not to worry about your life and what you are to eat, nor about your body and what you are to wear. Surely life is more than food and the body more than clothing!' **(verse 25)**

The disciples of Jesus were not paupers: they had adequate means of sustenance and shelter at the end of the day. Therefore they could be urged to set out trusting in God's Providence. It would have been cruel to urge starving people to forget about food and live like the lilies of the field. We are told to set our hearts on the kingdom and God's justice first, and all these other things will be given us as well.

✝ *Our Father, give us this day our daily bread.*

Friday February 4   Matthew 7:1–20

ACTIONS NOT WORDS   Raindrops falling on quiet water soon merge, rippling into each other, although each one is individual. The same could be said of all the elements in the Sermon on the Mount. There are many similarities between the Beatitudes and the Lord's Prayer, and both of these are echoes of the Hebrew scriptures, contrasting with and fulfilling those commandments which apply to human relationships. The Prophets spoke more about social justice, and our inner reality: our heart. Our Lord illustrates these teachings through parables and instruction on true morality. Since the heart of the law is perfect love, naturally all these examples come together in their effect.

> **'So always treat others as you would like them to treat you; that is the Law and the Prophets.'** (verse 12)

What is made clear to us is that cold-hearted observance of rules is not acceptable, but neither is devout but fruitless listening. Our actions will reveal our true state: are we working for God or for human approval? There is severity and condemnation in some of the statements, to show that leading others astray is totally unacceptable to God. We must be sensible people, building on goodness and truth, and not on the shifting sand of human esteem. Our Lord taught with authority; he did not qualify everything he said, as the scribes did because they did not have the assurance of faith, and for this reason he was heard – by some. Are we among them?

† *May we be sound trees, producing good fruit to delight the heart of God and our neighbour.*

Saturday February 5   Matthew 7:21–29

EVERYONE WHO ASKS WILL RECEIVE   The disciples are sent out, and we with them, to proclaim the kingdom of Heaven. For this we need wisdom, non-judgemental discretion, perseverance, trust and kindness, as well as a deep and abiding reliance on God. The first person to be converted must always be myself, though I do not always see this clearly! Then, with a chastened and contrite heart, we may begin to reach out to the poor in spirit – whoever they are. The parables in this section, seemingly disconnected, may be considered from this perspective. The people implied may be Gentiles, as later the 'scraps' given to 'dogs' are received by the pagan mother (*Matthew 15:27*). She showed the sort of perseverance required, expecting only good things. 'If you, then, evil as you are, know how to give your children what is good, how much more will your Father in heaven give good things to those who ask him!'

(*Matthew 7:11*). The Law and the Prophets are here summed up: do as you would be done by. And the rest flows from that. There is always the awareness that there is false teaching around, that we can choose the easier way, that we can be deceived by appearances, and that we can build on faulty foundations.

> **Therefore, everyone who listens to these words of mine and acts upon them will be like a sensible man who built his house on rock.** (verse 24)

† *Father, may we act with kind discretion, and learn to marvel anew at the confident teaching authority of your Son.*

For group discussion and personal thought

- How can we proclaim the spirit of the kingdom through our lives?
- What does it mean to be 'upright'?
- How can we build on firm foundations?

ESTHER

Notes by Jill Chatfield

based on the New Revised Standard Version

Jill Chatfield has worked as a teacher in England and in the West Indies. She is currently working in Theological Education by Extension in South Africa. She is also a self-supporting Anglican minister in a group of black township parishes in the Diocese of Christ the King in Southern Gauteng (formerly Johannesburg).

This story, much loved by Jews, claims to be one account of the beginning of the popular festival of Purim, which is a celebration of deliverance. It is a 'novella', a short work of fiction, possibly based on a historical memory of a real plot against the Jewish people. It was written to remind scattered groups of Jews living in an alien empire that their God would ensure the survival of their nation. Another theme is the contrasting uses of power for selfish and for selfless ends.

Text for the week: Esther 4:14

Sunday February 6   Esther 1:1–22

A DEFIANT STAND   King Ahasuerus (Xerxes) was the ruler of the Persian empire about 480 BC. He summoned his queen, Vashti, to display her beauty at the end of a great banquet held for all the people in the palace grounds at Susa. She refused. Why? Although this story is about Jewish nationalism, not about the rights of women, her refusal was interpreted by the powerful men of that time as a stand against male domination.

> 'Not only has Queen Vashti done wrong to the king, but also to all the officials and all the peoples ... For this deed ... will be made known to all women, causing them to look with contempt on their husbands.'   (parts of verses 16–17)

Perhaps this start to Esther's story reminds us that powerful men often ignore the rights of women in the twenty-first century. In South Africa a woman is raped every 33 seconds and women's inability to insist on safe sex is one factor in the increasing rate of HIV/AIDS.

† *Creator God, you have made all people, male and female, in your image. We pray for women throughout the world who suffer loss of dignity and self-worth at the hands of men. Raise up those who will take a stand against this oppression.*

Monday February 7   Esther 2:1–23

PAYING THE PRICE   The just often pay the price for any defiant stand against wrong and suffer in similar ways to those who pay the price for their criminal activity. Queen Vashti's refusal to obey her husband led to the loss of her royal position and to the selection of Esther, a secret Jew, as the new queen.

The king loved Esther more than all the other women ... and made her queen instead of Vashti.   (part of verse 17)

When Esther's uncle, Mordecai, overheard two eunuchs plotting to assassinate the king, Esther was in a position to pass on the information to the king. Although Mordecai received no reward, the two plotters paid the price of their treason. The new democratic and multi-racial South Africa has been built on the sacrifice of those who were willing to take a defiant stand and to pay the price with the loss of privilege, freedom and even of life itself. I am reminded of Peter's words: 'If you are reviled for the name of Christ, you are blessed ... But let none of you suffer as a ... mischief maker' (*1 Peter 4:14–15*).

† *Lord Jesus, help us to proclaim you, to stand for what is right and to be willing to pay the price.*

Tuesday February 8   Esther 3:1 – 4:17

UNBRIDLED PRIDE AND GREED   Haman's promotion led to unbridled pride which could not cope with Mordecai's refusal to bow down to him. He decided to use his power to destroy Mordecai and his people. Mordecai was a Jew. Haman was an Agagite, an ancient enemy of the Jews. The issue became a racial one; the whole Jewish nation was to be punished because of Mordecai's refusal to pander to Haman's pride.

'There is a certain people scattered and separated among the peoples ... their laws are different from those of every other people, and they do not keep the king's laws, so that it is not appropriate for the king to tolerate them.' (chapter 3 verse 8)

It is generalisations like this, made on the basis of race, that have fanned the flames of ethnic conflict throughout the world's history. It may have been the untold wealth promised by Haman that led the king to agree to issue a law allowing the Jews to be killed. Racial bigotry can be the result of active hostility (Haman) or of passive indifference by those who have something to gain (the king).

† *Almighty God, deliver us from the sins of pride, greed and racial hatred. We pray for people throughout the world who are the victims of racial and ethnic conflict.*

Wednesday February 9   Esther 5:1 – 6:14

RISKING ALL   Queen Esther, like Vashti, also made a brave and defiant stand, but she did it on behalf of her people. At first she refused to agree to Mordecai's plea for help. Maybe it was difficult for her to overcome the self-centredness of everyday life. However, his words, 'Perhaps you have come to royal dignity for just such a time as this' (*4:14c*), persuaded her to use her power to save the Jews from destruction. Esther risked her life by entering the king's court without being called.

As soon as the king saw Queen Esther standing in the court, she won his favour and he held out to her the golden sceptre.   (part of chapter 5 verse 2)

She also risked the king's displeasure by revealing her Jewish ancestry and asking him to repeal a law that he had himself proclaimed. Freedoms are often won by the people who are prepared to risk life itself. The greatest freedoms of all – from sin and death – were purchased by Jesus who laid down his life as a ransom for many. How much am I willing to risk for the sake of the gospel, for the freedom of others and on behalf of my brothers and sisters in Christ?

† *Lord of the cross, we pray for those who risk their lives day by day in order to proclaim Christ, to seek freedom and to protect their Christian brothers and sisters.*

Thursday February 10   Esther 7:1 – 8:2

POETIC JUSTICE   At the beginning of Esther, Mordecai used the little power that he had, the power of his knowledge, to ensure the survival of the king. Haman used his power to promote his own selfish ends. Esther used her power to seek the wellbeing of her people. Yesterday's reading told us of Esther and Mordecai's reward; today's tells of Haman's downfall.

Unbridled pride met its judgement and Haman was hanged on the gallows he had prepared for Mordecai.

So they hanged Haman on the gallows that he had prepared for Mordecai. (part of chapter 7 verse 10)

Mordecai was given Haman's signet ring, his goods and his position as the king's first minister. The roles were reversed and Haman's fall was balanced by the rise of Mordecai whom he had sought to overthrow. In this world evil so often seems to be victorious, but the day of God's judgement is coming. On that day, the first shall be last and the last first.

† *Holy and righteous God, help us to use what little influence we may have for the good of others and not for selfish gain.*

Friday February 11   **Esther 8:3 – 9:19**

SELF-DEFENCE   The villain of the piece, Haman, may have been disposed of but the law allowing the destruction of the Jews still stood. The king had absolute power and Esther once again used the power of her feminine charms to move the king to pass another law permitting the Jews to defend themselves.

Then Esther spoke again to the king; she fell at his feet, weeping and pleading with him... (chapter 8 verse 3)

Hardly a role-model for the twenty-first century woman who would prefer to wield the power rather than manipulate the men with the power! Likewise, her rather bloodthirsty request to allow the Jews to continue the slaughter arising from their self-defence makes her an unlikely heroine. However, we must remember that in those days women were treated as sexual objects and violence was used for political ends. Esther used the only power that was available to her and in so doing, she was revered as God's agent of salvation at a time when the destruction of the Jewish people was a real threat.

† *Lord Jesus, Alpha and Omega, help us to discern how you are working in our community and nation and to offer ourselves as willing agents of your salvation in our own day.*

Saturday February 12   **Esther 9:20 – 10:3**

CELEBRATION   Survival of the nation was followed by celebration and Purim became a joyous and not very solemn festival which involved much revelry.

> The Jews established and accepted as a custom for themselves ... that ... they would continue to observe these two days every year ... and these days of Purim should never fall into disuse. **(parts of verses 27–28)**

This entertaining story written for an oppressed minority became a symbol of national deliverance and of many lesser deliverances in different times in the political and personal lives of the Jewish people. In the story God is kept almost totally out of sight. So what is of value for twenty-first century Christians? God works through willing human agents; there are no miracles in this story. God saved his people through the actions of those who were prepared to risk their lives and take a stand against the powerful. Mordecai and Esther are examples of people who used the power they gained on behalf of their people and for the good of others. God calls us to be agents of his salvation in today's world, to fight against oppression in its many forms, to act without seeking reward and without fear, knowing that God is in ultimate control and that he is working his purpose out in our personal lives and in the world.

† *Almighty God, as you work out your plan of salvation in human history, help us to allow you to work through us for the good of all within the different communities in which you have placed us.*

___

For group discussion and personal thought

- Look carefully in the media for stories of modern-day Hamans and try to identify those who are risking their all to oppose oppression, greed, corruption and racial bigotry.
- How different is the position of women in today's society (and church)? Is there room for improvement? How can I help to bring this about?

___

LENT: JOHN'S GOSPEL 1
Who is this?

Notes by Kevin Ellis

based on the New International Version

Kevin Ellis is an Anglican priest in the Diocese of Carlisle. He was formerly Course Co-ordinator for the Open Theological College. He lives with his wife, Jennifer.

John introduces us to Jesus by setting his story on the wide cosmic canvas of time and space. We are introduced to Jesus as the Word made flesh, and as the Word who transforms the lives of others, from the Baptist to fishermen, from moneychangers to Nicodemus.

Text for the week: John 3:16

Sunday February 13   **John 1:1–18**

THE LIGHT   Words are dangerous. They have the potential to create hope and despair. The Word (many commentators use the original Greek word *Logos* for John's title for Christ in his first chapter) is also dangerous. The *Logos* comes into our world and creates hope and despair. Unlike Matthew and Luke, John begins his gospel not with the visit of angels and the pronouncement of birth, but by setting his gospel against time and space. For John the story of Jesus is one that is told on the cosmic stage. This should not surprise us. Stories, whether ancient or modern, are told on a wide canvas. For John there is no doubt about who will emerge victorious in the battle. There is no hint that the darkness will come close to winning.

> **The light shines in the darkness, but the darkness has not overcome it.**   **(verse 5)**

In the first chapters of John, we see the light shining in the darkness of people's lives. Are there areas of your life where you would rather the light did not shine?

† *Loving God, help me to shine as a light to your world. Holy God, help me to be willing to allow you to disperse any darkness within me. Amen*

THE ONE WHO IS GREATER THAN JOHN   Pointing to the Light is never easy. It certainly was not for John the Baptist, who endured hardship, deprivation and death for his ministry of proclaiming the kingdom. I often wonder how I would have coped with the difficulties of pointing to the Light if I had been John. Would I have been a tiny bit jealous of Jesus? Would I have found it easy to say what John did?

> **'He is the one who comes after me, the thongs of whose sandals I am not worthy to untie.'**   **(verse 27)**

I hope so. John had discovered a deep truth. He realised that when we step into the light of Christ, we discover not only who Jesus is, but also who we are. The Baptist knew himself to be loved and chosen by God. He also knew that part of his vocation, as a human being, was to point people to Christ. How easily do we point others to Jesus? Spend some time today thinking about the people you would like to point to him and pray for them by name.

> **'Look, the Lamb of God, who takes away the sin of the world!'**   **(part of verse 29)**

✝ *Lord Jesus Christ, Son of the living God, have mercy on me, a sinner. Amen*

THE ONE WITH TIME FOR OTHERS   In this passage, we are introduced to some of Jesus' disciples for the first time. Rather than look at them, however, focus today on how Jesus conducts himself. He has that rare quality: time. The Jews at the time of Christ – like many of us still today – wanted their Messiah to be a man of action, overturning the might of Rome. Jesus comes across quite differently. He is a doer, as we shall see over the next few days; but this doing arises out of his ability to be. Most of you, I suspect, are like me, wonderfully happy to be busy. I find it easier to do things for God rather than be with him. Yet, in response to the question posed by the Baptist's disciples, Jesus replies, 'Come, and you will see'. There was no particular manifesto offered or promises given, just an opportunity to spend time with Jesus. And as we know, when we spend time with God our lives change. Today, why not find a space within your diary to spend time alone with God? Try to do it within the next two or three weeks. It will be difficult, but rewarding.

They said, 'Rabbi' (which means Teacher), 'where are you staying?' 'Come,' he replied, 'and you will see.' So they went and saw where he was staying, and spent that day with him. **(part of verses 38 and 39)**

✝ *Loving God, help me to be as comfortable with who I am as with what I do. Amen*

Wednesday February 16   John 2:1–12

THE WEDDING GUEST   One of the most satisfying features of ordained Anglican ministry in England is the right to conduct weddings. A wedding is special. It is an important day in the life of a couple and their families. The thought of Jesus attending a wedding is both special and ordinary. It is as if John the gospel writer has moved us from the wide cosmic canvas to something which, although special, is still an event in everyday life. At first glance we have simply a story of Jesus intervening to spare the blushes of the bridegroom who has not provided enough wine for his guests. But there is much more in the story. There is the fact that Jesus has mastery over nature: he turns water into wine. He also overturns expectations; the best is saved until last. The story also contains a familiar theme from the other gospels: Jesus acts without wanting to draw attention to himself. But perhaps the most startling verse is spoken by Mary, Jesus' mother:

    'Do whatever he tells you.'   **(part of verse 5)**

The woman who gave birth to Jesus and watched him grow speaks these words: the mother who taught him to read and reached out for him when he fell as a toddler. And now she says simply, 'Do whatever he tells you'. She knows it is time for him to begin his ministry. She also knows it is time for her to let go of her dreams. The servants do as Jesus tells them. How willing are we to do whatever Jesus tells us? Can we let Jesus go rather than try to restrict him to our particular image of him?

✝ *Lord of all, meet us in the everyday and be Lord of our lives. Amen*

Thursday February 17   John 2:13–25

THE DEFENDER OF HIS FATHER'S HOUSE   John's Jesus in today's passage seems thoroughly human. It may be hard for us to imagine him deliberately weaving together a whip of cords in order to overthrow the tables in the Temple. For many western Christians this goes against the spirit of much of what we have been taught about the meek and mild Jesus, the nice Jesus. Even the words from the prophets that the disciples remember seem to fit uneasily with our imaginings about the Messiah:

His disciples remembered that it is written, 'Zeal for your house will consume me.' (verse 17)

This is an uncomfortable thought, that Jesus might be someone who is zealous for his father's house. Jesus may have loved the Temple and its architecture, but he was more concerned with what happened within it. The moneychangers operated in the so-called court of the nations, which meant that those who were not Jewish had nowhere peaceful to pray and worship God. We also find Jesus uncomfortable because he forces us to think again and understand at a deeper level. His response to his actions in the Temple takes us to that deeper level:

Then the Jews demanded of him, 'What miraculous sign can you show us to prove your authority to do all this?' Jesus answered them, 'Destroy this temple, and I will raise it again in three days.' (verses 18–19)

Here John introduces his readers to what is going happen. John's Jesus – like the Jesus of the other gospels – is born to die for us. Spend a few moments giving thanks for this.

† *Awesome God, thank you that Jesus cannot be put in a box. At times this makes me feel uncomfortable. Help me to accept this and to walk with you. Amen*

Friday February 18 **John 3:1–21**

THE MASTER COMMUNICATOR Jesus has met with fishermen, working people, and those attending a wedding. He now has a discussion with one of the leading rabbis of his time, Nicodemus. Nicodemus comes to Jesus by night, apparently because he does not want to be seen with Jesus, even though he seems to think that Jesus is 'a teacher who is sent from God'. Many people were unsure about what this Galilean teacher was up to. Jesus does not rebuke Nicodemus's uncertainty, but works with it. He draws the Rabbi into conversation and gently teaches one of Israel's masters about the necessity of new birth and the workings of the Spirit. John does not record Nicodemus's response to Jesus, but we know from later in the gospel that the Rabbi follows Jesus in secret, standing with Joseph of Arimathea after his death (*John 19:39*). John shows Jesus as the master communicator, but reminds his readers that he is much more than that, with words that have shaped the lives of many:

> **'For God so loved the world that he gave his one and only Son, that whoever believes in him shall not perish but have eternal life. For God did not send his Son into the world to condemn the world, but to save the world through him.'** **(verses 16–17)**

Spend some time today thanking God that Jesus' mission was to save rather than condemn.

† *Majestic God, thank you that Jesus welcomes all. Help us to welcome people in the way your Son did. Amen*

Saturday February 19   John 3:22–36

THE BRIDEGROOM   Finally, our attention switches back to the Baptist. On Monday we explored how John seems to have a right view of Jesus and himself. We return to that theme today.

> **'The friend who attends the bridegroom waits and listens for him, and is full of joy when he hears the bridegroom's voice. That joy is mine, and it is now complete. He must become greater; I must become less.'** **(part of verse 29 and verse 30)**

'He must become greater; I must become less.' These are words that have echoed down the centuries. It is the hope of all those who seek to serve Christ, but it is far from easy. Sometimes we cannot help getting in the way. Sometimes we cannot help detracting from the light at work in us. It is difficult because, like the Baptist, we are from below, whilst the Son is from above. The Good News is that the Son enables us all to share his light and become lights to the world. We should be as ready to join in this mission as the Baptist seems to have been.

† *Help us, Lord, to share with you in your mission, pointing people only to Jesus, your precious Son. Amen*

For group discussion and personal thought

● We have looked at many different pictures of Jesus this week: the light, the wedding guest, the Messiah, the communicator, and so on. Which picture of Jesus means most to you, and why?

LENT: JOHN'S GOSPEL 2
Signs and teaching

Notes by Supriyo Mukherjee

based on the New Revised Standard Version

Supriyo Mukherjee is an Anglican priest. He was ordained in the Church of North India in 1975. Since 1979 he has lived and worked in England and is now the Diocesan Adviser for Community Relations and Inter-Faith for the Diocese of Coventry.

John's gospel is a theological document. The writer uses the stories of Jesus' ministry and mission to reveal who Jesus is. In the early part of the gospel, after the prologue or introduction, individual disciples came to believe in Jesus as the Messiah. Through the incident of the Samaritan woman in chapter 4, John reveals his christological insight that Jesus is the saviour of the world. The early Christians were Jewish people who believed in Jesus as Messiah, so it is significant that the mass conversion takes place among the Samaritans, a non-Jewish community. Jesus is not just the Messiah for the Jewish people, he is now bringing salvation to others, even the ancient enemies of the Jews. And by talking to a woman alone, Jesus also breaks the social barrier between the sexes. God and his salvation are now available to all races, genders or nationalities.

Text for the week: John 4:10–14

Sunday February 20   **John 4:1–15**

THE GIFT OF GOD

> **Jesus answered her, 'If you knew the gift of God, and who it is that is saying to you, "Give me a drink," you would have asked him, and he would have given you living water.'** **(verse 10)**

'Gift of God' echoes John 3:16 ('God so loved the world that he gave his only Son, so that everyone who believes in him may not perish but may have eternal life'). Jesus, the saviour of the world, is the gift of God. By calling himself the 'gift of God' and the source of 'living water', Jesus implies that he is greater than

Jacob, and the woman asks him outright whether this is true (*verse 12*). In John 8:52–53 Jews ask the same question in connection with Abraham. Here in John 4:14, Jesus responds to the woman that he is not only greater than Jacob but is the continuous source of the living water which purifies souls and brings them eternal life. The woman still does not understand that Jesus is not talking about physical water but is implying that he is the Messiah or Saviour who gives eternal life.

✝ *Lord God, you have given us your Son Jesus Christ to be the source of eternal life. May we thirst for things eternal and not for things temporal.*

Monday February 21   John 4:16–29

JESUS BRINGS FREEDOM   Jesus asked the Samaritan woman to call her husband. John's readers would not be surprised that Jesus already knew that she had had five husbands, but this makes the woman believe in Jesus as a prophet. The mention of a sixth 'husband' who is no such thing implies that the woman was living a sinful life. Therefore Jesus is not only breaking with tradition by talking to someone belonging to a race hated by the Jews, and a woman – he is even talking to a sinful woman.

'You will worship the Father neither on this mountain nor in Jerusalem.'   **(part of verse 21)**

When Jesus says this, he doesn't mean that there will never be any worship of God in Samaria or in Jerusalem. The negatives serve the positive: God can be worshipped everywhere. We often attach ourselves to a place of worship or a 'holy' place. Church buildings developed much later than the time of the Johannine community, who never experienced worship in a church. A place of worship or a church may sometimes create an atmosphere which helps us concentrate but any attachment to or dependence on a 'sacred place' is contrary to Jesus' teaching. Jesus gives us freedom from all ritual, ceremony, sacred place or any visible and physical expression of religion. We can be with God and worship him without any of these things.

'God is spirit, and those who worship him must worship in spirit and truth.'   **(verse 24)**

There is no precondition either; both men and women can come to God even when they are sinners.

† *Father God, you are the omnipresent God. Forgive us when we*
seek your presence only in rituals, ceremonies or sacred places.

Tuesday February 22   **John 4:30–45**

SHARING OUR FAITH Jesus' disciples return while the
Samaritan woman goes into the town to bring others to Jesus.
Jesus urges his disciples towards their own task of 'harvesting'
– bringing to Jesus people who are not yet believers. The
Samaritan woman could be considered the first missionary. She
believed in Jesus, so she shared her faith with others.

> **Many Samaritans from that city believed in him because of**
> **the woman's testimony.**   **(part of verse 39)**

Her action of bringing others to Jesus also reflects the
discipleship stories (*John 1:40–49*). There, Andrew brought his
brother Simon and Philip brought Nathanael to Jesus. This is
the easiest way to bring other people to God. We are not all
capable of going out to preach the gospel to the public, but we
can all share our faith with others. When we experience
something good we share it with our friends. Similarly, we
should also share our religious experiences with others.

† *Lord, give us a willingness to share your good news with our*
friends and relations.

Wednesday February 23   **John 4:46–54**

THE POWER OF THE WORD

> **This was the second sign that Jesus did after coming from**
> **Judea to Galilee.**   **(verse 54)**

John refers to Jesus' miracles as 'signs'. For John, the signs of
Jesus led people into believing in him. But if this faith is based
only on signs and does not lead the believer into recognition
that Jesus Christ is the Son of God, then that faith is useless and
Jesus was often critical of this sort of faith (see for example *John
2:23–25*). However, for John the signs are the indicators that
Jesus is the Son of God. Near the end of his gospel he mentions
this: 'Now Jesus did many other signs in the presence of his
disciples, which are not written in this book. But these are
written so that you may come to believe that Jesus is the
Messiah, the Son of God, and that through believing you may
have life in his name' (*John 20:30–31*). Today's sign is a variant
of the healing of the centurion's slave in the synoptic gospels

(*Matthew 8:5–13; Luke 7:1–10*). In Matthew and Luke the petitioner is a centurion, a Roman official; but in John he is a royal official, probably a Jewish official of Herod's court, and the patient is the petitioner's son, not a slave. However, the main difference in John's gospel is that the man's 'belief in the word' of Jesus resulted in the conversion of his whole household (*verse 53*). He believed in the word of Jesus before he learned that his son had been healed (*verse 50*), therefore his conversion was not dependent on the sign. If our faith is dependent on miracles, it may be useless, because miracles do not always happen. If we expect God to perform miracles to show that he cares for us, it may not happen. The early Christians had to face this kind of challenge during persecution, God did not always save them from persecution or from death.

† *Forgive us, Lord, when we look for signs and miracles to strengthen our faith.*

Thursday February 24   **John 5:1–18**

JESUS IS THE SON OF GOD   Chapter 5 is an example of the long discourses by Jesus recorded by John. It begins with a healing miracle on the sabbath. At the time of Jesus there were many detailed regulations surrounding the observance of the sabbath. Modern Jews still have rules: for example, you should not turn on a switch on the sabbath, but a timer-switch can turn on the oven to cook your sabbath dinner. Mark and Luke both record incidents when Jesus' disciples were rebuked for 'harvesting' on the sabbath by plucking grain and rubbing it between their hands (*Mark 2:23–27; Luke 6:1–5*). In today's story, it is Jesus who seems to encourage breaking the rules:

Jesus said to him, 'Stand up, take your mat and walk.'
(verse 8)

So the cured man took up his mat and started walking. By carrying his mat he was breaking the law, he was working! Jesus knew the laws of his days, so why did he ask the man to 'work' on a sabbath? One reason for doing this is that Jesus gives us freedom from all sorts of mundane rituals. The other reason is that Jesus himself was also working on the sabbath – as his Father worked:

'My Father is still working, and I also am working' ... he was not only breaking the sabbath, but was also calling God his own Father, thereby making himself equal to God.
(parts of verses 17 and 18)

So here again we find John's insight that Jesus is the Son of God and equal to God.

† *Creator God, you work ceaselessly. May we never stop working for your kingdom and the world.*

Friday February 25   John 5:19–29

LIFE-GIVING AND JUDGING The discourse proper now begins. Jesus tells the Jewish people that he never acts on his own authority; he and his Father are in constant loving communion and his works are all motivated by the Father. Moreover, his Father has given him the twofold power of 'giving life' and 'judging'. God is the Creator, therefore he is the source of all life. By possessing the power of 'giving life' Jesus becomes equal to God. The term Son of Man is an early Christian image of the figure in Daniel: 'As I watched in the night visions, I saw one like a human being (son of man) coming with the clouds of heaven' (*Daniel 7:13–14*). So Jesus the Son of Man is the eschatological Judge. He is the judge of all – both the living and the dead:

> **The Father judges no one but has given all judgment to the Son ... the hour is coming when all who are in their graves will hear his voice and will come out – those who have done good, to the resurrection of life, and those who have done evil, to the resurrection of condemnation.**
>
> **(verse 22, part of 28, and verse 29)**

† *Lord Jesus, give us confidence to welcome you on the day of judgement when you come to judge the living and the dead.*

Saturday February 26   John 5:30–47

UNBELIEF AND CONDEMNATION Jesus' discourse now shifts to the issue of testimony to Jesus. The testimony of John the Baptist was a human testimony, although John was not an ordinary human being; he was a 'burning and shining lamp'. However, Jesus refers to his own 'works' as testimony superior to John's. Since his works are the direct doings of God, they are the divine testimony (see *verse 19*). This is confirmed here:

> **the Father who sent me has himself testified on my behalf.**
>
> **(part of verse 37)**

This refers directly to the cure of the crippled man at the beginning of this chapter. However, the Jewish people cannot hear God's voice because they do not believe in Him. The other reason for their unbelief is that they search the scriptures to find the path to eternal life, and fail to find it. But the scriptures themselves talk about Jesus, especially, in Jesus' view, the book of Moses, the Torah. Jesus is the source of salvation and through faith in him we also understand the meaning of the scriptures.

✝ *O Word of God, you are the perfect image of God. Give us enough faith to understand the meaning of the written Word.*

For group discussion and personal thought

● Do we really believe that God and his salvation are accessible to everybody – irrespective of their race, colour, gender or nationality?
● Is our faith dependent on miracles, sacred places, rituals or ceremonies?
● Do we make practical use of the scriptures as a guide for life or simply read them because they strengthen our faith?

LENT: JOHN'S GOSPEL 3
The Bread and the Light

Notes by Joan Stott

based on the New Jerusalem Bible

Joan Stott is a layperson in the Uniting Church in Australia and has served in a variety of leadership roles in Australia. She has also served extensively in the World Federation of Methodist and Uniting Church Women.

I attended a world conference on health issues where many people from affluent countries spoke of 'balanced' diets, and eating regular sustaining meals. Other people from impoverished countries spoke only of the need for clean water and the basic food requirements for survival. The bread of life that Jesus offers erases these barriers: it is sustaining food for the soul. A craving for sunlight develops within people who work for long periods at night, because artificial light does not have the same effect as real light. These workers long for the morning, when the real light comes. There is something special about sunlight; it nurtures the soul, revives the spirit, and ensures appropriate growth of the body and mind. So it is when the light of Jesus shines into our lives. Renewed daily, we grow to maturity as children of God.

Text for the week: John 6:35 and 8:12

Sunday February 27   **John 6:1–21**

THE SHARED BREAD

> **Then Jesus took the loaves, gave thanks, and distributed them to those who were sitting there.   (part of verse 11)**

At the 1986 World Assembly of the World Federation of Methodist Women in Nairobi, Kenya, the stage backdrop featured African women in a variety of traditional dresses, pouring mixed grains into a large bowl for crushing into flour. This symbolised women from all over Africa contributing their individual gifts to the whole, with the resultant flour being 'all-African'. The closing Holy Communion was served in front of this backdrop, which reminded me of the shared meal Jesus had with more than 5000 people long ago. Jesus distributed the bread that was offered to him by another, just as we received the bread offered to us by one nation from amongst many. The bread was blessed, broken and distributed to 'the multitude', a representative group of women from the whole world. When the 'multitude' of women had received of the grace of God poured out just like that grain into the bowl, they went away to their homes, sustained by that 'Bread of Life' which was to be shared again and again with others.

† *Jesus, Bread of Life, we thank you for your life shared with all who will receive it.*

Monday February 28 John 6:22–40

THE UNIVERSAL BREAD

**'I am the bread of life.
No one who comes to me will ever hunger.' (part of verse 35)**

The symbolism of the mixed grains from the Nairobi World Assembly has been special to me for years. When I was dedicated as a World Officer for the Federation of Methodist and Uniting Church Women, we had Holy Communion, with the local baker making a multi-grained loaf for me to be broken and shared during that service. This multi-grained bread was symbolic of the women from over seventy countries whom I represented in my role as a World Officer. There are many different types of grain; some are mixed together to be made into many different varieties of 'bread', depending on the regional and cultural background of the bread maker. It is truly a 'universal bread'. Jesus is the 'universal bread' of life, whatever the person's culture or circumstances. He comes into the lives of people to meet their particular need. Jesus sustains and renews them daily for their journey of life.

† *Jesus, Bread of Life, we thank you that you come to all people in response to their needs.*

Tuesday March 1 John 6:41–71

THE EMPOWERING BREAD

**'As the living Father sent me
and I draw life from the Father,
so whoever eats me**

will also draw life from me.' (verse 57)

After a week in Nairobi, spent looking at the imagery of the women grinding the mixed grains and becoming one flour and ultimately one bread, the empowering strength of that visual concept has become part of me. Fifteen years later, when I was back in Africa, I was invited to choose as a gift a carving that was symbolic of Africa. Through God's grace, I received carvings of a pair of women grinding grain into bowls. That imagery of many grains, one flour and one bread is now a daily reminder of the nourishing power of the Bread of Life that was broken for all humanity. Jesus drew life and power from God the Father to sustain him in his ministry of self-sharing, and we are called to do the same. The sacrament of Holy Communion, worship and prayer sustain and empower us in our daily pilgrimage.

† *Jesus, Bread of Life, you nourish our souls and bodies with your empowering love.*

Wednesday March 2 John 7:1–24

THE CHALLENGING LIGHT

The Jews were on the lookout for him: 'Where is he?' they said ... Jesus went to the Temple and began to teach. ... 'My teaching is not from myself: it comes from the one who sent me.' (parts of verses 11, 14 and 16)

Team sports provide special challenges with their interdependence on team members. In cricket, football, hockey etc., the challenge is to improve on past performances as a team and individually. The head coach is the one who has the 'big picture' and sets the patterns of play. Jesus challenged the people to see God in a new light, and spoke as one who knew God in an intimate and real way. The crowds who followed Jesus reacted to his words and actions with rejection or acceptance, or ignored him completely. Jesus' message about God was like a bright light, illuminating what had previously been an unclear message. An intimate relationship with God is available to all people through direct contact with God. Jesus is the 'Head Coach'. He not only sees the patterns of play, but is also part of the 'big picture'.

† *Jesus, Light of Life, illumine our hearts and minds with your challenging truths. May the light of your wisdom shine on us to inspire and renew us.*

THE UNRECOGNISED LIGHT

> **As Jesus was teaching in the Temple, he cried out:**
> **'You know me**
> **and you know where I came from.**
> **Yet I have not come of my own accord:**
> **but he who sent me is true;**
> **You do not know him**
> **but I know him...'**   **(verses 28–29)**

Studying the origins of their family background through the various branches of the family tree has become an obsession with some people. Family lineage was also important in biblical times, and it was the parents' responsibility to instruct their children in their heritage. People proudly followed their forefathers' line back into history, and Jesus would have been very conscious of his family background. He chose to claim his heritage from God rather than his human ancestors. The 12–year-old Jesus knew to whom he belonged when he replied: 'Did you not know that I must be in my Father's house?' (*Luke 2:49*). Jesus knew he had come from God, and was in God's Temple, doing God's will. Jesus was amongst people who knew of his human heritage; but they failed to recognise his true identity as God's promised light in a dark world.

† *Jesus, Light of Life, illumine our hearts and minds so that we see the truth of you in other people. Help us to follow their examples.*

THE LIGHT OF LIFE

> **'I am the light of the world;**
> **anyone who follows me**
> **will not be walking in the dark,**
> **but will have the light of life.'**   **(part of verse 12)**

In the crypt of Lund Cathedral in Sweden, light shines dimly through narrow windows, partially illuminating a number of burial tombs of famous people. Further along the crypt, there are an altar and a cross set before a window. The light shines through the window onto the altar, illuminating the empty cross, and because of the light, the cross becomes the main focus of attention. The contrast between the dim light surrounding the tombs and the light shining on the altar is very marked, yet each part of the crypt celebrates the life of significant people. The darker parts of the crypt illustrate the darker deeds of humanity. The light shining on the empty cross highlights the light-giving, life-giving path that the followers of Jesus must travel if they are to be true to their Lord. It is the path of self-giving, of service to other people, of bringing light and hope to a dark world.

† *Jesus, Light of Life, illumine our hearts and minds so that we may walk the path that Jesus followed, of self-giving love and service.*

Saturday March 5   John 8:21–47

THE COMMUNITY OF LIGHT

> **Jesus said:**
> **'If you make my word your home**
> **you will indeed be my disciples.'**   **(part of verse 31)**

Travelling in the deep darkness of the countryside in Ghana, West Africa, I was amazed at the beauty of the stars. There was no moon, but the entire sky blazed with stars, offering the only light apart from the car headlights. The dark quietness was eerie and still. In the distance there was a glow, and later on, another glow. As we came nearer to these lights, it became obvious that they were small family settlements, with people gathered around each lamp, forming communities of light. Family life continued as these 'people of the light' depended on their light and each other for companionship, comfort and security. Jesus is the light that draws people together, to be part of that light-sharing community, with a common aim of fellowship and mutual support. No matter what the dangers or threats that individuals experience, in that light-sharing community is security and sanctuary. Faith is renewed, courage is restored, and hope becomes a reality.

† *Jesus, Light of Life, illumine our hearts and minds through the community of your faithful people so that, strengthened by that community, we may be lights in the world.*

For group discussion and personal thought
- What other life-giving necessities did Jesus use as examples for his presence and purpose in this world?
- How do these life-giving necessities enrich our understanding of Jesus, and of God?
- What are the 'I am' statements of Jesus, and how do these compare with the Old Testament understandings of God/Yahweh?

LENT: JOHN'S GOSPEL 4
The world's life

Notes by Meeli Tankler

based on the New International Version

Meeli Tankler lives in Pärnu, Estonia where her husband pastors a Methodist church. She is a psychologist, and teaches part-time in the Theological Seminary of the Estonian Methodist Church. She is active in women's work both nationally and internationally, and in 2001 she was elected President of the Europe Continental Area in the World Federation of Methodist and Uniting Church Women. In her local congregation she is a local preacher, Sunday School teacher and Bible Study leader. She is also the mother of three grown-up children.

There is always something unexpected and thrilling happening when we walk with Jesus. He is not an ordinary person. He looks at things and persons in a very interesting and uncommon way, he chooses surprising solutions to serious problems, and his words are always worth listening to – even in very ordinary circumstances or while speaking about everyday matters he can reveal some extraordinary truths.

Text for the week: John 10:10b

Sunday March 6   **John 8:48–59**

WHO DO YOU THINK YOU ARE? This is the question rudely asked of Jesus here. There is no actual need for an answer – in fact, these people are afraid to hear it, because Jesus puzzles and irritates them and they would rather like him to disappear from their sight. At the same time they are secretly waiting for some kind of improper explanation from him so that they can accuse him of blasphemy. Jesus does not act according to their expectations. He does not reveal his identity to them or claim any glory for his deeds. He just keeps talking about his Father and all the glory he has and deserves. The only thing he directly says about himself is

'before Abraham was born, I am!'   **(part of verse 58)**

Even this seems to be too much for his listeners. They are thinking in totally different terms. They know dates well, and they are able to count months and years, so they say to Jesus: 'You are not yet fifty years old!'(*verse 57*). Their minds cannot understand Jesus as being the one through whom 'the world was made' (*John 1:10*). And they do not recognise in his words the ancient revelation of God, who often introduces himself by saying 'I am'. So instead of worshipping him they pick up stones. And this very word becomes true: 'his own did not receive him' (*John 1:11b*). Why is it so difficult to recognise Jesus as God incarnate?

† *Lord Jesus, yours is the glory. Thank you for being who you are – and for being here for me today. Amen*

Monday March 7   John 9:1–22

THAT THE WORK OF GOD MIGHT BE DISPLAYED   Who sinned? There are many people still asking this question when something goes wrong. We know that everything God has created is good, and that all problems and bad things originate from sin. But this is not always the sin that is visible before our eyes. Sometimes bad things happen for a very different reason:

'this happened so that the work of God might be displayed in his life.'   (part of verse 3)

In the life of this blind man on the road, this moment of God's work displayed in his life has come right now. He can suddenly 'go home seeing' (*verse 7*). Everyone considers it a miracle – and people keep asking all kinds of questions about it. So he has to testify about God's mighty work in his life many times, to many people, and not all of them respond to it in a friendly way. Through all these discussions about how and why Jesus healed him, his faith gradually grows. We can follow his testimony from speaking first about 'the man they call Jesus' (*verse 11*) to 'he is a prophet' (*verse 17*). The work of God is displayed not only in the miracle of healing but far more in the growing faith of this man.

† *Lord, help me not to look for sin when someone is hurting. Let me look for your mighty work happening in this person's life – and let me notice and believe it is happening. Amen*

YOU HAVE NOW SEEN HIM Our story from yesterday continues today. The man who has been blind is summoned to appear a second time before the Pharisees. His parents have meanwhile been questioned too, and for the Pharisees the case is still not clear. Perhaps they just do not want to believe what has happened before their very eyes. But by now the healed man's testimony about God's mighty work has grown even more courageous, as he declares:

'If this man were not from God, he could do nothing.'
                                                       (verse 33)

The result of his new courage is sad: the Pharisees throw him out of the synagogue. Now Jesus himself comes to him and offers him living faith – and the man worships Jesus in adoration and awe. When our eyes are open to see Jesus we can really fully worship him. And, for this man as for us, physical vision is only one of God's mighty works in his life. Much more important is his newly acquired spiritual vision – Jesus points out very clearly that we can sometimes be deceived like the Pharisees, claiming to have a vision when we are actually totally blind to the God-given miracles in our own or other people's life.

† *Dear Lord, help me to see things as you see them. Help me to worship you sincerely and with open eyes. Amen*

BECAUSE THEY KNOW HIS VOICE... It is interesting to think about sheep and their shepherd in the context of mutual relationship. A good shepherd talks to his sheep and calls each one of them by name. A good shepherd is one who knows all about the needs of his sheep and takes good care of them. So his sheep can really trust him, follow him, and always feel secure in his presence. Jesus here compares the good shepherd with the thief who 'comes only to steal and kill and destroy' (*verse 10*). The secret of God's love is in his abundant and sacrificial giving. Jesus declares that the good shepherd is willing to give everything, even his life, for his sheep. And what is the life he promises to his sheep – and for all of us who consider ourselves part of his flock?

'I have come that they may have life, and have it to the full.'   (part of verse 10)

I find the emphasis on the voice of the shepherd very interesting. There are many voices around us and it is not always easy to recognise the right voice. Yet Jesus makes it very clear how important this is, and that we should be careful not to follow a stranger whose voice we do not know. Perhaps we should spend more time with Jesus in order to know his voice better?

✝ *Dear Lord Jesus, help me to recognise your voice in the middle of all the voices of this world. Help me to follow you in full trust as sheep follow their shepherd. Amen*

Thursday March 10   John 10:22–42

WHO ARE YOU?

'What about the one whom the Father set apart as his very own and sent into the world?'   (part of verse 36)

This question which Jesus himself raises here seems to summarise all the other questions people have about Jesus. Who is he, what kind of relationship does he have with God, how does he perform all his miracles, who has given him the authority etc.? There is a willingness and openness to believe him, suspicions about him, and all kinds of rumours that cause some people to pick up stones (*verse 31*), and others to believe in him (*verse 42*). This is the serious question that we also face. What about the one whom the Father set apart as his very own? Do we recognise his distinctiveness, his very special position as God's incarnation, his extraordinary connection with his Father even during his earthly life? Do we value the gift of God in him? Do we see him as the one who is sent into the world for our sake? We need to face these questions from time to time. Otherwise we may become confused among all the opinions and theories that people around us offer about him, and lose sight of the real Jesus – the one whom the Father set apart as his very own.

✝ *Dear God, thank you for loving me so very much that you set apart your Son, and sent him into this world to save me. Help me to remember his sacrifice, and to cherish your love for me. Amen*

Friday March 11   John 11:1–27

IF YOU HAD BEEN THERE... We use this phrase very often – but here it is spoken in a very serious situation. There is really a question about life and death here. And Jesus clearly seems to be too late. For there is no hope for life any more – at least according to our human understanding. Lazarus has died and is buried, and there is only the future hope left. Martha says:

'I know he will rise again in the resurrection at the last day.' (part of verse 24)

No consolation for today. If you had been there in time... The Bible tells us that Jesus loves Martha and her sister and Lazarus. Why is he not present at the most difficult moment in their life, why is he absent, late, not involved? There is a beautiful Easter song which says:

After darkness, light;
After winter, spring;
After dying, life:
Alleluia! (F Pratt Green in *Hymns and Psalms*, 1983, number 186)

It may sound cruel but sometimes we really need to step into the darkness in order to recognise light and life. And only after this total darkness experience can we appreciate fully what Jesus can do in our lives – and what he has done. He cares even when we feel that we are forgotten and abandoned. He is always on his way towards us, bringing us hope, not going away from us.

† *Dear Lord Jesus, thank you for caring for us even when we do not believe that you do. Help us to trust you in big and small things, knowing that you are never late when we really need your help. Amen*

Saturday March 12   **John 11:28–57**

IF YOU BELIEVED YOU WOULD SEE THE GLORY OF GOD
Still on his way to Bethany, Jesus had told his disciples: 'Lazarus is dead, and for your sake I am glad I was not there, so that you may believe' (*verses 14–15*). The life he is going to give back to Lazarus is meant to strengthen many people's faith. His disciples see it happening and believe. Martha gives her amazing testimony, saying: 'Yes, Lord, I believe that you are the Christ, the Son of God, who was to come into the world' (*verse 27*) – even before seeing the actual miracle happening. Just the presence of Jesus influences her so powerfully that her faith grows so much. Many of the Jews, we are told, put their faith in him after he raises Lazarus from death (*verse 45*).

Faith and trust in Jesus can help us go beyond the accusation 'if you had been there' – toward new possibilities and solutions we have not even dared to dream about. The glory of God can become visible in the midst of the greatest grief and darkest night. Let us believe in the life that is in Jesus:

'Did I not tell you that if you believed, you would see the glory of God?' (part of verse 40)

† *Dear Jesus, let me believe so that I can see your glory even when it seems to be dark and hopeless around me. Strengthen my faith, and lead me on my path step by step. Amen*

For group discussion and personal thought

- Have you ever given a testimony about something God has done in your life, and felt your faith growing through this? Share your experiences of giving testimonies about your faith.
- How would you describe 'spiritual blindness'? What could you do to avoid it in your own life?
- Discuss the issue of familiar and strange voices. What can you learn from the warning not to follow the voice of a stranger? How could you better recognise Jesus' voice?
- Recall some situations where you have told God (perhaps only in your thoughts): 'If you had been there...' Looking back on these situations, can you understand them differently now?

LENT: JOHN'S GOSPEL 5
Jesus' farewell

Notes by David Huggett

based on the New Revised Standard Version

David Huggett is a Baptist minister with pastoral experience in the north of England and London, followed by work with the Bible Society and the Leprosy Mission and in adult Christian education. Now retired, he lives in Somerset and continues to be involved in preaching, writing and local church life.

The 'sons of the Law', as Jewish men were called, were required to journey to Jerusalem for the three main festivals each year – Passover, Pentecost and Tabernacles. Far from being just a duty, these pilgrimages were times of excitement and celebration. For Jesus, however, this was to be his last Passover shared with his friends. This week we consider some of the ways he prepared them for the parting.

Text for the week: John 14:21

Sunday March 13   **John 12:1–19**

GOD'S PERSPECTIVE   Just a week before the Passover and Jesus seemed to have attained celebrity status. He had performed an amazing miracle, so that everybody wanted to see him and the man restored to life. The crowds turned out to acclaim Jesus as their king as he approached the Holy City. Even his opponents admitted his popularity. But Jesus was not fooled. Not only did he recognise that fame is short-lived, but at a deeper level he understood that the clouds were gathering for him. The religious leaders felt threatened by his popular appeal; Judas felt cheated when Jesus condoned Mary's generous gesture; the crowds felt let down when he turned out to be a different kind of king to the one they wanted. Even his closest friends

> **did not understand these things at first; but when Jesus was glorified, then they remembered...   (part of verse 16)**

But Jesus never made any secret of the fact that he did not live according to other people's agendas. Doing the Father's will was all that mattered to him (*John 4:34*) – for himself and for his disciples.

✝ *Sometimes, Lord, I think I know better than you. Sometimes I don't understand what you are doing or why. Forgive me and help me to trust that you know best.*

Monday March 14   John 12:20–50

COSTLY DISCIPLESHIP   Jesus often returned to themes he had addressed before. The previous reference to a Passover is in chapter 6, where again Philip and Andrew were in the forefront of the action. Then Jesus fed a crowd of five thousand with bread and fish. Now he talks about meeting the needs, not of a crowd but of the world, not with bread and fish but with the bread of life – himself. The cost of doing this is enormous. It involves his own death.

Unless a grain of wheat falls into the earth and dies, it remains just a single grain; but if it dies, it bears much fruit.   (part of verse 24)

Little wonder his soul was 'troubled' (*verse 27*). Perhaps what troubles us is to realise that what is good for the master is good for the servant too. That doesn't mean that we shall all be martyrs (although statistics show that on average more than 400 people are martyred for Christ each day), but it does mean that true discipleship is costly. We need to let go of all those things that serve to indulge the self or the 'ego' in each of us.

✝ *As we approach Easter, Lord, help us to enter more fully into what your death signifies. We will follow you wherever you lead us, and want to let go of anything which hinders our true discipleship.*

Tuesday March 15   John 13:1–30

UNCONDITIONAL LOVE   The twelve disciples don't come out of this narrative very well. Peter failed to understand the meaning of the washing of his feet. He had also forgotten all Jesus' teaching about the need for humility. The 'beloved disciple' (whoever he was), surely intelligent enough to understand Jesus' sign about the betrayer, failed to do anything about it. And Judas presumably had his feet washed along with the rest, which makes his treachery all the worse. Remarkably, in spite of all this, Jesus,

Having loved his own who were in the world ... loved them to the end. (part of verse 1)

Honesty demands that we recognise ourselves in this story. We are guilty of the same sort of mistakes and misunderstandings. Humility, service, sacrifice are all difficult lessons for us to learn. As for following the Lord's example and 'loving to the end' those fellow disciples who let us down, who won't allow us to serve them, who misunderstand us, and who attribute false motives even to our best deeds – we have a long way to go. But that, says Jesus, is exactly what he requires of those who follow him.

† *I'm slow to learn, Lord, and quick to jump to the wrong conclusions about you and about others. As I give you thanks for loving me in spite of all this, I pray for help that I may be one who loves others to the end.*

Wednesday March 16   **John 13:31 – 14:14**

A CERTAIN FUTURE   Because Jesus knew what it was like to feel upset (*12:27* and *13:21*) he was able to encourage his disciples when they felt the same (*14:1*). When he was gone they were to remember the certainty of their destiny – not a fairytale castle in the sky at some vague future date, but a day-by-day living relationship through Jesus with God the Father.

Jesus said to him, 'I am the way, and the truth, and the life. No one comes to the Father except through me.'
                 (chapter 14 verse 6)

In the West, fewer and fewer people seem willing to follow Jesus, yet the majority still say they believe in God. Maybe the Indian Bishop was right when he pointed out that Jesus did not say that nobody comes to God except through Jesus, but rather that nobody comes to the Father except through him. God has revealed himself in so many ways – through creation, through science, through history, through the Jewish people of the Old Testament, but it is only when we come to Jesus that we discover God as Father.

† *Thank you, Father, that in your home there is a room with my name on it. I look forward to living there with you. Meanwhile, help me to live daily in you, and to allow you to live daily in me.*

JESUS' BEQUEST The Romans were respected for the large degree of stability they brought throughout their empire. The 'Pax Romana' (or peace of Rome) is the title given to it. But the peace they imposed by military means could only be maintained by power and brutality. It was quite different from the peace that Jesus bequeathed to his followers.

> **'Peace I leave with you; my peace I give to you. I do not give to you as the world gives.'**   **(part of verse 27)**

The Old Testament word for peace (*shalom*) means total wellbeing or wholeness – that experience when all the parts, whether of a community or an individual, work together for the good of the whole. Jesus knew plenty of conflict during his ministry, but in the midst of that conflict he experienced a deep sense of peace. It is that peace – 'my peace' – that he promises to those who both love and obey him (*verse 15*).

† *We pray for those who rob others of their peace;*
   for those who imagine that they can impose peace by force;
   for those who lack an experience of your wholeness;
   for ourselves that we may share your peace with others.

FACING THE WORLD Jesus' departure would inevitably make his followers more aware of what John calls 'the world'. By this he means the men and women and institutions that are opposed or indifferent to God. This world rejected Jesus (*1:10–11*), and also rejects, or at least ignores, his followers (*verse 18*). This world concentrates on amassing wealth, but increases the gap between rich and poor; it craves power, and is surprised when war and terrorism result; it invests heavily in extending the boundaries of knowledge, and damages our fragile earth by the overuse of its resources. This world is not altogether bad, but is fundamentally flawed because of its separation from God. It does not listen when he says,

> **'Those who abide in me and I in them bear much fruit, because apart from me you can do nothing.' (part of verse 5)**

Hence the picture of the vine. As the soil and rain and sun combine mysteriously to produce grapes, so God becomes a part of us and we of him when we put our faith in Jesus Christ. Dwelling, abiding, loving, obeying are key words in Christian experience. But because they are totally foreign to the experience of this world order, the latter can only respond with hatred and opposition.

† *Lord, thank you for calling me your friend. May that friendship grow daily through a deeper love and a more wholehearted obedience.*

Saturday March 19   **John 15:26 – 16:15**

GROWING IN TRUTH   One of the things I notice as the years go by is that I change my perspective on many things. Some things that were important to me become less so. Even things which once I believed in strongly no longer seem so significant. We change our minds as new factors come to light and as we experience things in new ways. That, says Jesus, is what should happen for us as we become more mature in our Christian faith.

'I still have many things to say to you, but you cannot bear them now. When the Spirit of truth comes, he will guide you into all the truth.'   **(verse 12 and part of verse 13)**

The disciple is someone who has embarked on the long process of seeking the truth. At the same time Jesus made it clear that it is not just about knowing more, it is also about being true. As he said, 'I am the truth'. It is the Spirit's task to carry on the ministry Jesus began and wishes to complete in us.

† *Lord, give me a sense of excitement today and each day that I may eagerly look forward to discovering new things about you. At the same time, may the integrity of my life support the truth of your gospel.*

For group discussion and personal thought

● How far do you think it is possible for someone to be a Christian and also a celebrity? What help and advice would you give to a modern celebrity who wishes to become a Christian?

● What do you think it might mean for you to live by the principle of the grain of wheat falling into the ground and dying?

● God loves the world. What are the practical ways in which your church community could translate that into action?

LENT: JOHN'S GOSPEL 6
Suffering and death

Notes by Sham P Thomas

based on the New Revised Standard Version

Sham P Thomas, a priest of the Mar Thoma Church, teaches communication at the United Theological College, Bangalore, India. At the time of writing, he is reading for a PhD at the University of Edinburgh. He lives with his wife Jolly and daughter Shyama.

In the last days and moments of his earthly existence, Jesus exemplified a way to face suffering and death and to bring glory to God. In this sense the passion narrative is comforting, encouraging and challenging. However, the crucial question that this week's readings place before us is, where do we stand in relationship to his cross and passion? Are we with him or not?

Text for the week: John 16:33

Sunday March 20   **John 16:16–33**

BE READY In his farewell discourse, Jesus prepares his disciples to face his impending suffering and death with assurance and hope. His death should not deter them from following his course. In addition we, like the disciples, are also to be ready to face pain and persecution for the sake of our faith. That we suffer should not surprise us because Jesus himself had to endure suffering and his followers are not exempt. We are not to succumb to suffering, because Jesus has conquered evil and death and as his disciples we are offered a share in that victory.

> **'I have said this to you, so that in me you may have peace. In the world you face persecution. But take courage; I have conquered the world!'**   **(verse 33)**

Because of this assurance, we can be cheerful in tearful situations. There is a certainty of pain and persecution but we are called to be at peace. This is the hope that makes people sing in their sufferings and dare to profess their faith even in the face of death. Faith is not an insurance against pain or death, but it strengthens us to endure and overcome.

✝ *Help us, O Lord, to believe that in any situation your presence is with us and you sustain us. Help us to serve you without counting the cost but counting on your promises. Amen*

Monday March 21 {.right John 17:1–26}

Monday March 21   **John 17:1–26**

PRAYER BEFORE THE PASSION Prayer was part of Jesus' preparation for his passion. The high priestly prayer in today's reading reflects his concern for God, his disciples and the church. In prayer, he entrusted himself to God. He prayed that his suffering should not be for his glory but for that of God alone. Glory, in this sense, is the gift of God alone and is not achieved by one's deeds or even one's suffering. Jesus also spoke for the future of his followers and his future followers.

 'I am not asking you to take them out of the world, but I ask you to protect them from the evil one.' **(verse 15)**

The disciples are to be kept faithful in a hostile world. Suffering and death can shatter and scatter the faith community. However, the disciples are not to draw away from the world but to live in the world. Without being one with the Father and in fellowship with one another they will not be able to remain united and committed to the mission of God. Isn't it comforting and encouraging that the risen Jesus continues to pray for us?

✝ *Triune God, help us to pray. Consecrate us so that sufferings may not stifle our faith and fellowship with you and our fellow followers. Amen*

Tuesday March 22   **John 18:1–18**

'NO' TO VIOLENCE Shakespeare described betrayal by a friend as the 'most unkindest cut of all'. How would we react if our close friends turned out to be aiding our enemies? For Jesus, one of his beloved disciples betrayed him; another denied him; and the rest deserted him. Judas, instead of fulfilling his own call to follow Jesus, called on his detractors and led them to arrest him. Peter promised to die with Jesus but ended up defending himself and denying him. In the midst of it all Jesus remained calm and composed; he was ready and prepared for his passion. He did not run away to save his own skin but even at the prospect of suffering he tried to protect others from suffering. He asked those who arrested him to let his disciples go and restrained his disciples from inflicting suffering on others.

'Put your sword back into its sheath!' (part of verse 11)

Peter wanted to defend Jesus by meeting the military on their terms, that is, with weapons. But Jesus knew well that the sword could bring only the sword and suffering, not salvation and peace. The world in which we live operates by Peter's logic, which leads to violence. Can we put the bombs away?

✝ *Crucified God, guard me from being carried away by my own sufferings. Help me to be sensitive to the suffering of others and not to join with those who perpetuate violence. Amen*

Wednesday March 23 John 18:19–40

UNJUST TRIALS Jesus was unfairly interrogated. He was tried by both the religious and the political leadership without regard for truth or justice. The religious leaders were determined to have him silenced and declared him guilty without adhering to their own set procedures for trial. Pilate's question,

'What is truth?' (part of verse 38)

seems to have many undertones in this narrative. The Jewish leaders wanted to keep ceremonial cleanness by avoiding entrance to a Gentile palace. They were afraid of defilement, but were not afraid of demanding death for an innocent man. In the same way, they handed Jesus over to Pilate, branding him a criminal worthy of capital punishment, but demanded the release of a known rebel, Barabbas. Pilate was told the truth about Jesus and that his kingdom is not based on force or violence, but he refused to recognise the truth. What had become conspicuous by its absence in these trials was a commitment to truth. Until and unless people dare to testify to truth and recognise it, many will continue to face unjust trials.

✝ *God of justice and truth, help us to be mindful of the pitfalls of our own truth claims and to be aware of the possible double standards in our lives. Strengthen us to demand justice for those who are detained illegally and denied their basic human rights. Amen*

THE CRUCIFIED KING   Jesus was an innocent victim. Pilate repeatedly asserted that there was no case against Jesus (see, for example, *John 18:38* and *19:4*) but no one was interested in his innocence. Prejudice, fear and the vested interests of the religious and political leaders contributed to his death.

> **He said to the Jews, 'Here is your king!' They cried out, 'Away with him! Away with him! Crucify him!'**
> **(parts of verses 14 and 15)**

Jesus was dressed as a king, only to be killed as a criminal. Pilate pronounced him the 'King of the Jews' but made that his prime offence. The soldiers hailed him as king, only to heap abuse and harm on him. On the other hand, the Jewish leadership and their followers rejected his kingship and affirmed their allegiance to Caesar as their king. In short, Jesus the king is a rejected and suffering king. They wanted him out of their way because the way he had shown was a challenge to their power, positions and prestige. Even today countless numbers of innocent people are being killed to protect the vested interests of religious and political leaders, but the crucified king becomes their companion in suffering.

† *Lord God, may your presence be power to us in facing rejection, humiliation and mockery for your sake. Amen*

SOLIDARITY IN SUFFERING Jesus was branded a blasphemer and condemned to the cursed death of a criminal. However, he endured the suffering and died in dignity because of his undying confidence in God.

> **He said, 'It is finished.'**   **(part of verse 30)**

For Jesus, suffering was part of accomplishing his mission. He was a martyr, offering himself as a sacrifice to bring glory to God. However, unlike suicide bombers, the modern-day martyrs, Jesus neither romanticised suffering nor sought to kill the maximum number of people along with him. He endured suffering to 'finish' its logic and threat and not to legitimise it or succumb to it. In spite of his agony on the cross, Jesus remembered his mother's wellbeing and future and initiated a new solidarity at the foot of the cross. The cross reveals another type of solidarity as well. There were two groups of people: four soldiers and four women. The soldiers were in solidarity in disposing of Jesus' clothes. They were together in sharing the spoil of an innocent victim without regard for his life. Unlike them, the four women stood there in solidarity with Jesus in his suffering. They dared to be there to share his pain and suffering. They acknowledged him in his most agonising moments of rejection and humiliation.

Standing near the cross of Jesus were his mother, and his mother's sister, Mary the wife of Clopas, and Mary Magdalene. (part of verse 25)

† *Crucified God, help us to share the pain of others. Amen*

Saturday March 26 **John 19:31–42**

OUT OF SECRECY   Except for the presence of the few women, Jesus suffered and died in isolation. Almost all of his followers deserted him to safeguard their own skins. When his followers went into hiding in fear, Jesus' passion prompted Joseph of Arimathea and Nicodemus to abandon their fear and secrecy and to come out into the open. If it had not been for their boldness, the soldiers and Jewish leaders might have dumped Jesus' body so as to denigrate him further. Joseph and Nicodemus turned out at the last and most crucial moment.

They took the body of Jesus and wrapped it with the spices in linen cloths. (part of verse 40)

Revealing their solidarity with Jesus was a politically incorrect move for them. Yet they risked their position by dissociating themselves from their peers and used their privilege and possessions to make sure that Jesus was given a decent burial. They acted out their love and reverence as his relatives ought to have done in his death. Discipleship is something that cannot be kept secret for ever. Jesus' suffering and death continue to challenge us to reveal where we stand: with him or against him!

† *Crucified and risen God, strengthen us to be like relatives to the lonely and needy, both in their life and in their death. Amen*

For group discussion and personal thought

● How do we face suffering in our own and others' lives?
● How do we understand martyrdom today?

EASTER FOR ALL 1
Hurry, everyone – he is risen !

Notes by Gillian Kingston

based on the New International Version

Gillian Kingston is a Methodist Local Preacher; she and her husband, a Methodist minister, have retired and live in Shinrone, County Offaly, Ireland. Moderator of the Church Representatives Meeting of Churches Together in Britain and Ireland and a member of the Methodist/Roman Catholic International Commission, she is committed to the vision of full communion among Christians in faith, mission and sacramental life.

A word which keeps appearing in this week's reading is 'running'. Everyone is running: there is a sense of urgency, immediacy. My mother was a sister tutor in hospitals in London and Nigeria. 'When we were nurses,' she used to tell us, 'we were only allowed to run for two things: fire and haemorrhage.' Matters of life and death – forget everything else and run! Resurrection is about life overcoming death. Go for it!

Text for the week : John 20:18a

Sunday March 27   **John 20:2–6**

COME QUICKLY, HE'S NOT THERE! That moment of blind panic: it's empty, nothing is there, where can he be? This is so unbelievable that it is absolutely necessary to share it with someone immediately, just in case, somehow, I'm the one who has got it wrong and I'm just not seeing properly. Run, get someone!

> **'They have taken the Lord out of the tomb, and we don't know where they have put him!'**   **(part of verse 2)**

Take time to read all the accounts of the empty tomb and see how each evangelist tells the story. Matthew (*chapter 28*) and Luke (*chapter 24*), like John, tell about the women, Mary Magdalene, perhaps another Mary, Joanna and others, making the startling discovery. An angel (or two) tells them what they most want to hear but can hardly believe. They must share it! Mark (*chapter 16*) gives a more muted story – did they or didn't they? The differences of detail aren't surprising: this was so amazing that it was unbelievable. It needed to be 'tested' with someone else – but then, perhaps not. They would be laughed at, told they were mad, maybe even reported to the Roman authorities or to the High Priest, and who knows what might happen then?

† *Loving God, help me to share this most amazing news of all: he is risen!*

Monday March 28   John 20:11–18

I SAW HIM – I WAS TALKING TO HIM! Is he there or isn't he? No one knows and everyone wants to know! Wild rumours are going around and people are asking questions – and then she comes running in saying she's seen him and she's been talking to him!

'Go ... to my brothers and tell them' ... 'I have seen the Lord!' (parts of verses 17 and 18)

Then they all went back to their homes and she was all by herself in the garden. A total anti-climax – no wonder she burst into tears. I would, wouldn't you? But, sometimes, in those moments of greatest grief and distress, when there seems to be nothing left, there comes a fresh insight, something new happens. I see things as I have never seen them before – he is there and he is with me, and he calls me by name. It is life-changing, but I cannot hold on to that wonderful moment. I must move on and, above all, I have a responsibility to share this revelation with other people. That is what he has asked me to do, because this isn't just for me, it's for everyone!

† *Lord Jesus Christ, give me such a powerful sense of your presence with me that I must tell everyone I meet that you are alive.*

Tuesday March 29   2 Kings 4:25–37

TIME TO ACT, NOT TO TALK   Things could not be worse. The unspeakable has happened and her hopes and dreams, once so high, are now completely dashed. This is beyond words and there is one person who may, just may, be able to help. Don't talk, just get him ... hurry! And Elisha too gets the command: 'Run!'

'Run to meet her and ask her, "Are you all right? Is your husband all right? Is your child all right?"' 'Everything *is* all right,' she said. (verse 26, our italics)

The perceptive pastor in Elisha recognised immediately that something was terribly wrong; the faith within the woman knew that now things would be all right. The presence of God in the situation was the deciding factor. And in this story the longed-for child is brought back to life through the decisive action of his mother and the man of God. Centuries later, through the active obedience of another mother and the love of God for God's world (*John 3:16*), all God's children will be offered new life through the death and rising of another child. (But we need, like Elisha, to be pastorally sensitive to those whose overwhelming grief at loss may blind them for a while to this truth.)

† *Saviour of the world, give me the grace to convey the sense of hope which your rising from death offers.*

Wednesday March 30   Luke 15:11–24

HE MIGHT AS WELL BE DEAD! After all we had done for him, he took what he could get and went off, leaving his brother to run the farm. We were devastated. We hear rumours of what he's up to, of course, and we don't like what we hear, so we say nothing. He's dead as far as we are concerned, really.

'This son of mine was dead and is alive again; he was lost and is found.' (part of verse 24)

He had hurt them, taken his inheritance, left – yet when he appears on the horizon, his father runs to embrace him and to welcome him back to his place in the family. Ready to forgive and restore, he does not wait for the words of repentance – his reaction is immediate and spontaneous and nothing is too much. This Forgiving Father is both an icon (image) of the heavenly Father who so loved us that he gave his only Son, and a model for Christian practice. We are deeply challenged, because the calculating reaction of the older son may come more naturally to us. However, the Resurrection teaches the profound truth that 'love conquers all' and that really is something to sing about!

† *Risen Lord Jesus, enable me to love those around me with your unreserved, accepting love.*

WHAT? EVERYONE? If something is available to everyone, then what's so special about it for me? I mean, who wants to be with the common crowd? It's better to be doing your own thing!

'Everyone who calls on the name of the Lord will be saved.'
(verse 13)

This is the tremendous all-inclusive message of Easter. The cynic who wants to be different is missing the point – this is about being part of the family of God, saved and redeemed by his Son. But belonging is not automatic: the offer needs actively to be accepted by each individual, by everyone. God, who has given his only Son, makes the offer of everlasting life through him, but I must trust (*verse 11*) and call on him (*verse 13*) to become part of that redeemed community. And there's another thing – we can't choose who else may respond. This is for all, even those we thought were outsiders altogether (*verse 12*), and that may be the most difficult thing to accept. God welcomes those who differ in their religious expression, in language, culture, skin colour, politics – you name it! The challenge for me is to acknowledge that my 'Gentile' is as welcomed by my Heavenly Father as I am.

† *Father in heaven, may I accept your offer of salvation – and accept those who accept it with me.*

WELL, I SUPPOSE WE'D BETTER DO SOMETHING It's better than doing nothing; at least you feel useful! It's a good way of stopping thinking too much, especially when you need to concentrate on what you're doing. Sometimes thinking is too painful to bear, so let's go fishing!

As soon as Simon Peter heard him say, 'It is the Lord,' he
wrapped his outer garment around him ... and jumped.
(part of verse7)

'The fishing did not go well, and it was maddening to have someone call from the lakeshore asking how we were getting on and telling us what to do! But hadn't he done this before on the same lake, with the same result? That time he had told me I was to fish for men (*Luke 5:4–11*). And now he had a meal prepared for us – and hadn't he done that before too? There could be no doubt about who was standing there in the early morning light. But faith requires that jump into the icy waters of doubt – and I had gone into the water before and nearly drowned (*Matthew 14:29–30*)! This time was different, I was ready to do anything to be right with him, to let him know how much I loved him ... I jumped!'

✝ *Loving Lord, keep me as faithful to you as you are to me.*

Saturday April 2 John 21:19b-25

CURIOSITY KILLED THE CAT Or so the proverb says! I sympathise with the cat – it is always interesting to find out what other people are up to, what they are being asked to do. Are they getting a better deal than we are, more prestige, a higher profile?

> **'If I want him to remain alive until I return, what is that to you? You must follow me.'** (part of verse 22)

Having denied Jesus three times, Peter has had the opportunity to re-affirm his love three times. His has been a tumultuous journey to faith and now he is in personal and intimate conversation with his Lord. Has he learned his lesson? Not quite! Not content with the commission to care for the lambs and sheep – the little ones and the mature ones – in the things of the faith and to exercise a personal discipleship, he wants to know about someone else, the one who had first recognised who it was on the lakeshore. It is tempting to look at someone else and see how he or she is doing; perhaps it deflects attention from our own discipleship, perhaps it is jealousy. Jesus wants none of this – our task, as it was Peter's, is to follow him, and no one else!

✝ *Lord, you have called me to follow you; keep me faithful to your calling.*

For group discussion and personal thought

● What difference does it make to my life to know that 'he is risen'?
● How best may I/we help those whose life experience tells them that death is the end of everything?

EASTER FOR ALL 2
Women with Easter tidings

Notes by Helen Van Koevering

based on the New Revised Standard Version

Helen and her husband are once again serving the Anglican Diocese of Niassa in northern Mozambique. They lived there before as missionaries for 10 years but spent the last 6 years in the UK, while Helen studied for ordination and then worked with the Diocese of Monmouth as World Mission Officer and curate in a housing estate in Newport, South Wales. They have three children.

Sometimes, the gospel message can seem so well-known to us and so well-rehearsed in our churches that we can be surprised by finding insights in new places. To be surprised by stories of faith is a joy and an opportunity to reflect afresh on our own stories and journeys. This week's readings draw our attention to some of the less well-known people of the Bible – women of faith, who point us towards remembering, seeing, hearing and living out our faith in the Easter news of life in Jesus Christ, the Son of God.

Text for the week: Luke 24:8

Sunday April 3   **Luke 24:1–11**

REMEMBERING HIS WORDS

Then they remembered his words, and returning from the tomb, they told all this to the eleven and to all the rest. Now it was Mary Magdalene, Joanna, Mary the mother of James, and the other women with them who told this to the apostles. But these words seemed to them an idle tale, and they did not believe them.   (verses 8–11)

Ours is a remembering faith. The Christian faith does not ask us to rely on what we feel and understand today, or just provide us with an ideology of what we must strive towards for the future. It is a faith based on our openness to the remembrance of Jesus – who he was and is, what he did and said – and what we have come to know of him in the journey of our lives. At the heart of our worship is the eucharistic celebration of the remembrance of Jesus, who came, died and rose again for us. The women who went to the tomb opened their hearts to the news of the Risen Christ and were made ready by their remembrance of what had been said, made ready to receive the word of resurrection for their lives. These women are examples for us of an openness to receive the life God constantly offers. It is this kind of opening up which is at the heart of the Easter story for us all.

✝ *God of the Resurrection, open me and hold me in the remembrance of your Word, the One who died and rose again, that I may live for you. Amen*

Monday April 4   Exodus 1:15–17

CHOOSING LIFE

The Hebrew midwives, one of whom was named Shiphrah and the other Puah ... feared God; they did not do as the king of Egypt commanded them, but they let the boys live. (parts of verses 15 and 17)

The ordinary people, the ones working at the margins, are not usually the named ones of history. It is the names of the strong and powerful that we are most often led to believe are the history-makers. Yet here, by naming Shiphrah and Puah, the midwives who chose to preserve life, they are honoured for their quiet stand against the power of such a one as the unnamed king of Egypt. Here, in today's reading, we are provided with a glimpse of the life God offers us with the Easter event. In choosing life, the God-fearing midwives let the boys live; in giving us the choice of life, God let his own Son die. In making our choices, we are known for who we are; when we choose life, God can be known for who he is.

✝ *Lord, I choose life, and I choose your life, today and tomorrow. Help me make these choices. Amen*

Tuesday April 5   1 Peter 3:1–4

BEING BEAUTIFUL

Let your adornment be the inner self with the lasting beauty of a gentle and quiet spirit, which is very precious in God's sight. (verse 4)

A testimony acted out through conduct is common in the New Testament, and today's verses provide us with the examples of the wives whom Peter is addressing. Peter encourages us to be pure and reverent towards God as these wives were, to allow these qualities to characterise the lives of all Christians. This advice is personalised by being asked to contrast outward adornment with the good deeds centred in the heart. Whatever the fashion, whatever the age, whatever the gender, the stillness and sincerity of a heart focused on a living relationship with God remains eternally beautiful and attractive. This 'heart' is who a person really is – it is the wellspring of the beauty of a Christian. It is the heart that God sees, the heart where God lives, and it is this humility of Christians that is the imitation of Christ in our lives. To accept the imitation of Christ with humility and reverence, gentleness and quietness, is to offer ourselves as living prayers to our God, who loves us.

† *Lord, help me to be open to your beauty and your presence, whatever the circumstances and situation, whoever I am with, wherever I am. Amen*

Wednesday April 6   1 Samuel 25:23–35

MAKING PEACE

David said to Abigail, 'Blessed be the LORD, the God of Israel, who sent you to meet me today! Blessed be your good sense, and blessed be you, who have kept me today from blood-guilt and from avenging myself by my own hand!'   **(verses 32–33)**

Yesterday, we read of a beauty in quietness. Today, we read of a beauty in speaking out. Abigail is the perfect heroine of any young child's imagination and story. Here she is, wise, sensible and beautiful, able to speak peace to an angry David so that bloodshed is avoided, reputations kept clean, and a better future kept in mind. The issues of peace and war so often seem to be in black and white, but wisdom and dialogue can prevent so much and add the colour and humanity to the picture which are so necessary to keep peace. Courage, and knowing when and how to speak, can open situations and people to the blessing of God, the blessing we know so often passes all understanding. Let us learn from Abigail, and take courage to speak for peace in the places where we find ourselves.

† *Give me courage and wisdom, Lord, to speak with words of peace, so that your world may know your peace. Amen*

Thursday April 7 1 Timothy 5:16

DOING GOOD

> **If any believing woman has relatives who are really widows, let her assist them; let the church not be burdened, so that it can assist those who are real widows. (verse 16)**

Doing good has a lot to do with being responsible. A few years ago, I was invited to represent a charity working with the Anglican church in Angola. Angola was still at war and Luanda, the capital, was overflowing with makeshift houses for the displaced. In every church, I met Mothers' Union groups, many of whom were widows. In one very poor church, I was asked to bless the offering of the MU, a washing-up bowl full of money. I was told that it would go to the poorest and neediest widows and orphans, the ones the MU visited and helped. I was humbled to tears, but also reminded of the millions in the world who really have nothing except a dependence on God. These are Timothy's 'real widows', the ones the church has a responsibility to support. What good are we truly doing if we don't help these?

† *Lord, melt my heart to see the real need around me, the real need of real people, and help me to get involved and make a difference. Amen*

Friday April 8 Joshua 6:22–25

INCLUDING OTHERS

> **'Go into the prostitute's house, and bring the woman out of it and all who belong to her, as you swore to her.' ... Her family has lived in Israel ever since. For she hid the messengers whom Joshua sent to spy out Jericho.**
> **(parts of verses 22 and 25)**

The prostitute Rahab and her extended family become part of Israel, the first recorded example of what seems to have been a quite frequent practice; Ruth is another example. The original Israelites were defined by kinship or shared experience, but Rahab (like Ruth) was included for her covenant-keeping loyalty, her solidarity with the experience of Israel. It was not her background, however bad (or, in the case of Ruth, however good) that defined her any more, but her inclusion and belonging with the people of God. This is what we can learn from Rahab's story today. Who do we include in our churches, in our fellowship? How do we judge a character – by the past, or by the present and future? Our covenant-keeping God chooses us and loves us out of our covenant-breaking lives. Let's choose to do the same for each other.

† *Jesus, your heart reaches out to the excluded of our world. Show us ways in which we can include and share your life with others, and heal our separations from one another and from you. Amen*

Saturday April 9   John 4:28–29

BEING A MISSIONARY

Then the woman left her water jar and went back to the city. She said to the people, 'Come and see a man who told me everything I have ever done! He cannot be the Messiah, can he?' (verses 28–29)

The Samaritan woman at the well has as much to teach people who live in rural, poorly resourced areas of our world as she does those who live in richly provided urban areas. Firstly, she meets with Jesus, the Son of God, as she is, at the place of her basic human need for water, alone and at midday. And she discusses questions of faith face to face with the one who is the Way, the Truth and the Life. This relationship, and her response to it, are for us all. In a way that echoes the calling of the disciples, this Samaritan woman shows herself to be the missionary that we should all be after we have met with Christ. She goes to others and invites them to see what she has seen, know what she has known, and learn more. God makes her the world's first missionary, an example to all those throughout the world who have met with the Living One.

† *Thank you, Lord, for the privilege of knowing you, and for the work you have left with us, with me. Help me to live your life with and for others. Amen*

For group discussion and personal thought

● Think of a significant Christian woman in your own life. Share with someone else what she taught you about God.
● How have the women in this week's readings created for you a personal image of the Easter life?
● From which of the women in these readings have you had to learn most?

EASTER FOR ALL 3
Young people living the Easter message

Notes by Chris Duffett

based on the New International Version

Chris Duffett is an evangelist based at Hoole Baptist Church in Chester. He works for The Light Project, a charity which aims to demonstrate the Christian message in a relevant way and to train others in evangelism. He is married to Ruth and has two children.

The message of Easter is not meant to be just another nice story with a happy ending. The stories written by the four evangelists have a purpose. Each writer recounts the death and resurrection of Jesus in the hope that their readers will share the impact that the risen Christ has made upon them. The Easter story is intended to transform the lives of those who read or hear it. Everyone who hears that Jesus is raised from the dead can have an experience of him. I have found that the best way to tell someone what I believe is by the way I live. If people cannot see Jesus' life in my life, then words alone will be ineffective in communicating the good news. D L Moody, the great hymn-writer, is reported to have said that one in a hundred people will read the Bible, ninety-nine will read the Christian. Each young person in our Bible readings this week met with the living God. Their lives were distinctive and those who watched them were able to say that 'the Lord (or someone like a son of the gods) was with them' (see *1 Samuel 3:19* and *Daniel 3:25*).

Text for the week: 1 Timothy 4:12

Sunday April 10   **1 Samuel 3:1–21**

SHUSH! The boy Samuel shows us that it takes time to learn the knack of hearing God's voice; God called his name three times before he knew what to do.

> **The LORD came and stood there, calling as at the other times, 'Samuel! Samuel!' Then Samuel said, 'Speak, for your servant is listening.' And the LORD said to Samuel:**

'See, I am about to do something in Israel that will make the ears of everyone who hears of it tingle.'   (verses 10–11)

There are three lessons in hearing God revealed by the story of the young Samuel. Firstly, God wants to communicate with his people. Prayer is not a one-way street. We need to be ready for God to speak to us, possibly in an audible voice like Samuel, but also through the Bible and through others. Secondly, Samuel shows us that we need to be quiet and still for the Lord to communicate with us. Psalm 46:10 says, 'Be still and know that I am God; I will be exalted among the nations, I will be exalted in the earth.' Thirdly, Samuel shows us that God doesn't limit his communication to people of a particular age. It doesn't matter how old or young you are, God wants to communicate with you!

✝ *Speak to me, Lord, for I want to hear you.*
Speak to me, for I need you.
Speak to me, because I want to do what you want of me.
Speak, as your servant is listening... Amen

Monday April 11   **1 Samuel 17:33–50**

'GO, AND THE LORD WILL BE WITH YOU'   It is in the going that we encounter the presence of God. Soon after Jesus' great commission to the disciples at the end of Mark's gospel, we read that Jesus was 'working with them' (*Mark 16:20*). But many of us have not yet experienced Jesus working with us. The great commission has sometimes rather jokingly been referred to as the great 'omission'. Many people find the prospect of speaking to others about their faith daunting. When preaching in different churches I often ask for a show of hands of those who find evangelism easy. Invariably only one or two people give me a wave! However, the knowledge that Jesus is with us can make the experience of evangelism less difficult. David was faced with a life and death issue, yet was confident of the company of God:

David said to the Philistine, 'You come against me with sword and spear and javelin, but I come against you in the name of the LORD **Almighty, the God of the armies of Israel, whom you have defied.'**   **(verse 45)**

The young David challenges us not to be people who are frightened by the very prospect of sharing our faith, but as we go out to others we should allow the presence and power of

Jesus to be with us. As a challenge for today, tell someone about what you believe; I guarantee you will have the feeling of not being alone!

† *Help me, Jesus, to know that you are with me.*
Help me to know that you will never leave me.
Help me to know that when I declare you, you are right there with me.
Thank you, Lord Jesus, for your wonderful presence and company with me. Amen

Tuesday April 12   Genesis 24:12–28

GOD OF THE DETAIL   The servant in today's story was anxious to fulfil his oath to Abraham and find a suitable wife for Isaac. His desperation could have turned into anticipation if he had believed that God delights to work in the small and big details of our lives. After a string of coincidences, the servant was able to say,

'Praise be to the LORD, the God of my master Abraham, who has not abandoned his kindness and faithfulness to my master. As for me, the LORD has led me on the journey to the house of my master's relatives.'   (verse 27)

Relationship with God is a twenty-four hour, seven days a week union with him. God led the servant on the journey; he also wants to lead us on our journeys, day in and day out. An awful and often prevalent attitude in the church is the separation of the sacred and the secular: God is only involved in church activities, rather than in the world and our day-to-day activities. However, the young man in the story shows us that God is involved in all things, not just a few select activities.

† *God of the detail, help me to know that you are very interested in all my life, including where I go today, who I will meet and the challenges that are set before me. Thank you that you are with me now and you will be with me throughout today. In your wonderful name, Amen*

Wednesday April 13   2 Kings 5:1–15

GOSSIPING THE GOSPEL, IN GOOD TIMES AND BAD Despite being snatched from her family and home, a kidnapped slave girl in her dreadful circumstances sought to share what she knew about the power of God.

Now bands from Aram had gone out and taken captive a young girl from Israel, and she served Naaman's wife. She said to her mistress, 'If only my master would see the prophet who is in Samaria! He would cure him of his leprosy.' (verses 2–3)

The extraordinary sequence of events that happened afterwards was due to the captured slave girl uttering nineteen words. Naaman was eventually healed and in verse 15 he says, 'Now I know that there is no God in all the world except in Israel.' He had come face to face with the reality of God and his terminal disease was cured. The words we share with others have great influence and often great potential for those who listen; like Naaman, people may act upon them. In 2 Timothy 4:2, Paul inspires Timothy to 'preach the word; be prepared in season and out of season'. This isn't a call for all Christians to speak the gospel in inappropriate moments, but for us all to be willing to share the gospel both when we feel like it, and when we don't! How will you open your mouth and share Jesus today?

† *My gracious Master and my God,*
assist me to proclaim
and spread through all the earth abroad
the honours of thy name. (Charles Wesley, 1707–88)

Thursday April 14 Jeremiah 1:6–10

THE BAD EXCUSE What stops you from helping others, serving in your local church or demonstrating the good news of Jesus? Jeremiah's defence for not being used by God was his age; however, God didn't seem to worry about that:

'Do not say, "I am only a child." You must go to everyone I send you to and say whatever I command you. Do not be afraid of them, for I am with you and will rescue you,' declares the LORD. (part of verse 7 and verse 8)

Do you think that you have an excuse for not being used by God? Think about the main characters in the Bible: many of them could have given God a good excuse for not using them. Noah got drunk, Abraham was too old, Isaac was a daydreamer, Jacob was a liar, Moses couldn't talk, Gideon was afraid, Samson was a womaniser, Rahab was a prostitute, David had an affair and was a murderer, Elijah suffered with depression, Jonah ran away from God, Peter denied Christ, the disciples fell asleep while praying, Mary Magdalene was demon-possessed, and the Samaritan woman had had five husbands! But yet God used all of them for his purposes. There is no apology from our past or present that will stop God using us, and, like Jeremiah, if we are willing God will put his words into our mouths (*Jeremiah 1:9*).

✝ *Here I am, for you, to be used by you, in any way, anywhere and anyhow. Amen*

Friday April 15   **Daniel 3:13–30**

'STAND UP, STAND UP FOR JESUS!' The three young Jewish men faced being baked in an oven if they persisted in honouring God amongst a whole city of people who did not believe. They chose the oven. What happened next? Today's reading narrates the amazing results of Shadrach, Meshach and Abednego standing up for God:

> **So Shadrach, Meshach and Abednego came out of the fire, and the satraps, prefects, governors and royal advisers crowded around them. They saw that the fire had not harmed their bodies, nor was a hair of their heads singed; their robes were not scorched, and there was no smell of fire on them.** **(part of verse 26 and verse 27)**

The three young men were willing to die for their faith; they believed that dying would be better than denying their God. Dietrich Bonhoeffer, who died for his faith, said, 'When Christ calls a man he bids him come and die.' Rachel Scott and Cassie Bernell were two of the students killed at Columbine High School in 1999. Both were committed Christians who expressed their willingness to suffer and die with Christ because they had experienced the joy of his resurrection life. Young people as well as old can witness to the power – and the cost – of the resurrection. Today's prayer was written by Cassie.

✝ *Now I have given up on everything else. I have found it to be the only way to really know Christ and to experience the mighty power that brought him back to life again, and to find out what it means to suffer and to die with him. So, whatever it takes I will be one who lives in the fresh newness of life of those who are alive from the dead. Amen*

LOOK AT ME! God's goal for your life is that you will increasingly become like Jesus. In today's reading Paul shows us that one of the best ways of doing this is by watching and then emulating others. Timothy had learned how to live the Christian life through the example of Paul. Now it was his turn to be an example to the people around him:

> **Don't let anyone look down on you because you are young, but set an example for the believers in speech, in life, in love, in faith and in purity ... Be diligent in these matters; give yourself wholly to them, so that everyone may see your progress. Watch your life and doctrine closely. Persevere in them, because if you do, you will save both yourself and your hearers.**   **(verses 12 and 15–16)**

Think of someone you know that you can emulate. It will need to be someone who is an example to you – perhaps your church leader. However, it may be someone younger than you, like Timothy. Here are some questions which I find it useful to consider when deciding to emulate someone in order to become more like Jesus; you might like to use them as well. How do they handle worry and stress? How do they deal with 'difficult' people? How do they spend their money? Their time? How do they learn more about God – do they have favourite books or patterns of Bible reading that I could try? What events in their life have taught them most about God? No matter how old we are, or what experience we have had, we can always learn more about being like Jesus.

† *Father God, thank you for sending your precious Son.*
Father God, thank you for giving him for me.
Father God, thank you that you want me to grow.
Father God, thank you that each day I can become more and more like Jesus. Amen

---

For group discussion and personal thought

● Where in your life could you create an opportunity to tell someone what you believe?
● Is God calling you to do something specific for him which you have made an excuse not to do?
● Would you be willing to lay down your life for Jesus?

EASTER FOR ALL 4
Can men believe the Easter news?

Notes by John Holder

based on the Revised Standard Version

John Holder was born in Barbados and for several years was deputy principal of Codrington College, the Anglican theological college for the province of the West Indies. He is now the Anglican Bishop of Barbados, and is married with one son.

Can men believe the Easter news? The evidence of this week's readings might suggest the answer 'No'! The male disciples certainly show much more resistance to belief in the resurrection than Mary Magdalene and the other women. But they get there in the end, and it may be the very slowness of their journey which results in well-laid foundations and deep roots for their subsequent life of faith.

Text for the week: John 20:29

Sunday April 17   **Mark 16:9–14**

THE ESSENTIAL JOURNEY   This final episode in Mark's gospel is brim-full of life and hope. Like the other Easter stories, it begins early in the morning on the first day of the week. New light ushering in a new day repels the darkness with its haunting stories of pain, death and a cold tomb. The episode has a personal dimension to it. We meet people who are struggling out of the darkness into new light, moving from doubt to faith. There are Mary Magdalene, the two disciples and the eleven. It is Mary, however, who reaches the point of conviction. She experiences the Risen Lord in a way that no one else has. Indeed, verse 9 tells us she was the first to do so, and this may reflect an element of female intuition that can very often lead women to see and even experience things in a way that men cannot. It is yet another case of the priority given to women in the Easter stories. Mary shares her story but is met by the men's refusal to believe:

She went and told those who had been with him, as they mourned and wept. But when they heard that he was alive

and had been seen by her, they would not believe it.
(verses 10–11)

However, this obstacle, like others, is finally overcome and at last the eleven have their Easter experience. There is movement from doubt to faith. The new-found faith is not simply a story to be told, it has to be transformed into missionary action. Those who experience this blessing of light and life are to share it with others; the Risen Lord issues the command: 'Go into all the world and preach the gospel to the whole creation' (*verse 15*).

The movement from doubt and darkness to faith and light is a journey we are called to make at several points in our lives. A faith-shattering experience, like the sudden and unexpected death of a loved one, can be a great challenge to make this essential journey – a journey we make sustained by the power of God. Let us rededicate ourselves to be an experience of light and hope for others.

† *Give us grace, O Lord, to go and share the faith.*

Monday April 18   **1 Corinthians 15:1–11**

A LAUNCHING PAD TO HOPE   This well-known passage is Paul's personal testimony. We cannot enter into it completely but there is no doubt that Paul did experience a transformation which made him into the great apostle he became. He describes himself as someone who was unworthy of such an experience of the risen Lord:

> **Last of all, as to one untimely born, he appeared also to me. For I am the least of the apostles, unfit to be called an apostle, because I persecuted the church of God.**   **(verses 8–9)**

Just as he is not afraid to confess his unworthiness, so he is humble enough to admit that any achievements of his are only through the grace of God (*verse 10*). Paul's confession reminds us that our belief in the resurrection of our Lord should take us beyond mere words into action. Resurrection is transformation. The transformation is not only of our lives, but of other lives through our work and witness. Paul is honest about the obstacles we may encounter, but emphasises that we are not alone in the struggle. God is with him and with us. The confession of the faith is like a launching pad to move on and do great Christian things. We can begin by telling of our experiences of the Risen Lord and we move on like Paul to guide others to these experiences through simple acts of love and compassion that can dispel doubt and fear and engender hope. Be a source of hope for someone today. Think of someone who may be struggling with a problem that they are not handling too well. Be their experience of the Risen Lord.

† *O God of resurrection hope, let me be a source of this hope for someone today.*

Tuesday April 19   Mark 8:31–34

BEARING THE CROSS TOGETHER   At the centre of the Christian faith stands the cross. We have attached several layers of theology to this symbol of one of the crudest forms of capital punishment, and this can transform the cross into a symbol of sentimentality, far removed from how Jesus saw it. In today's passage Jesus spells out for his disciples the consequences of his ministry. He had taught, healed, helped, admonished, but also offended. His message and actions often went against the traditional accepted view. He was not afraid to pay the price for his convictions, the consequences of his message, which could be death; this was what his heavenly father wanted him to do. Saint Mark tells us in our passage that he shared all this with his disciples. But Peter was not convinced and Jesus had to pull him up sharply and make him face reality:

And Peter took him, and began to rebuke him ... [Jesus] rebuked Peter, and said, 'Get behind me, Satan! For you are not on the side of God, but of men.' (parts of verses 32 and 33)

For Peter it probably did not make sense that someone kind, gentle, loving and generous, who had dedicated his life to God, should be abused and killed. God should protect those who work for him. We can all side with Peter here. But our Lord adds another dimension to the discussion. His retort emphasises the point that his ministry, and indeed a life lived for God, carried painful consequences that Peter could not and should not ignore. We cannot ignore the consequences of our ministry as Christians. We may be tempted like Peter and pretend that all will go smoothly. We would all like to live our Christian lives free of the hurdles that will appear as we stand up in the name of our Lord for what is right and just. But there will be a cost, symbolised by the cross. How well are you bearing your cross at this time in your life? With the grace of God we can do so. His grace will always be sufficient for us.

† *O Lord, give me grace to bear my cross and to help others to do the same.*

STEPPING OUT IN FAITH   This passage identifies some of the heroes of faith that stand as models for Christians. They are heroes because they followed the path to God even when the way ahead seemed unclear. Abraham is the supreme model:

> **By faith Abraham obeyed when he was called to go out to a place which he was to receive as an inheritance; and he went out, not knowing where he was to go.   (verse 8)**

He is a model because of his belief that God could sort out what seemed a very uncertain future. Faith leads us to conclude that what is unclear for us is surely not the same for God. This passage reminds us that we walk by faith rather than by sight. This is not simply pious Christian talk but a realistic understanding of life in general and the Christian life in particular. As Christians we do not need to fear the future but acknowledge our total dependence on God, the one who controls the present and determines the future. But this is not an easy path to walk. We would all like to know every detail of the future, as the continuing attraction of horoscopes indicates. The future can often be a source of fear and uncertainty; walking by faith is not walking in the dark or going on a blind date, but rather living out the conviction that God is in charge of time and history and we can rest assured of his grace and goodness. Faith can work miracles and produce life where there seems to be a forecast of death (*verse 12*). There may be an experience of death in our lives that can only be transformed into an experience of life through steps of faith. Take that step like Abraham. There will be life waiting for you at the end of the journey.

† *O God, grant us faith to follow where you lead.*

CONFESSING THE FAITH   In this passage Paul offers his defence against the accusation that he is a threat to the law and order so treasured by the Roman empire. Paul's convictions and his teachings as a Christian ran counter to much of the official Roman religion. He proclaimed Jesus rather than the Roman emperor as his Lord and God. The price was arrest and trial. Here Paul is doing far more than giving a speech in his defence. He is also confessing his faith in Jesus as Lord. He recalls his Damascus experience (*verses 12–14*) and tells of his encounter with the one whose servant he is and whose gospel he preaches. In this encounter with Rome, Paul also tells of his mission, which is :

> 'to open their eyes, that they may turn from darkness to light and from the power of Satan to God, that they may receive forgiveness of sins and a place among those who are sanctified by faith in [Jesus].' (verse 18)

Here Paul moves beyond his personal conversion and focuses on what God wants him to do for him. His conversion was not about making him a better person but about strengthening the mission of bringing others to confess Jesus as their Lord. But even in his defence which becomes a confession, Paul is still on a mission to convert. He shares his faith and hope that others, even governor Agrippa, will respond and be converted to Christianity. This reminds us that as Christians we are always on the job. We must keep sharing the faith and, like Paul, use every opportunity to help others to understand our belief in Jesus as Lord. Some will hear and remain unmoved. But others will hear and be touched by our confession. Confessing the faith is not simply about words, but about displaying those Christian qualities that can make a great difference in any life. When last did you confess the faith?

† *Grant me the courage, O God, to share the faith today.*

Friday April 22   Luke 24:36–43

This story comes after the encounter of two disciples with the risen Lord on their way to the village of Emmaus. It is another appearance story that is used to emphasise that God has conquered death through Jesus our Lord. Again, it happens in the context of a meal; it is in sharing and fellowship that the resurrection is experienced. But the disciples, after all the previous encounters with the risen Christ, are still initially 'startled and frightened, and supposed that they saw a spirit' (*verse 37*). But there are words of assurance:

> **And he said to them, 'Why are you troubled, and why do questionings rise in your hearts?'** (verse 38)

The faith of the disciples is stretched to breaking point, so Jesus reassures them of his reality by asking for something as ordinary as food. Their experiences of their risen Lord have not been figments of their imagination. In our crises of faith we need the assurance that God is still alive and available. If you know someone who is going through a crisis, can you bring to them the assurance that Jesus brought to the doubtful disciples by reminding them of God's eternal presence and care?

✝ *Help me, O God, to be like my risen Lord and respond in love to those who have lost their faith.*

Saturday April 23   John 20:24–29

BELIEVING WITHOUT SEEING   Walking by faith rather than by sight is never an easy task, as Thomas knows very well. All the confessions of his fellow disciples cannot move him from the realm of doubt to that of faith. He is adamant. He will only move on if there is irrefutable proof (*verse 25*). Like Thomas, we can become stuck at this point in our journey of faith, scared to make the leap that will lead us to a better understanding of God. But this is the journey that we are called as Christians to make in this life. It is a journey of faith rather than sight – which runs completely contrary to our modern world's insistence on evidence and proof. The journey of faith is not easy in such a world. It can be an uphill task to hold on to the belief that God is present and in control when the experiences of life may seem to suggest the very opposite. By the grace of God Thomas moves beyond this point. He confesses 'My Lord and my God' after he has seen the evidence. But the Christian journey of faith is primarily about trust, not evidence:

> **Jesus said to him, 'Have you believed because you have seen me? Blessed are those who have not seen and yet believe.'**   **(verse 29)**

There can never be irrefutable proof of God's presence, but this does not mean that his presence is not with us. Yes, like Thomas we shall have our doubts, but these cannot sever the link we have with God through Jesus our Lord.

✝ *Strengthen my faith, O Lord, when I am besieged by doubt.*

For group discussion and personal thought

● The men in the gospels take some convincing about the reality of the resurrection; today in many parts of the world, men are in a minority in the church. Do men find it more difficult to believe in the good news of Easter than women? If so, why do you think this might be?

REMEMBERING 1
God remembers...

Notes by Marcel V Macelaru

based on the New Revised Standard Version

Marcel V Macelaru is a Romanian evangelical preacher and teacher of the Bible. At the time of writing (2004) he is living in Oxford, England, where he is studying the Old Testament. He is also a visiting lecturer at the Evangelical Theological Seminary in Osijek, Croatia, and at Elim Evangelical Theological Seminary, Timisoara, Romania.

Most of us connect remembering with the universal human experience of forgetfulness. Therefore, the very notion that God also remembers, which is the theme of this week's reflections, must come as a startling idea. Theologians used to speak of God as being omnipotent, meaning: all-powerful; omnipresent, meaning: present everywhere; and omniscient, meaning: knowing everything at all times. In this light, why would God need to remember anything? If he never forgets, and all knowledge is ever before him, how is it then that the Bible portrays him as a God who remembers? The readings chosen for this week are informative in this sense.

Text for the week: Leviticus 26:43–45

Sunday April 24   **Genesis 9:1–17**

THE PARADOX OF 'GOD REMEMBERS'

> **'I will remember my covenant that is between me and you...'** (part of verse 15)

The idea that God remembers is the centrepiece of today's reading and it points to God's grace. In the midst of divine wrath and judgement of sin, there is remembrance – a wonderful expression of divine mercy that brings hope and provides for the future through the establishment of a covenant. This passage also gives us some insight into the things that God considers important to remember. These are Noah's obedience and faithfulness on the one hand, and God's covenantal promises on the other hand. Today, in a similar way, God remembers us, and this gives us assurance in the cataclysms we experience. In the midst of destruction and judgement, when everything seems to fall apart, God remembers; and because he remembers, there is hope for each one of us.

✝ *Thank you, Lord, for your grace and for the hope you bring in our lives. Please remember us in the midst of our cataclysms.*

Monday April 25   Genesis 17:1–22

A CHAIN OF MEMORY

'I will establish my covenant between me and you, and your offspring after you throughout their generations.'
(part of verse 7)

Christian living has been described in many different ways throughout the years. For instance, some have compared it with a journey, and others have described it as a fight. Here, however, Christian life can be seen as a chain in which each link represents yet another memory, or act of divine remembrance. Today's reading introduces to us exactly such a picture. The covenant God made with Abraham, and his promise to bless Abraham's offspring on the basis of this covenant, are shown in the Bible to continue from generation to generation; and what ensures this continuity is the fact that God remembers his covenantal promises again and again. As Christians, we share in the blessings brought about by this chain of divine remembrance. Together with those before us and those that will follow after us, we are beneficiaries of God's covenantal love and of every promise that accompanies it.

✝ *I praise you, Lord, and I thank you for making me a beneficiary of your love and of all the promises you have made.*

Tuesday April 26   Genesis 30:22–24

REMEMBERING AS DEED

Then God remembered Rachel, and God heeded her and opened her womb.   **(verse 22)**

When God remembers, gracious things happen in the world! This is the amazing message of the story of Rachel. Indeed, both humans and God remember. However, unlike human beings, God's way of remembering is not reduced to a simple memory exercise; rather, it always involves acting on behalf of and for the good of those remembered. In Rachel's case, God's 'deed of remembrance' meant that the barren woman gave birth to a child. In our case, God's deed of remembrance may mean restored relationships, health, financial recovery and/or provision for any other need we may have. Nothing is impossible when God remembers.

† *Heavenly Father, thank you for your concern for every detail of my life. Remember me, Lord, and act on my behalf according to your grace and according to my needs.*

Wednesday April 27   Exodus 2:23–25
WHEN GOD REMEMBERS (1)

God heard their groaning, and God remembered his covenant with Abraham, Isaac, and Jacob.   (verse 24)

The values upheld as normative in our societies today usually allow for the remembrance only of the powerful and the highly productive. Today's reading, however, reveals different values. God chooses to remember the weak, the poor and the suffering. The persecuted Israelite slaves were probably the lowest and humblest group in Egypt at that time. Yet it is exactly these people that God hears crying, remembers who they are, and takes notice of. For us, this reading brings a twofold message. On the one hand, this is a message of hope – regardless of how little valued and how forgotten people may be within their community, God will not devalue or forget them. He will hear, remember and take notice of even the least among us. On the other hand, this reading is a challenge for each one of us to reconsider our values and the criteria according to which we relate to and value others.

† *Heavenly Father, we recognise that the way in which we have related to others has been wrongly influenced by the standards of our contemporary world. May we be influenced by the example you set before us and begin to notice the unnoticeable.*

Thursday April 28   Exodus 3:7–17
WHEN GOD REMEMBERS (2)

Then the LORD said, 'I have observed the misery of my people who are in Egypt; I have heard their cry on account of their taskmasters. Indeed, I know their sufferings, and I

have come down to deliver them from the Egyptians.'
(verse 7 and part of verse 8)

Divine deliverance is always connected to divine remembrance. The cry of the Israelites prompts God to remember the past and his covenantal promises; and when God remembers, the present and the future are acted upon in light of the recollection of this past. Thus, divine remembrance turns out to be a powerful experience for the ones remembered. Also, observe that 'coming down' is God's initiative. The Israelites do not do, and cannot do, anything to persuade God to act. Their only cry is one of anguish on account of their persecutors. God is the one who decides to 'come down' and rescue them from Egyptian slavery. This gracious divine initiative is the same today. In the midst of our misery and pain, when we can only cry in anguish, God will come down once again to rescue us and give us the hope of a new beginning.

† *Lord, in our moments of anguish, when nothing is left but a cry, we trust that you will deliver us from all evil.*

Friday April 29   **Leviticus 26:40–45**

A TIME TO REMEMBER

[I]f then their uncircumcised heart is humbled and they make amends for their iniquity, then will I remember my covenant with Jacob; I will remember also my covenant with Isaac and also my covenant with Abraham, and I will remember the land.   (part of verse 41, and verse 42)

The reading today reveals a conditional aspect to divine remembrance – it occurs where there is repentance and humility. Today, this message is of utmost importance. We live in times when pride and self-sufficiency have made talk about sin and repentance an unwelcome subject. We do not like to feel remorse and are not used to taking full responsibility for our evil doings. However, if our land – meaning our families, our cities, our countries, and even our world – is to be healed, our attitudes have to change. We need to become truthful to ourselves and to others, we need to acknowledge and unmask the wickedness in our lives, and we need to turn our back on old ways of life and embrace honesty and humility. Then God will remember the land!

† *Lord, we have sinned against you and against our fellow men. We have lived proudly and uncaringly. Forgive us, Lord, and heal our land.*

Saturday April 30   Ezekiel 16:59–63

AN EVERLASTING COVENANT

I will establish my covenant with you, and you shall know that I am the LORD.'   **(verse 62)**

Observe the form of this promise. The emphasis is not on our memory, which is fickle and frail, but upon God's memory, which is infinite and immutable. It is not us remembering God, but God remembering us that is the ground for safety; it is not us laying hold of his covenant, but him laying hold on us on account of his covenant that is the basis for freedom and knowledge of God as Lord. So even the remembrance of the covenant, which means salvation and deliverance for us, is not left to our memories. It is God's doing and God's remembering. It is God establishing his covenant. Hence, this is an everlasting covenant, a secure salvation, and an assured deliverance for each one of us.

† *Lord God, thank you for establishing my deliverance on your memory, not on mine.*

For group discussion and personal thought

● What is 'divine remembrance'?
● What does God remember?
● Whom does God remember?
● What happens when God remembers?
● Are there any conditions to God's remembrance? When will God act to heal our lands?

REMEMBERING 2
Memories are made of this...

Notes by Sister Christopher Godden OSB

based on the New International Version

Sister Christopher Godden is an enclosed Benedictine nun living in the suburbs of Chester. She is an ordinary sort of person and is content to seek God within community life under the Rule of Saint Benedict.

Most weekends, for a short period after our midday meal, my community gather together for recreation. Apart from our services in chapel, meals in the refectory and the occasional community meeting, this is the only time we are all together as a monastic family. News and notices are given out. So are sweets. We relax together. Often the conversation will turn to the past and memories will emerge. Our oldest sisters will regale us with tales of 'how things used to be' and events they can remember from long ago. This is important. It helps in the bonding of our group of individuals, and gives us a sense of community identity. Sometimes drawing on history helps us with present-day life or even hope for the future. And what is true for a monastic family and its individuals is true for everyone everywhere.

Text for the week: Psalm 95:1

Sunday May 1   **1 Corinthians 11:23–32**

THE WRONG MEMORY

Therefore, whoever eats the bread or drinks the cup of the Lord in an unworthy manner will be guilty of sinning against the body and blood of the Lord.   (verse 27)

The trouble was, the Corinthians were focusing on and emphasising the wrong part of the memory. Saint Paul had spent 18 turbulent months with them (*Acts 18:11*) but as time went on after his departure things began to slip. The church in Corinth would have consisted of one or more small house groups, not a large group in a purpose-built hall. Surrounded by pagans indifferent to the new Christian way of life, who probably still worshipped their gods with the bacchanalian type of feast described, it would have been hard going for these new Christians, who were possibly mocked and ridiculed for their 'new faith'. How would we have done? Following his tirade (*verses 11–17*) Paul emphasises the heart of his teaching. We do not remember just words of preaching and teaching, we remember a person, Jesus, the Son of God, who actually came and lived on earth. Knowing how it is to be human, just before a painful, shameful and humiliating death he gave us an act to perform by which to remember him and the meaning of what he stood for. Living as I do in a monastery with a daily celebration of the Eucharist, I especially need to take note of what Saint Paul says next (*verses 27–32*). It is all too easy to come to the Lord's table unprepared or distracted by the worries and concerns of everyday life. Thank God there is then something and someone we can remember, which brings our lives back into focus.

† *Lord, you renew us at your table with the bread of life. May this food strengthen us in love and help us to serve you in each other.*
(Collect from the Weekday Missal, week 22)

Monday May 2   **Luke 22:14–20**

MAKING A MEMORY

When the hour came, Jesus and his apostles reclined at the table.   **(verse 14)**

Have you ever read a book or watched a film and become so engrossed that you felt you were present as the story unfolded? Saint Luke may never have visited the Holy Land at all and he would not have been present at the Last Supper, yet by the time he wrote his gospel these happenings had become so real to him that he wrote as if he had witnessed the event itself. His gospel and the Acts of the Apostles are both addressed primarily to Theophilus, 'Lover of God' (*Luke 1:3* and *Acts 1:1*), so his unknown disciple already had some knowledge of scripture. Perhaps it was this that made Saint Luke unique among the gospel writers in referring to two cups of blessing. The first could refer to the Jewish Feast of Passover, part of the Old Covenant which was soon to be finished. The second refers to the New Covenant soon to be brought into being, although not completed, by Jesus' death. And Saint Luke sees this 'hinge' moment of the ending of the Old and beginning of the New Covenants as central to his portrayal of the Last Supper. Traditionally, covenants were ratified by the spilling of blood. In biblical times blood was understood to contain the life of a living being and belonged only to God. The New Covenant would be ratified in the same way – except that this time the blood of the sacrifice belonged to both God and man. 'Take up your cross and follow me,' Jesus invites in Luke 9:23. We are lucky. We know the end of the story. Jesus didn't. But he had faith in God and a love for humanity that not only made him see his Passion through to the end but also prompted him to give us a way of renewing and refreshing ourselves as we remember him and try to follow in his steps.

† *Lord, we thank you for the nourishment you give us through your holy gift. Pour out your Spirit upon us and in the strength of this food from heaven keep us single-minded in your service.*

(Collect from the Weekday Missal, week 32)

Tuesday May 3   **Psalm 95:1–11**

SHAMEFUL MEMORY

**Today, if you hear his voice,
do not harden your hearts as you did at Meribah.**
(part of verses 7 and 8)

Today's psalm has two distinct parts: a joyful hymn of praise, and the reminder and warning of a shameful memory. What went wrong at Meribah? After the events leading up to the Exodus, (*Exodus 7:1 – 11:10*), the miracle of the Red Sea (*Exodus 14:15–31*), the miracle of water at Marah (*Exodus 15:22–25*), the provision of manna and quails to eat (*Exodus 16:1–26*) – after all that, when the Israelites arrived at Meribah and found no water, did they turn to Yahweh with trust in the providence he had shown them before? No, they did not. Instead, they turned on Moses and each other and began to grumble and grouse. Just how much more was Yahweh expected to do for them before the lessons he was teaching them finally sank in? He was there guarding, guiding and teaching them. To remind them of his continued presence there was a cloud going before them by day and a pillar of fire at night (*Exodus 13:21–22*). Did the wonders and the lessons he had given them mean nothing? Sometimes a display of anger is the only way a message can sink in. Pulled up short, shocked out of ourselves, there's a chance we might see beyond our small expectations. And the shame felt when the realisation dawns that we are in the wrong can engrave itself on the memory in such a way that a lesson is finally learned. Worship is about praising God; it is also about remembering and thanking him for all he has done and hopefully will do for us in the future, providing we remember to ask.

✝ *Lord, help us when the grumbles start, both our own and others'.*
Let us turn to you in faith when things do not turn out as we
expect. Open our eyes to see your answers and give us grace and
faith to accept them.

Wednesday May 4   Isaiah 49:14–16
HOPE FOR THE FUTURE

I will not forget you!   (part of verse 15)

In today's reading Isaiah speaks to the exiles of Jerusalem, once
their pride and joy but now in ruins and desolate. He has the city
speak, lamenting her fall: 'the Lord has forsaken me, the Lord has
forgotten me' (*verse 14*). This powerful symbol speaks to all for
whom life has taken a downswing and God seems far away, if he is
there at all. How can God, the creator and giver of life, forget what
he has made? He cannot. He remembers us even when we forget
him. This was perhaps the most important lesson for the exiles to
learn. Everything that has life carries within it a part of God. Closer
to us than even our mothers when we were born, God cannot
abandon or forget us. Only we can deliberately turn from him and
even then he will not go away. Beautiful though the words and
image of this passage are, they cannot explain fully how God can
and does care for his creation. Words, like ourselves and like
Jerusalem with her city walls, have limits. God has no limit or end.
When prayers seem to go unanswered, when things go wrong and
keep going wrong, when we feel abandoned or forsaken, there is a
lesson to remember from these two verses. The words may not
solve anything but they do remind us we are not alone. Ever.

✝ *Lord God of light and life, we remember today all for whom the*
way is dark and lonely. We pray for all who live as exiles or
refugees and are separated from their families, friends and homes.

Thursday May 5 (Ascension Day)   Acts 1:6–11
STOPPED IN THEIR TRACKS

'Men of Galilee,' they said, 'why do you stand here looking
into the sky?'   (part of verse 11)

Was the Ascension expected then? Probably not. The Apostles had
known, seen and been with Jesus when he was alive, preaching,
teaching and healing: they knew he had been crucified, they had
seen him on more than one occasion since the resurrection,
although his appearances do seem to have been a bit unpredictable.

Also, they were slow on the uptake with much of what was being taught them, so it is hardly surprising they were rooted to the spot, left gazing skywards, as Jesus ascended. A sudden shock can have a paralysing effect on both body and mind and a second jolt is often needed to get us going again. For the Apostles it was the 'two men dressed in white' (*verse 10*). (Were they the same as those mentioned at the empty tomb in Luke 24:4?) As the Apostles walked back to Jerusalem I wonder what they said – or were they silent? Once back at their lodgings we are told they prayed (*verse 14*). Probably they also spoke and discussed amongst themselves, rehearsing again all that they could remember since they first met and followed Jesus. It must have been puzzling, exciting, disturbing and not a little frightening when viewed in retrospect. Good for the prayer-life, as we say! Often we can only learn a lesson by looking back and trying to remember. Then, by replaying and occasionally pausing and stopping the memory tapes of the mind to look deeper, we can see what at the time we were too caught up in events to see. Maybe see things from a different and better perspective. And maybe at the same time see a possible way ahead.

† *Lord God, who travels behind, before and within us, give us the grace to look for you in each event of the day. Help us to move forever onwards until your kingdom comes.*

Friday May 6   Luke 24:13–32

LONG SIGHT/SHORT SIGHT

Then their eyes were opened and they recognised him, and he disappeared from their sight.   (verse 31)

Every member of my community wears glasses. Some of us are long-sighted, some short-sighted, others something else. We all have defective vision and do not see things clearly or correctly without help. The two disciples on the road to Emmaus were also having problems with seeing things correctly. They still misunderstood the true nature of the kingdom of God (*verse 21*). The shock, horror and pain of the crucifixion had ruined their hopes and, despite the fact they had heard of the resurrection (*verses 22–24*), they decided to move away from Jerusalem and put distance between the pain and themselves. But there was another way of looking at the events and another way of remembering and interpreting them. This they are given by the stranger who joins them along the way and walks with them. As the distance from Jerusalem increases, their pain and confusion decrease, until they see things in true perspective.

Eyes 'opened', they understand and finally recognise Jesus as he breaks bread with them. We see with our minds as well as with our eyes. Sometimes our minds need correcting just as much as the lenses in our spectacles correct our eyesight.

† *Lord Jesus, just because I see things one way does not mean I hold all the truth. Help me to be open to the attitude and way others have of seeing the same thing, so that together we shall all find the truth.*

Saturday May 7   Mark 14:3–9

NEVER THE SAME AGAIN

She broke the jar and poured the perfume on his head.
(part of verse 3)

Life was hard in the early church. Persecution was rife, imprisonment a real possibility, torture probable. Yet still people were coming and inquiring about the new faith, the Christian Way. Saint Mark does not go in for lengthy explanations in his gospel; he does not tell his readers or hearers what to think, or justify his words with quotations from the Old Testament. He deals in facts. (I once read that his gospel could be described as 'being written on postcards – short and to the point'.) And he leaves his readers or hearers to form their own conclusions or judgements. The Messiah had long been expected to 'free' the Jewish people from oppression, but was this Jesus, son of the carpenter, the one? Messiah means 'Anointed One'. In today's passage we hear of the anointing of Jesus. No grand ceremonial occasion fit for a king, no pomp and circumstance. A simple, quiet act of love. Misinterpreted by many present. Big things in life can happen in small, quiet and unexpected ways, yet afterwards, as we look back and remember, we see their significance. Afterwards, life was never the same for Jesus, a corner had been turned. What did the readers of Mark's gospel eventually decide? Truth or not truth? How do we decide?

† *Lord, at the end of each day, help me to remember all you have done for me, been for me and will be for me.*

For group discussion and personal thought

● Think back to memorable occasions in your life and the life of your church; how did God intervene and what were the results?
● Do we ever learn lessons from the past?
● What is it best to forget?

REMEMBERING 3
Called to remember

Notes by Ngozi Okeke

based on The New Living Translation and New King James Version

Ngozi Okeke is the wife of Ken, the Anglican Bishop of the Diocese on the Niger in the Province of the Niger of the Church of Nigeria. Theologically trained, she has been actively involved in Christian work for over thirty years. Apart from having to travel and support the work of the Bishop, she is also the President of the Women's Ministries in the Diocese. She has four children.

The God whom we love and serve is an ever-present God. He calls us to live in the present where he is and operates, rather than in the past with its mistakes and regrets, or the future with its problems and fears. However, he also wants us to always stop and take stock of the past; to remember his goodness and mercy in past situations because we can learn useful lessons that will enable us to make better use of the present and the future. There is also another kind of remembering that we need to do as God's people. He wants us to remember people – the less privileged in our midst – to care for them and share their burdens. Today marks the beginning of Christian Aid Week and we must share God's concern for the poor and other people on the margins. My prayer is that this week will help us to remember in all sorts of ways and that through this we will realise that we have great cause to be thankful to God for the whole of life in all its ramifications.

Text for the week: Psalm 105:4–5

Sunday May 8   **Galatians 2:9–10**

EAGER TO CARE

> They encouraged us to keep preaching to the Gentiles ... [and] suggested ... that we remember to help the poor, and I have ... been eager to do that.
>
> **(parts of verses 9 and 10 – NLT)**

This injunction is set within the context of the early church's struggle to understand, accept and affirm the ministry of Paul to the Gentiles. It is as if Paul was being asked to show solidarity with the leadership in Jerusalem by sharing the burden of providing for the welfare of their poor. However, with Paul, loving care for the disadvantaged was not a bargaining tool in the struggle for acceptance. This was something he was 'eager to do'. Today, the church still operates in societies where the gap between the rich and the poor is very wide. As we challenge ourselves to meet these physical needs, we must address the more covert spiritual poverty that comes from not knowing and responding to the importance of the death and resurrection of Christ for our eternal destiny. We must help people commit their lives to Christ so they can experience that abundant life he promises (*John 10:10b*), and be assured of a place in eternity hereafter (*John 14:1–3*).

† *Father, thank you that you remembered us in Christ. Help us to remember others in their needs, whatever they are.*

Monday May 9   **Psalm 105:1–5**

SPIRITUAL PUBLICITY CAMPAIGN   What sort of reputation does God have among your friends, neighbours and wider community? Do they know about the wonderful things he has done? Secular institutions spend millions to protect their public image with a well-ordered publicity strategy, to ensure their continued existence, growth and success. Are we as astute in presenting God to the world? This whole psalm encourages us to remember and publicise the goodness of God.

Make known His deeds among the peoples ... talk of His wondrous works ... Remember His works ... His wonders, and the judgements of His mouth. (parts of verses 1, 2 and 5 – NKJV)

We can then go out and tell others through our music (*verse 2*), our retelling of stories of God's goodness in our lives (*verse 2*) and our worship (*verse 3*). We must also do this by living lives of integrity which will convince others of the credibility of the faith we profess and share. Remembering and recounting will achieve two things. First, through such witness we shall enable others to respond to God in commitment; and second, it will inspire gratitude in us, greater loyalty to God, joy for today and hope for the future.

† *Father, we thank you that you are faithful and consistent in your goodness, love and care for your children. Help us to share this truth with others, to enable them to come to know you personally.*

Tuesday May 10   **Exodus 20:8**

TIME OUT   How to spend Sunday has exercised both Christians and trade unionists alike, though for different reasons. Today's passage has been quoted by some sections of the Christian community in support of their belief that we should not work on Sundays. Observing the Sabbath is one of the few spiritual disciplines specifically commanded in scripture. God said:

Remember the Sabbath day to keep it holy. (verse 8 – NKJV)

Why? God decreed the Sabbath to be a day of rest for all sections of the community (*Exodus 20:9–11*), as well as a holy day set apart for worship. Rest is an important ingredient for spiritual renewal and is linked to effective worship, which is the primary means of refreshing the soul. Through worship, we meet with the living Christ and are released from the grip of worldliness. We become available to God and, in return, he blesses us with his presence, purposes and power. That experience of God will enable our lives to exhibit the characteristics outlined in the rest of the Ten Commandments. Consequently, we will be effective ambassadors for Christ to our world.

† *Father, thank you because you cared enough about our spiritual and physical wellbeing to decree rest from our labours. May we learn the benefits of rest in our relationships with you and others.*

Wednesday May 11   **Joshua 1:12–18**

PROMISES, PROMISES   How often do we make promises when we are in tight corners, only to renege on them when things improve? In my experience, students especially seek God's help with their exams in return for more spirituality and commitment on their part. However, many go back on their word as soon as they get their results. Joshua, however, would not allow the tribes of Reuben, Gad and Manasseh to forget the promise they made to Moses.

You shall pass before your brethren armed ... and help them, until the NKJV has given your brethren rest ... Then you shall return to your possession and enjoy it.   (parts of verses 14 and15 – NKJV)

This instruction was given on the basis of the promise they had made to Moses when they received their inheritance (*Numbers 32:20–28*). They could so easily have reneged on it, resulting in internal conflict or discouragement among the people. Ecclesiastes 5:4–7 warns us to think before we make promises, because failure to keep them will offend God and militate against our wellbeing. Therefore, as Christians we must be watchful to remember our promises and keep them, as failure to do so may have far-reaching consequences for us and others.

† *Lord, teach us always to remember to honour the promises we make, so that we may in truth be children of our heavenly Father.*

Thursday May 12   Isaiah 64:1–9

LORD, REMEMBER MERCY   Crisis has this quality of focusing our minds on things that are truly important. In the passage before us, Israel is again in trouble because of their disobedience. Their cities, including Jerusalem, are in ruins; the Temple, the symbol of God's presence, is destroyed along with all its beautiful things (*verses 10–12*). Their present crisis forced them to stop and think, to look back and remember; to pray with a better understanding of the God they worshipped. They remembered among other things:

That God did awesome things beyond our highest expectations ... And ... the mountains quaked! For since the world began ... no eye has seen a God like you who works for those who wait for Him! (parts of verses 3 and 4 – NLT)

They also remembered that God welcomes 'those who cheerfully do good and follow godly ways' (*verse 5*) and that none of them could be justified in his sight because of their sins, so they pleaded for God to forgive their sins. We do well as Christians to also stop, think and remember. God's previous dealings should increase our faith and our awareness of our need to depend on his grace for the future.

† *Lord, thank you because your mercies are new every morning. Teach us to come to you daily for cleansing and grace to live obedient lives that please you.*

Friday May 13   Colossians 4:15–18

IDENTIFY WITH THOSE WHO SUFFER

Remember my chains.   **(part of verse 18 – NKJV)**

Christians suffer for their faith through persecution, or the very harsh conditions in which they serve. One-third of our Diocese, which still needs primary evangelism, is very difficult to access for much of the year and the living conditions for the workers are dire, as there are no basic amenities. When the Bishop arrived in his new diocese, he declared the place a mission area, so that the church would remember the plight of those who have to work there. Now he can pour in centrally-provided resources to improve the living conditions, mobility and general welfare of the workers. We also show support through visits to encourage and affirm the work they are doing. Other Christians, like the Apostle Paul, daily suffer physical inconvenience, imprisonment, torture and death for the sake of the gospel in our world. We must pray for them and, where possible, act to change the situation. We must show through our love and care an appreciation of the sacrifices they make.

† *Father, we thank you because your Son made the ultimate sacrifice to redeem us from sin. Help us to remember and care for those who suffer much personal inconvenience as they seek to share that good news. Bless and preserve those also who suffer and die for believing it.*

Saturday May 14   **Revelation 2:1–7**

FIRST LOVE   The Bible likens our relationship with Christ to that of a husband and wife. Just as marriage as an institution is under great stress, the church is going through a bad patch. The problem is largely the same – we forget what the relationship was like at the beginning. We begin to take it for granted, and before too long it begins to unravel at the seams. There is an air of normality, but all is not well. Part of the Spirit's message to the Ephesian church was:

I know your works, your labour, your patience ... You have persevered ... and have laboured for My name's sake ... Nevertheless ... you have left your first love. Remember ... from where you have fallen, repent.   (parts of verses 2, 3 and 4 – NKJV)

They served God whole-heartedly, rejecting evil people and false apostles, but they had left their first love. The Lord counselled them to discover where the slide in affection started. We too can be guilty of losing that love which originally motivated our service. We seek to be faithful to the Lord, but he reminds us here that faithfulness is no substitute for passion.

† *Father, help us to understand that you have made us primarily for fellowship, not service. Help us to maintain our relationship with you as the basis of our service to you.*

For group discussion and personal thought

● Does your church have an effective welfare scheme that cares for the poor among you?
● Do you remember to pray for and, if possible, care for Christians persecuted for their faith?
● How fresh is your love for the Master you serve?

FRUIT OF THE SPIRIT 1
Love

Notes by Gloria Barrett-Sobers

based on the Revised Standard Version

Gloria Barrett-Sobers lives in Kingston, Jamaica. An active Methodist who gives leadership in her home church, Providence Methodist Church, she spent the academic year 1999–2000 in retreat at the College of the Ascension, Selly Oak. She is now back at the University of the West Indies where she is Director of Administration and University Registrar.

The Greek word for fruit, *karpos*, is used in the singular in Galatians 5:22. The NEB translates it as 'the harvest of the Spirit', conveying a certain unity in the graces listed. Each fruit is an aspect of the character of Christ and reinforces the others. All cohere to form a composite outcome. This week's focus is on love: humble, gentle, patient, kind love whose most excellent way and whose centrality in the Christian life and character are stressed in the readings from 1 Corinthians 13. As we read we should understand more clearly that love, rather than being the soppy, sentimental, self-gratifying emotion often portrayed in novels and the movies, is an active, practical and impactful grace without which none of the others makes any sense.

Text for the week: 1 Corinthians 13:4

Sunday May 15   **Galatians 5:22–23**

THE FRUIT OF THE SPIRIT   The six attributes of a godly, Spirit-filled life, though many, are referred to as the 'fruit' of the Spirit, in the singular. This suggests a single outcome. We do not choose one as the fruit we will bear as against the others, for none makes sense without the others. If you are loving, kind and patient, you will know and reflect joy and peace. The exercise of self-control will reveal itself in gentleness and faithfulness. The fruits are many yet the fruit of the Spirit is one, intimately bound together in love. Read the verse aloud and as you mention each fruit reflect on how it is evidenced in your life and whether you can afford to be without it.

But the fruit of the Spirit is love, joy, peace, patience, kindness, goodness, faithfulness, gentleness, self-control; against such there is no law. **(verse 22)**

† *Holy Spirit of God, come dwell in me, work on the soil of my heart and make it produce a good harvest so that by my fruits I can be known to be your child and collaborator.*

Monday May 16   **1 Corinthians 13:1–3**

THE MORE EXCELLENT WAY   John Wesley referred to love as the highest gift of God – 'all visions, revelations, manifestations whatever, are little things compared to love; all the gifts mentioned above are either the same with or infinitely inferior to it. There is nothing higher in religion.' The Bible reading is uncompromising in its pronouncement.

> **And if I have prophetic powers, and understand all mysteries and all knowledge, and if I have all faith, so as to remove mountains, but have not love, I am nothing.**   **(verse 2)**

The faith which moves mountains, the supreme price of martyrdom, prophetic powers: none of these can match the impact of love unless they are based on and accompanied by love. Note that God, who first reaches out to us in love, becomes the source of our love. The sign of the presence of God's love in our hearts is that we love others. The world has had to recognise and celebrate this more excellent way in, for example, the life and leadership of Nelson Mandela. Not only has he graciously forgiven but he has been prepared to accept his erstwhile enemies as partners in building a better South Africa and a better world. May we earnestly seek the fruit of love.

† *Teach us the lessons of love so well, Spirit of God, that this more excellent way becomes as natural to us as breathing and eating.*

Tuesday May 17   **1 Corinthians 13:4 -7**

LOVE IS PATIENT AND KIND   These verses clearly outline the behaviours which reflect love and those which do not. Patience, kindness, forbearance, trust, hope and endurance are the evidence of love. On the other hand, love does not co-exist with arrogance, boastfulness and rudeness, selfishness and jealousy or joy at others' plights or the triumph of evil. Gentleness and courtesy have been replaced by crudeness and a lack of civility in my own country, even as violence and crime have become a serious threat to our society and our economy. We have perhaps missed the connection made in this passage between love and some simple, ordinary civil behaviours like common courtesy.

Love does not insist on its own way; it is not irritable or resentful. (part of verse 5)

Preparing these readings has been a blessing for me as I have been reminded that my own irritability sometimes in dealing with my noisy, energetic young grandchildren belies my love for them, which I strongly proclaim in their less boisterous moments. I have to pray specifically for patience, kindness and endurance. Maybe as you read this passage again, you may recognise which of these characteristics of love you need to work on. Perhaps you have no difficulty being patient and kind but just can't seem to help jealous and resentful reactions towards your partner, your colleagues at work or even your church brother or sister who seems to gain the love and respect of the fellowship. Let the Spirit have his way in you.

† *Holy Spirit of God, take charge of the garden of my heart and make it fruitful with love. Let patience, kindness, gentleness and forbearance come to me as naturally and easily as they do for you. Erase all arrogance, irritability, jealousy and resentment, so that I can reflect your love to all.*

Wednesday May 18   1 Corinthians 13:8–13

LOVE NEVER ENDS   If ever we need a modern-day example of the faithful, unending, covenant-love of God for the loveless as demonstrated in Jesus, we would do well to consider the life and witness of Mother Teresa of Calcutta. In much the same way that God gives his love unreservedly to all humankind, so this remarkable woman embodied the love of God as she took abandoned babies out of dustbins and loved them back to life. For her, every single person was of infinite value. Mother Teresa spoke with authenticity when she affirmed that 'Love is a fruit that is in season at all times, and within reach of every hand. Anyone may gather it and no limit is set.'

Love never ends. (part of verse 8)

How transformed our world would be if each of us who professed Christianity and claimed the indwelling of the Spirit reflected this fruit of unending mother-love to all, however poor, however unlovely. If we really believe and love 'because he first loved us' (*1 John 4:19*), we too could change the world for the people who cross our paths, even if we do not, like Mother Teresa, launch religious orders to serve the poor.

† *Holy Spirit of God, teach us to reach out in love to everyone whom you send into our lives today.*

Thursday May 19   **Luke 6:27–36**

LOVE YOUR ENEMIES   Does Jesus really expect us to love our enemies? The uncompromising answer to that question rings out in verse 27. Jesus then goes on to give practical ways in which we must show this love. If someone strikes you on one cheek, offer him the other as well; do not hesitate to give your shirt to the person who steals your coat. What tough instructions! But the principle is summed up in the golden rule he articulates:

> **And as you wish that men would do to you, do so to them.**
> **(verse 31)**

In 1965 Dr Martin Luther King, preaching at the Valedictory Service of the University of the West Indies, reminded us that 'Somewhere along the way we must be willing to meet hate with love, and to meet physical force with soul force, recognising that an old "eye for an eye" philosophy ultimately leaves everybody blind.' Responding to the difficulty of loving those people who were bombing their homes and churches, he explained that 'Love is understanding, creative, redemptive goodwill for all men and it is the kind of love which causes you to look at that man and say, "He is misguided. He was taught this way."' Can we work on loving our enemies today?

† *Holy Spirit of God, only you can work the seemingly impossible feat of helping me to love my enemies, those who do me wrong and those whom I find difficult to love. Help me today, Lord, to seek out occasions to show love for any such person with whom I deal or work.*

Friday May 20   **2 Corinthians 6:3–7a**

GENUINE LOVE   It is often easier to substitute nice-sounding words for difficult actions. This passage speaks to love as a sacrificial commitment which will ensure that we put no obstacle in anyone's way. What does this commitment entail?

> **As servants of God we commend ourselves in every way:**
> **through great endurance, in afflictions, hardships,**
> **calamities, beatings, imprisonments, tumults, labours,**
> **watching, hunger.** **(verses 4–5)**

Paul knew what he was talking about. He had undergone all the sacrifices listed here, including imprisonment, for the sake of the gospel and out of love for those whom he sought to bring to Christ. Do we really have to go so far today? We have so often compromised on our commitment that the real demands of genuine love seem unreasonable and unrealistic. But Paul is adamant that this is what genuine love demands – purity, forbearance, truthful speech and the power of God.

† *Lord, help me to be unswerving from the sacrificial commitments which genuine love demands. You did not shrink from the ultimate sacrifice for me. Strengthen my resolve and my love.*

Saturday May 21   Ephesians 5:25–33

LOVE IN EVIDENCE Over the past few days we have confronted the nature and demands of love. Nowhere is love put more keenly to the test than in the marriage covenant. This is no doubt why Paul uses it as the analogy for the love between Christ and his church. As Christ gave himself up for the church, husbands are called upon not to be self-serving (*verse 25*) but unselfish and generous (*verse 28*). Wives are called upon to be holy and pure and to offer respect to their husbands (*verses 27, 33*). There should be no betrayal of trust (*verses 27–28*). Daily care and loving actions should be the evidence of love (*verse 29*). There can be no love without commitment (*verse 31*).

Even so husbands should love their wives as their own bodies. He who loves his wife loves himself. For no man ever hates his own flesh, but nourishes and cherishes it, as Christ does the church, because we are members of his body. (verses 28–30)

If each of us brought to the marriage relationship the gentle, patient, kind, courteous, respectful love referred to in 1 Corinthians 13 and the selfless, caring actions referred to in this passage, what a difference it would make to our homes and marriages and, of course, to the church and its witness.

† *Holy Spirit, thank you for the inspiration and revelation on love which you have shared with us this week. Help us now to put these things into practice and give evidence of your love in us.*

For group discussion and personal thought

● Identify two or three well-known world figures who have exemplified love in their lives and reflect on what they did and how they came to achieve these things. Can we emulate them?
● Is love really the most powerful force in all the world? Why then do not more of us practise it to the fullest?

FRUIT OF THE SPIRIT 2
Joy

Notes by Philip Wadham

based on the New Revised Standard Version

The Revd Canon Philip Wadham is a Regional Mission Co-ordinator for the Anglican Church of Canada. He travels regularly in Latin America and the Caribbean. He recently spent 4 months living in the West Indies, the setting for this week's reflections.

A correcting word – Paul contrasts 'the works of the flesh' (*Galatians 5:19–21*) with 'the fruit of the Spirit' (*verse 22*). Does that mean our bodies are bad? No. As the first creation story affirms, 'God saw everything that he had made, and indeed, it was very good' (*Genesis 1:31*). It is true that we regularly betray this goodness and fall into sin (*Genesis 3*). Yet our bodies are the temple of God's Spirit, a channel of God's love to his creation. We should always try to use them as such.

Text for the week: Isaiah 35:1–2a

Sunday May 22   **Galatians 5:22–23**

LUCINDA'S GARDEN   In the heart of the small island of Saint Vincent in the Caribbean is Mesopotamia. The name is appropriate: it is a rich fertile region. Lucinda lives there. Now 75 and a widow, she still lives in the home where she and her husband began their life together. Her large garden has a wide variety of fruit trees and fruit fills her kitchen.

The fruit of the Spirit is love, joy, peace, patience, kindness, generosity, faithfulness, gentleness, and self-control.(verse 22)

Lucinda's home has a constant stream of visitors throughout the day. Some come seeking advice, others need comforting, the majority come just to spend some time with her. 'How come, Lucinda, when I leave here I feel better than when I came in?' asks a neighbour. 'I don't know,' admits Lucinda, 'perhaps after all these years the good soil has got into me and you get a bit of it when you're here.' Jesus knew the value of good soil. Recall the story of the farmer sowing seeds. The seed that fell into good soil bore much fruit (*Matthew 13:1–9*). Lucinda knew the story very well and could recite it by heart. More important was the fact that she lived out the truth of the story, and it showed.

✝ *Holy Spirit, live in me that I may bear good fruit.*

Monday May 23   **Isaiah 12**

RORY'S CELEBRATION   Rory made sure that he arrived on time for the lunch-hour meeting, because today was an important anniversary. So different to five years ago when his constant rum drinking had meant that arriving on time, or even arriving at all, had been of no consequence to him. Only the rum bottle demanded his attention. The stern words of a Christian neighbour helped him see his problem. 'Can't you see, man,' he had said, 'you're a captive to the drink and it is going to kill you.'

> **Surely God is my salvation;**
> **I will trust, and will not be afraid,**
> **for the LORD GOD is my strength and my might;**
> **he has become my salvation.**   **(verse 2)**

His first lunchtime meeting at Alcoholics Anonymous had been difficult. To his surprise he saw the same neighbour across the table from him. As people were invited to tell their stories of addiction his neighbour shared his. It was a story as painful as Rory's. Now, 5 years later, it is a time to give thanks. Thanks for the presence of God in his journey to healing (salvation). Thanks also for a good friend, a neighbour who walks the same journey as Rory. It is a time to rejoice.

✝ *God of liberation, free us from all that prevents us from joyfully living for you.*

Tuesday May 24   **Isaiah 35**

JOHN'S PAPAYA   'They told me I was wasting my time, that nothing would grow here. "The soil is shallow and too poor." But come and see this.' That's John speaking, a seminary teacher living in Barbados. He takes me to his garden where a young papaya tree is growing in a car tyre. 'Place a tyre on its side, fill the centre with whatever soil there is, plant the seed, keep it watered and fed and watch it grow.' John had watched it grow for the last ten months and now the first fruits were ripe.

> **The wilderness and the dry land shall be glad,**
> **the desert shall rejoice and blossom;**

like the crocus it shall blossom abundantly,
and rejoice with joy and singing ...
Then the eyes of the blind shall be opened,
and the ears of the deaf unstopped;
then the lame shall leap like a deer,
and the tongue of the speechless sing for joy.

(verses 1–2 and 5–6a)

I asked whether we would be eating the ripe papaya for breakfast. 'No, later,' said John. 'First I'm taking it to teach my students an Old Testament principle. God's people believed that though things looked unpromising, with God's help and their labour good things could happen. We need to believe the same, and work for it.'

† *God of hope, open our eyes to your possibilities and use our hands to work for them, that we may share your joy in good things happening.*

Wednesday May 25   Luke 10:17–20

FLORENCE'S DISPUTE   She had not been to church for two months now, but why should she return when the priest had been so offensive? 'If he wants to change the service that's up to him, but don't let him think I support him,' Florence had complained to Charlene, also a member of Saint George's. That week Charlene talked with the Reverend Hastings. He was sympathetic but said that he couldn't go back on the decision agreed by the church council. 'At least go and see Florence and explain,' Charlene pleaded.

The seventy returned with joy, saying, 'Lord, in your name even the demons submit to us!' ... [Jesus said] 'Nevertheless, do not rejoice at this, that the spirits submit to you, but rejoice that your names are written in heaven.'

(verses 17 and 20)

Some days later Charlene saw Florence at her market stall. She was smiling and humming a tune. She saw Charlene. 'I had a visit from Father Hastings last night. We talked for a while and I promised I would see him on Sunday, at church.' 'Good, so you like the new service now!' 'No, but at least he came to visit and have tea.' As she walked away Charlene recalled the tune that Florence was again humming: it was from the new service.

† *God of reconciliation, help us to defeat the demons that seek to divide your people and to know the joy of unity.*

NATHAN'S DILEMMA Nathan's work unloading and loading cargo boats docked at Saint Vincent satisfied him. His wages provided for his family, though there was little to spare. It was the constant mocking from one of his workmates that troubled him. 'Do you really believe all that stuff about Jesus, about dying, rising and going to heaven?' At first Nathan had tried to defend his beliefs but he learned that his tormenter was not interested in discussion. He simply enjoyed provoking him, so now Nathan remained silent when goaded.

> **Repentance and forgiveness of sins is to be proclaimed in [Jesus'] name to all nations ... You are witnesses of these things ... And [Jesus' close friends] worshipped him, and returned to Jerusalem with great joy.**
>
> **(parts of verses 47, 48 and 52)**

Talking at work with a Christian friend, Nathan confessed that the taunting annoyed him, yet he felt that staying silent was a poor witness. 'I don't think responding will make any difference,' said his friend. 'But let me tell you, I see you at work. You are honest, you are considerate of others, they share their problems with you because you listen and care what's happening. It seems to me that's a fine witness to what you believe.' Nathan thought about this, and smiled inside.

† *Lord Jesus, risen Saviour, when I find it difficult to talk about you let my actions and my joy speak for me.*

BESSIE'S GIFT Dinah had always loved going to visit her grandmother. It was because she always felt so welcome there, Great-grandma Bessie hugging her, showing Dinah her 'special things' and telling her stories. She was sad when Great-grandma could no longer walk very well, even sadder when she had to stay in bed. 'Not to worry,' said Great-grandma. 'You can be my legs now. Bring me those "special things" and we'll look at them together.' In some ways those times with Great-grandma had been the best of all.

> **May [you] lead lives worthy of the Lord ... May you be made strong with all the strength that comes from his glorious power, and may you be prepared to endure everything with patience, while joyfully giving thanks to the Father.   (part of verse 10, verse 11 and part of verse 12)**

Dinah had cried a lot when her mother told her the news, and now at the funeral she was crying again. The priest talked about Bessie being 'a faithful minister of God'. She wasn't sure what that meant. Great-grandma took her to church when she was small but she never heard her preach. Though there were all those stories about Jesus and the coloured pictures in Great-grandma's Bible – now the most important of Dinah's 'special things'.

† *May we be filled with the joyful knowledge of God and live lives worthy of the Lord.*

Saturday May 28   **Luke 15:3–10**

JASON'S RETURN   Jason wondered why he had come. He hadn't planned on being there and he could feel the eyes of other people cutting into him like knives. He was tempted to get up and leave, but that would have been to give in to their judgement of him. Of course what he had done was wrong, but he had paid a price for it. Three years locked away in the prison on the hill. Was he now condemned to be locked out of people's lives also? People who were once his friends.

> **'When he has found [the lost sheep] he ... rejoices ... he calls together his friends and his neighbours, saying to them, "Rejoice with me, for I have found my sheep which was lost" ... I tell you, there will be more joy in heaven over one sinner who repents than over ninety-nine righteous persons who need no repentance.'**   **(parts of verses 5–7)**

He endured the service, though when others went forward for communion he stayed at his pew, kneeling. The footsteps of communicants stopped, there was a pause and then solitary footsteps once more. A figure standing next to him, the priest, wafer in his outstretched hand. 'The body of Christ, broken for you', he said. And Jason replied, 'Amen'.

† *Forgiving and including God, help us to forgive as we have been forgiven, and so know the joy of heaven.*

For group discussion and personal thought
● Paul tells us that one of the fruit of the spirit is joy. How do you experience this joy in your life?
● Think of some of the gifts that other Christians have given you. Which of them were given and received with most joy?

FRUIT OF THE SPIRIT 3
Peace, patience

Notes by Selina Samuel

based on the New International Version

Selina Samuel is from India. She is a housewife and a freelance editor.

The theme for this week continues to talk about the fruit of the Spirit, with emphasis on peace and patience. The fruit of the Spirit is the character of the person who lives by the Spirit. It is both something that we 'are' and something that we 'do'. It is from within us. Each of us will express this fruit in different ways and in different measures but all components of the fruit have to be seen as we grow deeper in our relationship with Jesus Christ and receive the help of the indwelling Holy Spirit.

Text for the week: Isaiah 26:3

Sunday May 29   **Galatians 5:22–23**

THE CHARACTER OF THE CHRISTIAN   The apostle Paul talks of the fruit of the Spirit in the other epistles too but Galatians 5:22–23 is the most familiar passage. The fruit of the Spirit is a description of the character traits of people who have the Holy Spirit indwelling them. This list is in total contrast to the list in verse 19 which depicts the character of a sinful person. But when we live by the Spirit we 'will not gratify the desires of the sinful nature' (*verse 16*). On the contrary we have an overflow of 'love, joy, peace, patience, kindness, goodness, faithfulness, gentleness and self-control' (*verses 22–23a*). This fruit is the mark of a life which is the 'new creation' in Jesus Christ. We are called to be free:

Against such things there is no law.   **(verse 23b)**

But that freedom is not a licence to indulge the sinful nature (*verse 13*). Those who belong to Christ Jesus have crucified the sinful nature with its passions and desires (*verse 24*). The fruit of the Spirit is from within; it is a depth of character, not any display of outward miraculous deeds. Christian character or life in the Spirit or the fruit of the Spirit needs nourishment, pruning and a lot of care. We need to allow this process to happen in us and learn to 'be' and 'walk' in the Spirit. We need to learn to keep in step with the Spirit (*verse 25*). It is not automatic. It is the Holy Spirit who makes good fruit or good character come from within us.

✝ *Lord, I pray that you will help me to live by the Spirit and may my character be marked by the outworking and overflowing of the fruit of the Spirit.*

Monday May 30   **Revelation 12:7–12**

REJOICE AND BE AT PEACE BECAUSE GOD IS IN CONTROL

They overcame him
by the blood of the Lamb
and by the word of their testimony.   **(part of verse 11)**

This passage helps us realise that although peace as a fruit of the Spirit is something within us, yet peace is experienced even more completely when wars cease and the heavens rejoice and we know God is in control. Evil is no longer powerful. Satan is not strong and has lost his place in heaven. Satan has been hurled to the ground and overcome by the blood of the Lamb. He can no longer lead people astray. There will be no more temptation. No more hostility and wars. The one who constantly accuses us has been hurled out of heaven. There is a sense of victory and great jubilation. This passage also talks of peace not just because evil is no longer, but also because there is rejoicing in heaven. Peace as a fruit of the Spirit is about being at peace because we know God is in control and because Satan has been defeated.

✝ *Lord, we thank you for the peace that rules in our hearts because we belong to you. We wait, Lord, for the day when we can have this complete peace not only in us but around us too.*

Tuesday May 31   **Ephesians 2:13–18**

NO MORE DIVISIONS AND HOSTILITY

For through him we both have access to the Father by one
Spirit.   **(verse 18)**

If one of the fruits of the spirit is 'peace', it is because the Lord Jesus himself is our peace. On the cross he destroyed hostility. He made access to the Father in heaven possible for all people. He is the reconciler of human beings with God and with each other. He destroyed the hostility between the Jews and the Gentiles. This can be applied to breaking down the barrier of hostility between class, caste, colour and nationalities. No one is superior. We can live in peace with each other because we are all equals in his sight. We all access the Father by the same Spirit. This peace and this sense of equality are only to be found among those for whom the Lord Jesus himself is their peace (*verse 14*). In the world we have too many barriers and too much hostility. But his purpose for the church is to create in himself one body that lives in peace because we access the Father by the one Spirit.

† *Lord Jesus, help me to accept your work on the cross of breaking down all barriers. Help me not to have any hostility in my relationships and to live in peace because you are my peace.*

Wednesday June 1   Isaiah 26:1–4

PERFECT PEACE

> **You will keep in perfect peace**
> **him whose mind is steadfast,**
> **because he trusts in you.**   **(verse 3)**

Perfect peace, a steadfast mind and trusting in God go hand in hand. Steadfast minds come not because we have a lot of self-control but because we trust in the Lord. We place our trust in a God who is the Rock eternal. He is the Lord for ever. It is in thinking and reflecting that we realise that God's work in our midst is to put together a strong city, a nation whose walls are made of salvation and whose inhabitants are the righteous ones. It is a nation that keeps faith. When we belong to such a nation our mind will naturally be focused on the Lord and perfect peace is absolutely possible. This peace is not just because the sounds of war around us have ceased or because there is no more oppression, but because in the midst of all these we put our trust in God. The mind is steadfast because we trust in him. This kind of peace is possible not when we do exercises and meditation but when we put our trust in God, the Rock eternal. The work of God for us is to 'keep' us in perfect peace. He will keep and not allow us to be shaken. This is a peace that the world will not understand and this is not the kind of peace that the world will give. This is his peace and it is perfect.

† *Lord, help me to learn to trust in you and know what it is to have a steadfast mind. May your perfect peace be my portion too.*

Thursday June 2   **1 Thessalonians 5:12–14**

PATIENT WITH EVERYONE 'Patience' is another of the fruit of the Spirit. When our life is marked by love and perfect peace, and the dividing walls of hostility are broken down, patience is another character trait that should naturally develop. This entire epistle is about Paul's love and desire for the Thessalonian church to continue to walk in the Spirit, in faith and in love. He encourages us to respect people, to live in peace with each other, to accept admonition and live in order to please God. As I wrote on Sunday, the fruit of the Spirit is expressed in different measures in each of our lives, and patience is what helps us to accept everyone at their own level. Accepting does not mean we leave them at that level but it means that we urge, encourage and warn each other to work, to respect, to help the weak and encourage the timid to be bold. We respect people and we respect those who work hard and those who admonish us in the Lord. We encourage each other to live in peace.

> **Warn those who are idle, encourage the timid, help the weak, be patient with everyone.**   **(part of verse 14)**

The ability to be patient is the character of the person who lives by the Spirit and is in step with the Spirit.

† *Lord, help me to be patient with all those I meet today and not to expect everyone to be perfect. Help those I come in contact with to be patient with me also.*

Friday June 3   **Luke 13:6–9**

FRUIT, THE EXPRESSION OF THE LIFE WITHIN

> **'Leave it alone for one more year, and I'll dig round it and fertilise it.'**   **(part of verse 8)**

The fruit is the sign of life in a fruit-bearing tree and when that does not happen the tree is a waste of space. The gardener's efforts and time are wasted. A fruit tree has to bear fruit. If we walk by the Spirit, our lives will naturally produce or exhibit or express love, joy, peace, patience, kindness, goodness, faithfulness, gentleness and self-control. If we do not produce fruit or we do not have the character of the Christian, then we need to be cut down. It is a proof that we are not walking in the Spirit, that we do not take seriously the requirements of our life as a Christian. A tree whose roots are not deep and which does not receive any nourishment will not produce fruit and will dry up fast. Read the passage again. The Lord waited for three years to see fruit. He gives us time. He is very patient. He prunes us and gives us the Holy Spirit to indwell us in order to help us. We need to grow deep in our relationship with the Lord. The Word of God is the nourishment. If despite all this we do not bear fruit he has no option but to cut us off.

✝ *Lord, help me to be rooted and grounded in you so that my life may bear much fruit.*

Saturday June 4   Romans 12:14–21

LIVE IN HARMONY AND OVERCOME EVIL WITH GOOD
This passage is full of instructions for a peaceful and positive way of life. Some of the things we do are to bless, to rejoice, to mourn, to live in harmony, to associate with people of low position, to live at peace with everyone, leave room for God's wrath, feed the hungry enemy and satisfy his thirst and overcome evil with good. Some things which we should not do are: curse, be proud, be conceited, repay evil for evil, take revenge and be overcome by evil.

Do not be overcome by evil, but overcome evil with good.
(verse 21)

It is easier to mourn with those who mourn and be at peace with our friends. It is very easy to be angry and curse those who persecute us, and to feel justified and conceited about these feelings. But those who are walking by the Spirit have a totally different agenda for their lives. They bless and take care of the enemy. They are able to rejoice in others' joys and accomplishments. They trust in a just God and so are able to leave room for God's wrath. They are the people who make peace and harmony a possibility in this world. And the root of much of this peace is patience: patient acceptance of what others do to us, patience in the face of extreme provocation, patient putting good into evil situations.

✝ *Lord, help me to overcome evil with good and may my life be a life of patience that builds peace and harmony with everyone and in every situation.*

For group discussion and personal thought

● When do you most experience God's peace in your life?
● Are there any situations in which you could be a peacemaker? How could you set about creating peace?
● What tests your patience? What could you do to nourish the fruit of patience in yourself?

FRUIT OF THE SPIRIT 4
Kindness, generosity

Notes by Elisa Gusmão

based on the New International Version

In a world often described as a global village, Brazil has been, since its discovery in 1500 by the Portuguese, a multicultural and multi-faith society, where people arrived from different continents bringing along their different ways of worshipping God. Elisa Gusmão, for example, is descended from German Lutheran immigrants, Portuguese Catholic farmers and Amerindian natives. She grew up in the Presbyterian Church, where she was a youth leader in the 1950s. For many years, she worked as a language teacher and then as a bilingual Personal Assistant. In 1987 she moved to the UK where she runs her own translation office, serving the United Reformed Church as an elder and lay preacher.

This week is dedicated to two other fruits of the spirit, kindness and generosity. There are so many ways in which these wonderful gifts can be expressed that our notes could never cover them all. We will try to examine some of them. Note that the NIV translates the sixth fruit of the Spirit as 'goodness'; most other translations have 'generosity' and that is the meaning we shall follow here.

Text for the week: 1 Timothy 6:18

Sunday June 5   **Galatians 5:22–23**

GENEROSITY AROUND THE TABLE   As the young bride of a Methodist minister, I lived for a while in a cattle-breeding area in Brazil, where I supplemented our income by working as a language teacher. One of my schools was 16km away from home, so I had to stay there most of the day. Knowing this, the local Methodist minister and his wife told me I was always welcome at their meals. When I showed up at their house, I realised that they normally gave the same invitation to several people, and that there was always a surprising group of different faces around their table every day – the food, in some mysterious way, always being enough for everyone!

But the fruit of the Spirit is ... kindness, goodness.   **(verse 22)**

Today, in a world riddled with economic problems, the generosity I found in that small town seems to be disappearing. Who would still issue an invitation like that? It seems quite understandable that, with food prices as they are, we find it sensible to 'count our potatoes' carefully instead of being too generous in sharing them. Still, something makes me yearn for that generosity. That family made their guests feel at home in a warm and happy place. I remember we used to laugh a lot together! Isn't this what a Christian home is all about?

† *I thank you for all the generous people that have come my way and I promise you, my Lord, to try and share with others the things you generously give me.*

Monday June 6   Romans 2:1–11

KINDNESS LEADS TO TOLERANCE   In this initial part of his letter to the Romans, Paul is telling them that no one is righteous. Later on, he will show them that we are made righteous by faith. In this chapter, he addresses Christian Jews who draw attention to the Gentiles' moral failure. They criticise and condemn acts practised by the Gentiles, although often guilty of the same faults themselves. Paul goes on to show them that God's kindness and generosity should lead them to repentance and tolerance. The letter to the Romans was probably written in AD 56 or 57. Yet it seems we still need its teaching, as we often act in the same way, pointing our finger towards other groups, other people – as if we were the only paragons of virtue and perfection.

> **So when you, a mere man, pass judgement on them and yet do the same things, do you think you will escape God's judgement? Or do you show contempt for the riches of his kindness, tolerance and patience, not realising that God's kindness leads you towards repentance?**   **(verses 3–4)**

In the eyes of our Eternal Father there are no differences between Jews, Gentiles or any other culture. 'For God does not show favouritism', concludes the Apostle (*verse 11*).

† *Dear God, we recognise that before you, all the peoples in the world are equal. Teach us to show the same kindness and lack of prejudice of which the Bible speaks.*

Tuesday June 7   Colossians 3:12–17

KNOWING HOW TO FORGIVE   Forgiveness is at the heart of Christian faith and is the great secret of a lot of the kind, happy people we meet. As human beings, we are always hurting each other – no matter how much we try not to do it. The resulting resentment often sours relationships, even if it does not destroy them completely. How many neighbours, relatives, and friends lose each other because of unfortunate words, unresolved quarrels, deep hurts?

Bear with each other and forgive whatever grievances you may have against one another. Forgive as the Lord forgave you. And over all these virtues put on love, which binds them all together in perfect unity. (verses 13–14)

Christ freed us from all resentment by inaugurating a new era of love and forgiveness, giving himself as the example. He was the one who taught us to pray 'Forgive us our debts, as we also have forgiven our debtors' (*Matthew 6:12*). Forgiving is a liberating experience. Just ask those who have forgiven or been forgiven: they can tell you how wonderful it is!

† *Lord, who forgave your torturers on the cross where you died for us all, teach me to forgive my debtors. Fill my heart with your kindness and love, I pray.*

Wednesday June 8   Romans 12:6–13

GIFTS ROOTED IN LOVE In this chapter Paul starts writing about Christian living and relationships. The seven gifts of the Spirit he lists here are all meant for the good of the community: prophesying, that is, inspired preaching; serving, which refers to the distribution of help to the needy; teaching the Christian doctrine; encouraging, that is exhorting fellow Christians to faith; contributing by sharing our own means with others; leadership, which applies to the head of the community who, very significantly, is one of the last in the list. Finally, showing mercy cheerfully – and this makes us think how important is the spirit of our acts of mercy!

Never be lacking in zeal, but keep your spiritual fervour, serving the Lord. (verse 11)

And love is mentioned again, like the eternal theme of a 'New Testament Symphony':

Love must be sincere ... Be devoted to one another in brotherly love. (parts of verses 9 and 10)

There is no other way to follow Paul's teachings. His words are valid today because they are rooted in love, Christ's love for him and the faith that it generated.

† *Lord, thank you for the Christian community in which I live.*
Bless us with the eternal gifts of inspired preaching, serving,
teaching, encouraging, contributing, leading, and showing mercy.
May we be bound together by our loving kindness for each other.

Thursday June 9   **2 Corinthians 9:6–15**

WITNESSING BY BEING GENEROUS   A few weeks before I
professed my faith in Jesus Christ, I had to face and be questioned
by the Elders' Meeting of my church. I was then 12 years old, but I
can still remember a scene from that day: I felt rather nervous,
standing in front of the table where the Elders sat. The most vivid
image in my mind is of old Ishmael, a remarkable man of faith.
Very thin, he was sitting upright, his dark skin making a striking
contrast with his white hair; I can see him shaking his head to and
fro whilst stressing his words by carefully enunciating them: 'I
have only three words of advice to you, my daughter:
witnessing, witnessing, witnessing.'

> **Because of the service by which you have proved
> yourselves, men will praise God for the obedience that
> accompanies your confession of the gospel of Christ, and
> for your generosity in sharing with them and with
> everyone else.**   **(verse 13)**

In today's reading Paul tells the church in Corinth that our
generosity, among other things, will result in people praising
God. In other words, generosity is also a form of witnessing.
People will know us (and listen to us) by our fruits.

† *Dear God, may the actions I perform today show people how much I love*
you. May their hearts be warmed by your grace reflected in what I do.

Friday June 10   **1 Timothy 6:17–19**

GENEROSITY MEANS SHARING   There have always been rich
and poor people, say some – that's the way things are. For us
Christians, though, the command is to share. It is all over the gospels,
in Acts, in the epistles, and it is crystal clear in today's passage:

> **Command them to do good, to be rich in good deeds, and
> to be generous and willing to share.**   **(verse 18)**

Every time Christian congregations in Christian countries repeat
the sentence 'Thy kingdom come' in their prayers, they are
asking for a world where there will be peace and justice. This
could be translated as bread, shelter, health, education and so on,

for everyone. The thought is extremely attractive, and so are the words. The Bible teaches us that we should put into practice what we say with our lips. How different then will our world be!

† *Jesus, my Saviour, forgive me when I conform to ways of thinking that are different from what you taught. Give me your sense of justice and make me willing to share.*

Saturday June 11   Acts 9:36–42

A GENEROUS LIFE   The town of Joppa sat on a coastal cliff, where Tel Aviv is today. It is from this enchanting place that the story of Dorcas comes to us – commemorating her life of generous service.

He took her by the hand and helped her to her feet. Then he called the believers and the widows and presented her to them alive.   **(verse 41)**

A recent article in the British newspaper *The Independent* was about the work of Martin Seligman, an American professor of psychology who studies happiness in human life. He says the first level of contentment concerns satisfying one's body and physical pleasure. The second is about what we need as social beings: enjoying activities like games, and so on. The third and highest level of happiness, though, is reached when we give a wider meaning to our lives – by helping others. The story of Dorcas shows us yet another thing: people like her have realised that there is something more important than themselves. They are not only happier – they are needed.

† *Lord, thank you for stories like this, which are still an inspiration for Christians today. Give us the spirit of Dorcas, who knew how to serve and be happy, who was so wanted that she was brought back to life.*

For group discussion and personal thought

● What opportunities for kindness do you find in your own life?
● 'Forgive us our debts, as we also have forgiven our debtors' – is generous forgiveness part of daily experience in your family or community?
● Do you think a person can be brought to faith by observing the life of a Christian? How could you improve your own witness in this regard?

FRUIT OF THE SPIRIT 5
Faithfulness

Notes by Peter Cotterell

based on the New Revised Standard Version

Peter Cotterell is a retired Uniting Church minister living in Wynyard, on the northwest coast of the beautiful island of Tasmania, Australia. Ordained in 1977, he has ministered in a number of rural parishes. He has also served the Uniting Church on local, regional, state and national committees. He was Moderator of the Synod of Tasmania 1993–95. He is married to Sally and they have four children.

God is faithful in all his dealings with us and calls us to be faithful too. But this is only possible through the presence and the power of the Holy Spirit.

Text for the week: Galatians 5:22

Sunday June 12   **Galatians 5:22–23**

MIRROR THE FATHER

By contrast, the fruit of the Spirit is love, joy, peace, patience, kindness, generosity, faithfulness.   **(verse 22)**

It is the work of the Spirit to lead us to Christ, convict us of sin, seal us as God's children, gift us for ministry and make us more like Christ in our daily living. These are all signs of God's faithfulness toward us. It is indeed wonderful that our God keeps his promises. Our response should be to strive to mirror the nature of our heavenly Father. We need to be faithful as he is faithful. But this is not something we can achieve on our own. It is the work of the Spirit. The Apostle Paul says that the fruit of our natural self is at odds with the life that God would have us lead (*Galatians 5:17*). If we are to be like Christ we must open ourselves to God and allow the fruit of the Spirit to be developed in us. During this week we shall focus on one quality of that fruit – faithfulness. We shall recognise that our faithfulness impacts on the lives of others, enriches our relationships and binds us together. Our faithfulness is nurtured by the Word of God, brings honour to our Lord and must be maintained to the end of our lives. This is a holy calling. As such, our faithfulness can only be maintained through a close relationship with the one who produces his fruit in us – the Holy Spirit.

† *O Holy Spirit, produce the fullness of your fruit in me.*

Monday June 13   Ruth 2:8–12

A BLESSED IMMIGRANT When I was twelve years old my family emigrated from England to Australia. We knew no one in this new land and it was months before my father was able to get work. On our arrival the Methodist Church helped us find a home and generally helped us to settle in. They were not obligated to do this but it is evidence of the fruit of the Spirit in their lives that they cared for us with such faithfulness. As a result I had my first experience of attending church and Sunday school. It left a lasting and positive impression on my life, which I believe contributed to my conversion to Christ at the age of sixteen. Because we moved house after three months none of the people of that church were ever aware of the lasting impression they made. When Ruth arrived in Bethlehem with her mother-in-law, Naomi, the fruit of the Spirit was clearly evident in this foreigner. The quality of her love, patience, kindness and faithfulness, her willingness to be a servant in the fields, attracted the attention of Boaz, the owner of the fields. Boaz was a deeply spiritual man in whom the fruit of the Spirit was also evident. He responded to Ruth's faithfulness with love, kindness and generosity of his own.

But Boaz answered her, 'All that you have done for your mother-in-law since the death of your husband has been fully told me, and how you left your father and mother and your native land and came to a people that you did not know before. May the LORD reward you for your deeds, and may you have a full reward from the LORD, the God of Israel, under whose wings you have come for refuge!'

(verses 11–12)

The story goes on to relate how they were later married and became ancestors of the great king David. The Lord certainly blessed this Spirit-filled migrant abundantly.

† *O Holy Spirit, may others see my faithfulness and rejoice.*

Tuesday June 14   **Luke 12:42–48**

BE FAITHFUL IN RELATIONSHIPS   On the surface this
parable seems very negative. It seems to be all about
punishment of those to whom the master has given
responsibility. If we see the master as Jesus then this becomes a
parable of his coming. Those who are condemned are those
who have acted arrogantly, selfishly, or abusively towards their
fellow slaves. However, those who faithfully fulfil the task
assigned to them will be given even greater responsibility.

> **And the Lord said, 'Who then is the faithful and prudent
> manager whom his master will put in charge of his slaves,
> to give them their allowance of food at the proper time?
> Blessed is that slave whom his master will find at work
> when he arrives. Truly I tell you, he will put that one in
> charge of all his possessions.'   (verses 42–44)**

It is the presence of the Spirit that enables us to live faithfully in
relationships. But we can always choose to ignore the
prompting of the Spirit. When we are unfaithful we grieve the
Spirit and destroy the trust that enables us to live creatively in
relationship with others. I have seen congregations torn apart
by the unfaithful behaviour of their leaders. I have seen families
destroyed through unfaithfulness in marriage. How faithfully
we care for our fellow 'slaves' is an indication of how mature
the fruit of the Spirit is in our lives.

† *Spirit of God, bring your fruit to maturity in me.*

Wednesday June 15   **Psalm 119:30–37**

FAITHFUL STUDY OF THE WORD   We have been living at our
present address for about a year. In the backyard there is an apricot
tree. When we went to harvest its fruit we found that the branches
were so long and high that the fruit was very hard to reach. After
we had gathered what fruit we could, we pruned the tree to make
the fruit more accessible in the future. The primary purpose of the
fruit tree is to bear fruit. It is wonderful that it is decorative and
provides shade but its primary purpose is to be fruitful. We make
the fruit accessible by pruning the tree and nurturing its growth.

> **Teach me, O Lord , the way of your statutes,
> and I will observe it to the end.
> Give me understanding, that I may keep your law
> and observe it with my whole heart.
> Lead me in the path of your commandments,**

for I delight in it.
Turn my heart to your decrees,
and not to selfish gain.
Turn my eyes from looking at vanities;
give me life in your ways.   **(verses 33–37)**

We are pruned and nurtured by the word of God. We need to be faithful in our study of God's word. We need to delight in God's word. We need to allow our lives to be conformed to the will of our God. The Spirit will give us understanding but we must then put it into practice in our daily lives. As we faithfully and diligently do this we will find ourselves becoming more fruitful and that fruit will become more accessible to others.

† *Word of God, nurture me that I may bear more fruit for your glory.*

Thursday June 16   Titus 2:9–14

BE AN ORNAMENT   One of the major national sports in my country is Australian Rules football. At times, when a player has had an outstanding career, he is described as an ornament to the game. This means that he is not one who has brought the game into disrepute, but is a player to be admired and emulated.

Tell slaves to be submissive to their masters and to give satisfaction in every respect; they are not to talk back, not to pilfer, but to show complete and perfect fidelity, so that in everything they may be an ornament to the doctrine of God our Saviour.   (verses 9–10)

How we live our lives reflects upon the God whom we serve. We are always witnesses, twenty-four hours a day, seven days a week. Our faithfulness in the power of the Spirit helps us to be ornaments to our God. Our daily lives may be demanding and difficult. But we are no worse off than the ones to whom Titus was writing. It was not easy to be a slave always at the beck and call of the master. Titus instructs the slaves of his time to be faithful, respectful and obedient. They were to be ornaments to the doctrine of God their Saviour. Whatever our circumstances, the Spirit enables us to live lives worthy of our Saviour, lives filled with faithfulness, respect and obedience.

† *Help me, O Lord, when times are hard, to rely upon your Spirit.*

Friday June 17   Philippians 1:27–29

STAND FIRM FOR HARMONY We live in a broken and bruised world. Everywhere we look there is tension, discord and conflict.

Elections often bring out the worst in people as opposing parties or groups criticise, blame and vilify one another. In some cases this results in open violence and destruction. We wonder if there can ever be any hope of harmony. Yet, as Christians, we are called to be living witnesses to the harmony our Lord desires. There is to be unity in community.

Only, live your life in a manner worthy of the gospel of Christ, so that, whether I come and see you or am absent and hear about you, I will know that you are standing firm in one spirit, striving side by side with one mind for the faith of the gospel. (verse 27)

Paul tells his readers to 'stand firm in one spirit, striving side by side with one mind'. This is only possible through the power of the Holy Spirit. Faithfulness to our calling in Christ results in harmony as we love one another, rejoice in one another, live peaceably, patiently, generously and kindly with each other. This does not mean that we all have to think the same, share the same political beliefs, or be of one culture. Rather, it is the diversity of the church that makes our faithful witness to harmony all the more powerful.

† *Help us, O Lord, to celebrate our diversity and not allow it to become a source of discord or division.*

Saturday June 18   **Revelation 2:8–11**

BE FAITHFUL UNTO DEATH The churches of the Revelation were either undergoing, or about to undergo, severe persecution. John wrote to encourage them in their faith and urged them to stand strong. The church at Smyrna was pleasing to the Lord, but this would not preserve them from persecution. The church at Smyrna was encouraged to be faithful until death.

I know your affliction and your poverty, even though you are rich. I know the slander on the part of those who say that they are Jews and are not, but are a synagogue of Satan. Do not fear what you are about to suffer. Beware, the devil is about to throw some of you into prison so that you may be tested, and for ten days you will have affliction. Be faithful until death, and I will give you the crown of life. (verses 9–10)

I have never undergone persecution of the kind suffered by Smyrna but I have seen many faithful Christians severely tested in their faith by sickness or tragedy. One friend's last words to me shortly before she died from a cruel cancer were 'Beat ya!', meaning that she would be in the glorious presence of the Lord

Jesus before me. Another friend's faith grew stronger in the midst of the tragic loss of her son in a motor accident. What enables such strength in overcoming the most terrible of circumstances? It is the faithful presence of the comforting Spirit and the character-enhancing fruit the Spirit has produced in their lives. Someone has said, 'It is the faith we have at the end of life that saves us.' Let us be faithful throughout our lives, even unto death.

† *O Holy Spirit, thank you for your presence; please keep me faithful to the end.*

For group discussion and personal thought

● Reflect on the occasions in which you have recognised God's faithfulness to you.
● In what contexts do you find it most difficult to be faithful to your calling in Christ?
● Have you thought of yourself as an 'ornament' to the doctrine of God the Saviour?
● How does this impact on your life?

FRUIT OF THE SPIRIT 6
Gentleness, self-control

Notes by Carol Mouat

based on the Jerusalem Bible

Carol Mouat is a Roman Catholic Dominican Sister who was involved in Theological Education by Extension in South Africa throughout the 1990s. Currently she is on the staff at Hawkstone International Pastoral Centre in Shropshire, England.

Gentleness is not a fashionable virtue today. Yet it is one of the hardest to practise. It is much easier to become angry, to insist on having our own way, to make sure that our views and our needs are attended to. So it is appropriate that the writer of Galatians links it with self-control, because gentleness – indeed, all the fruit of the Spirit – requires very great self-control. It is not a weak and easy option.

Text for the week: 1 Corinthians 9:25

Sunday June 19   **Galatians 5:22–23**

DISCERNING THE SPIRIT

> **What the Spirit brings is very different: love, joy, peace, patience, kindness, goodness, trustfulness, gentleness and self-control.**   **(verse 22 and part of verse 23)**

As we travel on our spiritual journey, Paul invites us to gaze inward and reflect on our actions. It is a common feature to seek rewards when we have performed a task well. The tendency is to seek affirmation. No matter how hard we try to please everyone, there will always be some people who are not happy with our performance. This is a fact of life. If we seek to receive praise and rewards for our actions we will be disappointed. It does not help to criticise, to become judgemental towards others, or bitter and angry. We want to be 'all-perfect', and we tend to get upset when we realise that we are not perfect. The secret is to recognise that we belong to the human race, and we too have our weaknesses. Then we shall react to failure both in ourselves and in others with gentleness and self-control. The fruit of the Spirit is the result of true discernment of God's Holy Spirit. It is very simple really: if we live a good life and obey God's commandments, all this fruit will not only flourish in our lives but will enrich our relationships and all with whom we come into contact.

† *Lord, you know how often I lose sight of you in my life. I strive after perfection and then feel let down by myself and others. Help me to react to these failures with gentleness towards myself and others and with a renewed self-control. Then I shall not waste my energy on fruitless bitterness and self-reproach but will be able, by your Holy Spirit, to bring forth fruit for myself and others.*

Monday June 20   **Ephesians 4:1–6**

LOVE AND UNITY We all want to be loved and cherished by someone. We long for peace and harmony in our lives. During our faith journey we 'wind in and out' of people's lives, and as we form new relationships we continually experience a variety of different emotions. Sometimes the experience is that of joy, happiness, fulfilment, gratitude, peace, love; but sometimes the relationship is fraught with pain, disappointment, and unhappiness. Love does not always come easily, it costs and sometimes involves challenge – challenge to trust. Preserving unity in various groups of people does not mean absence of conflict. Sometimes we will experience the hurt and pain in a relationship and then we are encouraged to work towards a healing and forgiveness that are based on the gentleness that respects all people in the relationship. The bond of unity can therefore be restored when conflict is addressed in relationships.

Do all you can to preserve the unity of the Spirit by the peace that binds you together. **(verse 3)**

Bishop Desmond Tutu instituted the Truth and Reconciliation Commission in South Africa. The gifts of love, peace, healing and unity were experienced by many people as they expressed their pain and anger towards one another. They publicly asked forgiveness for their sinful behaviour towards each other. The Holy Spirit was indeed at work during this time, and a strong bond of unity was experienced by a great many people from the different racial groups living in South Africa. Unity is a tender plant which requires patient and gentle nurturing.

† *Thank you for the gifts you have given me. Help me, Lord Jesus, to approach others with gentleness so that I can share with them your gifts of love and unity.*

Tuesday 21 June   **1 Peter 3:13–16**

COURTESY AND RESPECT

[A]lways have your answer ready for people who ask you the reason for the hope that you all have. But give it with courtesy and respect and with a clear conscience.
                              (parts of verses 15 and 16)

I am very privileged in my ministry at Hawkstone International Pastoral Centre to meet a very wide variety of people from all over the globe. Many of them are missionaries who serve God and his people of many different faiths, often in very difficult situations and in spite of war, poverty, crime and seeming hopelessness. Joy emanates from them. These people willingly give their lives for the poor, the homeless, the sick and the dying in the face of deep suffering and humiliating conditions. In their gentleness and respect, people of all faiths or none see the face of Christ.

† *Help me, O Lord, in all my dealings with others to approach them with the courtesy and respect which is the essence of your gentleness.*

Wednesday June 22   **Titus 3:2–7**

GENTLENESS AND UNDERSTANDING   Our journey with the Lord is an invitation to become a pilgrim – to become gentle in our dealings with ourselves and our relationships with others, and above all to be understanding. It is sometimes very difficult to comprehend why people do the things they do, especially when we would do things differently from them.

Remind them ... to be ready to do good at every opportunity; not to go slandering other people or picking quarrels, but to be courteous and always polite to all kinds of people. **(part of verse 1 and verse 2)**

We journey alongside the one who leads and guides us along the rough paths, sometimes across muddy waters, or through the desert or along dark tunnels. It is God who has saved us from darkness, the love of God which has been poured generously into our hearts. The Word has become flesh in us. If our lives are an expression of God's love we can be a healing power to others. The Word can gently express itself in us and enable our hearts to understand the faults and weaknesses of others. It is Jesus who will give us his understanding and prevent us from harbouring condemnation of others in our hearts. What a powerful means of healing and reconciliation the Lord invites us to enter!

† *Thank you, Lord, for your spirit of gentleness. Help me to have the self-control to show this gentleness towards all kinds of people, however different or difficult they may seem to be.*

Thursday June 23   **Philippians 4:4–7**

TOLERANCE   Tolerance is an important part of being gentle. So often we see others doing what seems wrong and we want to rush in and stop them or set things right. But often what people need is not zealous correction but understanding of their need for healing. We know from our own experience that healing is a slow process; the wounded need gentle handling. We may need to tolerate the weeds in others until the time is right for God to reap his harvest; we have our own weeds as well, and these also need to be tolerated until the Lord comes to deal with them (see *Matthew 13:36–43*).

Let your tolerance be evident to everyone: the Lord is very near.   **(verse 5)**

It can take a lot of self-control not to rush in and hustle people into change for which they are not yet ready. We don't necessarily know what is best for them, we don't know what God is planning for them. If the Lord needs our help, he will ask for it; meanwhile, our task may simply be to gently love and support the other with our presence and our prayer. The approach of gentleness and self-control brings its own peace (*verses 6–7*).

† *Lord, you tolerate so many faults in us, and handle us with such gentleness; help us to do the same to others.*

Friday June 24   **1 Corinthians 9:24–27**

RUN THE RACE   But above all finish the race! We are all invited to 'run the race', and this can be very challenging.

All the fighters at the games go into strict training; they do this just to win a wreath that will wither away, but we do it for a wreath that will never wither.   **(verse 25)**

Paul very cleverly uses the metaphor of the race: strict training is emphasised, and this is the same for each of us who are 'running' the faith journey. Our eyes are focused on the Lord and not on 'a wreath that will wither away'. If we keep our eyes and ears focused on God's love for us we will not give in to tiredness and aching limbs. We will not allow any trivialities or weaknesses to deflect us from running the race to the end. The training beforehand and the tactics of the actual race require great discipline and self-control. These are only possible because we think the goal is worth it.

† *Dear Lord, run beside us as our pacemaker as we train and race towards the great goal of heaven. Give us your grace and strength to continue following you, especially during the weak moments when we feel like giving up.*

Saturday June 25   Titus 2:1–8

LIVE A GOOD LIFE Most of us want to be channels of God's love. We want to spread God's love to our families, our friends, those with whom we work, all with whom we come into contact. Our best way of showing this love is through our own behaviour:

in everything you do make yourself an example to them of working for good.   **(part of verse 7)**

The last in Paul's list of fruit of the Spirit is in reality the basis for them all. We cannot be loving, joyful, peaceful, patient, kind, good, trusting and gentle unless we are also self-controlled. Paradoxically, of course, we are not really called to be self-controlled in the sense of controlling ourselves by the force of our own will. We cannot control ourselves; we need to be Spirit-controlled, so that the power of the Spirit can control the self which would prefer to be unloving, depressed, aggressive, impatient, unkind, doubtful and domineering. The result, or fruit, of the Spirit's power in our lives will be the characteristics we have been studying over the 6 weeks of this theme. These are not virtues to be worked at; they are the by-products of allowing the Holy Spirit to take over our lives.

† *Come, Holy Spirit, fill the hearts of your faithful people, that they may display your fruit in their lives.*

For group discussion and personal thought

● How difficult do you find it to be gentle? Why is gentleness so difficult?
● In which areas of your life do you particularly need to grow in self-control?

MATTHEW 3
Healing encounters

Notes by Marian Strachan

*based on the New Revised Standard Version
and the Good News Bible*

Marian Strachan has taught in Papua New Guinea, Western Samoa and Britain. She is a part-time lecturer and freelance writer. Marian is the wife of a minister of the United Reformed Church, and in her spare time works with international students, children and young people in the church.

Healing encounters are something we all understand. Treatment from a doctor or a friend's encouraging word, look, or touch can be healing and enabling. And when we open our lives to God, we experience his forgiveness, love and healing presence. In Matthew chapters 8 and 9, the gospel writer places a large number of healing miracles immediately after the Sermon on the Mount. Jesus' words are followed by his deeds. These healing miracles go beyond physical healing, and show us that Jesus seeks to bring wholeness to every part of a person's life.

Text for the week: Matthew 9:2

Sunday June 26   **Matthew 8:1–4**

CHRIST'S HEALING TOUCH

> 'Lord, if you choose, you can make me clean.' [Jesus] stretched out his hand and touched him, saying, 'I do choose. Be made clean!' Immediately his leprosy was cleansed.   (part of verse 2 and verse 3, NRSV)

When Jesus reached out to touch the leper (the word 'leper' covered various skin diseases), everyone who saw it would have been horrified and amazed. This man was a Jew and the Jewish Law ordered that, 'A person who has a dreaded skin disease must wear torn clothes, leave his hair uncombed, cover the lower part of his face and call out, "Unclean, unclean!" He remains unclean as long as he has the disease, and he must live ... away from others' (*Leviticus 13:45–46, GNB*). This rejection by society, and the gulf between clean and unclean, was bridged by Jesus; his touch brought healing and acceptance. Jesus found it necessary to defy the Law in order to bring healing, but also showed respect for it by sending the man to the priest to be examined and to make a gift as proof to everyone that he was cured and ready to return to his community. With humility, and recognising Christ as Lord, the man had opened himself to receive healing and wholeness, and we are challenged to do the same.

† *Loving Lord, help me to be open to receive your healing; make me whole.*

Monday June 27   Matthew 8:5–13

THE HEALING WORD   The Roman officer, a Gentile, recognises Jesus' authority and calls him 'Lord'. He was certain that Jesus could heal his servant (the word Matthew uses can mean either a servant or a son, see *John 4:46–54*). To enter the Gentile's house, as Jesus offered, would have made him ritually unclean, but again, as in yesterday's reading, we see that Jesus never hesitated to help those excluded by Jewish Law and practice. The officer said to Jesus,

> **'I do not deserve to have you come into my house. Just give the order, and my servant will get well...' When Jesus heard this, he was surprised and said to the people following him, 'I tell you, I have never found anyone in Israel with faith like this.'** (part of verse 8 and verse 10, GNB)

Matthew records Jesus' stern warning against the complacency of the Jews, who assumed that, because they were descendants of Abraham, they were sure to be favoured by God. But he praises those who live their faith, like the Roman officer, in the problems and necessities of everyday life.

† *Lord, help me to have confidence and faith in you as I face the practical needs and tasks of daily life.*

Tuesday June 28   Matthew 8:14–22

COSTLY HEALING   Jesus' third healing involved another marginalised person in Jewish society. Jesus went into Peter's home and found Peter's mother-in-law in bed with a fever. He touched her hand to heal her. No Rabbi or teacher would usually touch a woman. Jesus did. No one asked him to do this; he saw her need and responded to it.

> **That evening they brought to him many who were possessed by demons, and he cast out the spirits with a word, and cured all who were sick.** (verse 16, NRSV)

Through the healing miracles Matthew sees Jesus fulfilling God's promises in the Old Testament. It was written that God's Servant would take away, and himself bear, the sicknesses of the people (*Isaiah 53:4*). He would suffer and be broken to make people whole. The importance of the healing miracles lies not only in what they tell us about Jesus' actions, but in what they say about the person of Jesus. The gospels often link together following Jesus, trusting him, healing and wholeness. Two men who want to follow Jesus are asked to think carefully about the cost of what that might mean. Perhaps forgoing comfort, or following without delay, even though that might be difficult.

† *Lord, help me not to shrink from following you and serving those in need.*

Wednesday June 29   Matthew 8:23 – 9:1

HEALING FEAR   Fear is something we all face again and again at different times in our lives, whether it is fear for loved ones or ourselves, fear of new experiences, failure, and so on. The disciples feared for their lives when their boat was caught in a terrible storm on the Sea of Galilee. They woke Jesus, saying,

'Lord, save us! We are perishing!' And he said to them, 'Why are you afraid, you of little faith?'   (parts of verses 25 and 26, NRSV)

The disciples, like many of us, had 'little faith'. They had started out on their journey as followers of Jesus but they were not yet properly aware of his power. The boat is often used as a symbol for the church. My own church advertises itself as a place for people of much faith, little faith, or no faith. We believe that even when our faith is weak, we are never abandoned or alone (*Matthew 28:20*). Having amazed the disciples by calming the sea, another kind of fear awaits Jesus on the other side of the sea. Two mentally and emotionally disturbed men were causing fear in the area. They lived among the graves and were described as being possessed by demons, or an unclean spirit (*Mark 5:2*). Recognising Jesus' authority and power, they shouted, 'What have you to do with us, Son of God?' Much of Jesus' ministry was about releasing people from the evil which seemed to surround them, from fear, from unhelpful traditions and from rejection by their communities.

† *To all who live with storms in their life, with rejection, fear, mental illness, or who feel evil around them and within, Lord, bring your healing and peace.*

Thursday June 30   **Matthew 9:2–8**

HEALING AND FORGIVENESS

> Some people were carrying a paralysed man lying on a bed.
> When Jesus saw their faith, he said to the paralytic, 'Take
> heart, son; your sins are forgiven.' Then some of the scribes
> said ... 'This man is blaspheming.'
>
> **(parts of verses 2 and 3, NRSV)**

The faith and effort of the man's friends are noticed by Jesus. In
Mark 2:1–12 and Luke 5:17–26, more detailed accounts tell how
they let the paralysed man down through the roof of a house to get
him to Jesus. Jesus spoke to the paralytic about forgiveness. Many
of the Jews of Jesus' day believed that suffering and sin were linked,
so perhaps this was something he needed to hear. Or perhaps Jesus
knew that some unforgiven problem in his life needed to be sorted
out. But the Jewish scribes or teachers were angered by Jesus'
words and they accused him of insulting God – forgiving sin was
God's job, something only he could do. Jesus told the paralytic to
get up and walk, to show that he really was able to forgive sin. His
actions backed up his words and authority. They were part of his
message. God's kingdom, or new society, had come, and the sick,
weak, helpless, and rejected were to share in it and find wholeness.
The faith, prayer and support of friends, and the work of those in
healing and caring positions, contribute in so many ways to healing
today. But it is God's forgiveness that brings his gift of wholeness to
all who will receive it.

✝ *Compassionate Lord, show me how to share in your work of bringing
healing and wholeness, and strengthen all who work to reduce
suffering.*

Friday July 1   **Matthew 9:9–17**

HEALING FRIENDSHIP   One of the most loved stories in the
gospels is that of Jesus calling Matthew, a hated tax collector, to
follow him. If Jesus loves sinners, that means he welcomes all who
are open to him, and he gladly shared a meal with Matthew. This
was too much for the religious Pharisees, who kept themselves
separate and aloof from common people and 'outcasts'.

> 'Why does your teacher eat with tax collectors and sinners?'...
> But when [Jesus] heard this, he said, 'Those who are well have
> no need of a physician, but those who are sick. Go and learn
> what this means, 'I desire mercy, not sacrifice.'
>
> **(part of verse 11, verse 12 and part of verse 13, NRSV)**

Jesus was reminding them that all their religious observances and sacrifices to God in the Temple meant nothing if they failed to show mercy and kindness to their fellows (*Micah 6:8*). John's disciples were puzzled that Jesus' disciples did not follow the practice of fasting. But Jesus says that whilst he is with them, it is a time for celebration. He makes everything new. His presence and teaching transform old ways and attitudes.

† *Lord, help us to celebrate and share your healing friendship.*

Saturday July 2   **Matthew 9:18–34**

COMPASSIONATE HEALING   In today's reading, five people with very different problems are restored to health. As we read and try to understand the stories of Jesus' healing miracles, we are challenged by his compassion, mercy and care for people. Today, more than ever, in a world ravaged by AIDS, where poorer people in every country have limited access to care and medicines, we need to remind ourselves daily of our responsibilities towards others. We do not all have medical training, but we should pray for and support those who do, and we can all be healers. Christ's gift to us is his love, compassion and power for ourselves and for those in special need. Whether we share a loving and healing word or touch, or put aside time to help and care for the sick, or give a share of our income to support healing, our task is to share in Christ's work.

> **The blind men came to him; and Jesus said to them, 'Do you believe that I am able to do this?' They said to him, 'Yes, Lord.' Then he touched their eyes and said, 'According to your faith let it be done to you.' And their eyes were opened.**
> **(part of verse 28, verse 29 and part of verse 30, NRSV)**

† *Merciful God, thank you for those with special skills who work in many parts of the world with people who have difficulties in seeing, speaking and walking.*

For group discussion and personal thought
● When we think about healing and wholeness, we are concerned with body, mind, emotions, faith, and relationships. What areas in your life may need healing?
● How can your church be more involved in helping people in your community to experience Christ's healing and wholeness?

MATTHEW 4
Instruction to the twelve

Notes by Emmanuel Asante

based on the New International Version

Emmanuel Asante is an ordained minister of the Methodist Church in Ghana and an Associate Professor of Theology at Trinity Theological Seminary, Legon in Accra, Ghana.

Commitment to Jesus Christ leads to participation in his life and ministry. Followers of Jesus share in his compassionate ministry to the lost and needy. But they also share in his suffering and rejection. Those who follow Jesus are exhorted to do so in total commitment. In this week's readings, Jesus invites the readers to participate in his life and ministry.

Text for the week: Matthew 10:16

Sunday July 3　　　　　　　　　　　**Matthew 9:35 – 10:4**

COMPASSIONATE MINISTRY　　When we are called to follow Jesus we are summoned to participate in his compassionate ministry to the sick, the poor and the needy. We read in today's passage that, deeply moved with compassion as he saw the multitudes with no one in Israel to guide them aright, Jesus directed the attention of his disciples to the great harvest fields of the harassed and helpless multitudes.

> **When he saw the crowds, he had compassion on them, because they were harassed and helpless, like sheep without a shepherd. Then he said to his disciples, 'The harvest is plentiful but the workers are few. Ask the Lord of the harvest, therefore, to send out workers into his harvest field.'**　　　　　　　　**(verses 36–38)**

The central message of today's reading is that our ministry, as followers of Christ, is defined and informed by our Lord Jesus Christ who, out of compassion for the many who are hopeless, harassed and helpless, has called us to service. Believers in Christ have been called to participate in the compassionate ministry of Christ, which brings fullness of life to all. Jesus calls for workers who have the heart to deal with people's problems.

† *Lord Jesus, grant that, as we minister to people, we may see them as you see them and feel for them as you feel for them.*

Monday July 4   Matthew 10:5–15

MINISTERING TO THE LOST SHEEP Jesus, having identified the lost, the helpless, the poor and the needy of Israel as sheep without a shepherd, commissioned his disciples to minister to them and gave his followers specific instructions. The disciples were instructed to present to the lost the message concerning the accessibility of the kingship or lordship of God over their lives. The Jews eagerly expected this kingship of God, in the firm belief that, under the kingship of God, they would enjoy fullness of life – including good health and material and spiritual prosperity – in short, the peace of God. In sending his disciples with the specific instruction to go to the lost sheep of Israel and proclaim to them the message that 'the kingdom of God is near', and also to heal the sick among them, Jesus was offering to the materially and spiritually impoverished, the lost and the hopeless, the possibility of life, health, hope and the peace of the kingdom.

> **'Go ... to the lost sheep of Israel. As you go, preach this message: "The kingdom of heaven is near." Heal the sick, raise the dead, cleanse those who have leprosy, drive out demons.'   (part of verse 6, verse 7 and part of verse 8)**

As followers of Jesus, we have been called and sent to the lost. We have been sent with the specific instruction not to condemn but to woo them. We have been called to bring the message of hope to the hopeless, life to the lost, the acceptance of the Lord and the people of God to those who feel rejected and alienated.

† *Lord, grant us the grace to respond positively to your calling to seek out the lost with your message of love, forgiveness, acceptance and newness of life.*

Tuesday July 5   Matthew 10:16–23

SHEEP AMONG WOLVES The call to serve is a call to go through suffering, rejection and persecution for the sake of the kingdom. Jesus was fully aware of this and would not have his followers under any illusion about what was involved in carrying out his mission to the hostile lost who have a history of persecuting the prophets and rejecting Jesus as their lord and master. The disciples had been sent to face people who would be hostile to them. They would be among the lost as sheep among wolves. Therefore they needed the wisdom of God, they needed to be blameless and they needed the spirit of endurance as they ministered among the hostile lost.

'I am sending you out like sheep among wolves. Therefore be as shrewd as snakes and as innocent as doves. (verse 16)

Ministry to the lost involves the suffering of persecution, rejection and, in some extreme cases, even death. Nevertheless the followers of Christ are not to court persecution or needlessly expose themselves to danger in a foolhardy way. The disciples must do all they can to avoid persecution. If it did come, however, the disciples should not despair but take courage, for the Lord would not abandon them.

✝ *Dear Lord, strengthen us to stand firm in the midst of persecution, the suffering of rejection and threats of death for the sake of your name and kingdom.*

Wednesday July 6   **Matthew 10:24–36**

SHARING THE MASTER'S FATE   Followers of Christ have been called to participate in his ministry. But participating in the Lord's ministry is also sharing his fate. In spite of the good things Jesus did, his own people rejected him and called him names. The Pharisees even called him 'Satan'. If they did this to Jesus, they would do it to his followers. For they share in his fate:

'A student is not above his teacher, nor a servant above his master. It is enough for the student to be like his teacher, and the servant like his master. If the head of the house has been called Beelzebub, how much more the members of his household!'   **(verses 24–25)**

Followers of Christ should not forget that the inevitable outcome of committing their life to Christ and what he stands for is suffering what he suffered in his rejection. Believers in Christ should not think that because they are available to Christ they will not suffer personal threats or difficult trials. 'Blessed are those who are persecuted because of righteousness, for theirs is the kingdom of heaven' (*Matthew 5:10*).

† *Lord, grant us the grace to know that commitment to you may lead to the suffering of persecution, rejection and threat. In the midst of all things, help us to know that you are with us.*

Thursday July 7   **Matthew 10:37–42**

TAKING UP YOUR CROSS AND FOLLOWING JESUS Christian commitment may lead to the separation of friends and loved ones and even of families. Confronted with a choice between Jesus and our friends, loved ones and family, we are enjoined to choose Christ. We should not neglect our families, friends or loved ones. But also we should not neglect our commitment to the Lord because of our concern for our families, friends or loved ones. In other words, our love for our families and friends should not be self-serving and an excuse not to give undivided commitment to God. We should take up our cross and follow Jesus.

> **'Anyone who loves his father or mother more than me is not worthy of me; anyone who loves his son or daughter more than me is not worthy of me; and anyone who does not take his cross and follow me is not worthy of me.'**
>
> **(verses 37–38)**

Following Jesus calls for total commitment, laying down other cares and priorities, and a willingness to suffer persecution and even death for his sake.

† *Dear Lord, grant us the grace to love you above all and to stand firm in our commitment to you even when we face persecution for your sake.*

Friday July 8   **Matthew 12:1–8**

THE SPIRIT AND NOT THE LETTER OF THE LAW   In order that the Law might be kept to the letter, the Pharisees had erected a hedge around it. An example of this hedge is today's passage. The Law insists that no work should be done on the Sabbath (*Exodus 20:8–10*) because the Sabbath was a day God had set aside for rest and worship. To ensure compliance with this law, the Pharisees established thirty-nine general categories of work forbidden on the Sabbath. Harvesting was one of those forbidden works. On one Sabbath, the disciples of Jesus, hungry as they were, picked some grains of wheat, rubbed them in their hands and ate them. In doing this, the motive of the disciples was not to harvest for profit on a Sabbath day. They were hungry and they found something to eat. So they were not working on the Sabbath. However, the Pharisees could not see beyond the letter and the technicalities of the law and thought otherwise. To the Pharisees, Jesus' disciples had crossed the hedge they had erected around the substantive law and that was enough to constitute an illegality on the Sabbath. In response to their charge of illegality against his disciples, Jesus made it known to them that, as Lord of the Sabbath, he was concerned with the spirit, not the letter or the Pharisees' technicalities of the Law.

'If you had known what these words mean, "I desire mercy, not sacrifice," you would not have condemned the innocent. For the Son of Man is Lord of the Sabbath.' (verses 7–8)

For Jesus the Law was intended for the good of the covenant community; it was not an end in itself. The Law is at the service of humanity and not humanity at the service of the Law. What God demands is mercy, love and compassion, not uncompassionate legalism and condemnation.

† *Lord, give us a heart that will observe the spirit and not the letter of the Law.*

Saturday July 9   **Matthew 13:1–17**

THE KINGDOM WILL TRIUMPH   Jesus, in his teaching, used parables or illustrations which help us to understand the unknown, spiritual truth, through the known, the familiar. Today's reading presents one of Jesus' popular parables, the 'Parable of the Sower', sometimes called the 'Parables of the Four Soils'. These alternative names indicate that this parable can be considered from two main perspectives: that of the 'sower' who sows the seed and that of the soil which receives the seed that is sown. In addition, this parable could also be considered from the perspective of the seed that is sown, and so given a third title – the 'Parable of the Seed'. If we take this latter view, a farmer who loses 75 per cent of his seed might consider himself a failure and become discouraged. Yet the parable encourages the sower not to be discouraged by the seeming loss of 75 per cent of the seed he sowed, because the remaining 25 per cent compensated for the loss:

Still other seed fell on good soil, where it produced a crop – a hundred, sixty or thirty times what was sown. (verse 8)

People who faithfully lead others to Christ through teaching and preaching of the Word should not be discouraged if the message they proclaim and teach seems to fall on deaf ears. No matter what loss the seed of the gospel suffers, some will germinate and produce fruit. The kingdom of God will surely triumph.

† *Dear Lord, strengthen us not to be discouraged if the message we preach and teach seems to be falling on deaf ears. Grant us the grace to see beyond the seeming failure to the triumph of the kingdom.*

For group discussion and personal thought

● Have you experienced suffering, rejection or persecution in your ministry? If so, how did you feel about it and how did you deal with it?
● 'For Jesus the Law was intended for the good of the covenant community; it was not an end in itself.' How far is this true of your local Christian community?
● In what sense is the 'Parable of the Sower' an encouragement to a discouraged church?

LAMENTATIONS
The loneliness of the city

Notes by Peter Cotterell

based on the New International Version

Lamentations is a series of five carefully constructed laments over the destruction of Jerusalem. It is an outpouring of grief and a terrible description of the horrors that engulfed the nation. It is read today by the Jewish community on the anniversary of the destruction of the Temple in AD 70. We will use these poems to reflect on terrible events of our own time.

Note that the two stories in this week's notes (about H G Spafford and David and Svea Flood) are adapted from *Stories of Faith* by Ruth A Tucker (Daybreak Books, Zondervan Publishing House, Grand Rapids, Michigan, 1989).

Text for the week: Lamentations 3:22–23

Sunday July 10   **Lamentations 1**

NATIONAL CALAMITY Still fresh in my memory, as perhaps it always will be, are the scenes of destruction in the aftermath of September 11 in New York. So many dazed, bewildered people wandering the streets, covered in grey dust. Heartrending images of families seeking frantically for sons, daughters, husbands or wives. The TV networks constantly replayed the moment of impact and the collapse of the Twin Towers, perhaps to convince themselves that it had really happened. It was unbelievably painful, yet we sat hour by hour glued to the TV. We now understand a little of how the writer of Lamentations felt as he witnessed the collapse and destruction of Jerusalem.

> Bitterly she weeps at night,
> tears are upon her cheeks ...
> Her enemies looked at her
> and laughed at her destruction ...
> 'This is why I weep
> and my eyes overflow with tears.
> No one is near to comfort me,
> no one to restore my spirit.

My children are destitute
because the enemy has prevailed.'
                              (parts of verses 2 and 7, and verse 16)

But the destruction of Jerusalem was not just the collapse of the capital city, it was also the destruction of the spiritual confidence of Israel. 'How could this be?' 'Where is our God?' 'Are the gods of Babylon more powerful than our God?' These and many other deep questions were asked as Israel grieved in the aftermath of this national calamity.

† *In the midst of tragedy, O Lord, help us to seek your face.*

Monday July 11   Lamentations 2

IT IS THE LORD'S DOING   'How could this be?' 'Where is our God?' In this second lament the writer of Lamentations begins to address these questions. He recognises that the terrible tragedy of Jerusalem's destruction is the Lord's doing. Israel's God is the sovereign Lord; he is never caught unawares, or found to be impotent. In fact, the Lord is the author of their destruction.

How the Lord has covered the Daughter of Zion
with the cloud of his anger!
He has hurled down the splendour of Israel
from heaven to earth;
he has not remembered his footstool
in the day of his anger.
                                                    (verse 1)

The writer's appreciation of God's sovereignty does not ease the grief or lessen the pain. A common element of profound grief is to hurl accusations at God, and this writer does it with passion:

'Look, O LORD, and consider:
Whom have you ever treated like this?
Should women eat their offspring,
the children they have cared for?
Should priest and prophet be killed
in the sanctuary of the Lord?

'Young and old lie together
in the dust of the streets;
my young men and maidens
have fallen by the sword.
You have slain them in the day of your anger;
you have slaughtered them without pity.'   **(verses 20–21)**

155

To speak in such passionate terms is paradoxically a sign of honest faith. Even as he kicks against the judgements of God he is demonstrating his belief in the One who is the sovereign judge of all the earth.

✝ *Truth of God, help us to be honest in our faith.*

Tuesday July 12   Lamentations 3:1–20

IT BECOMES PERSONAL   How poignant are the personal accounts of a tragedy. In the aftermath of September 11 we heard many deeply moving first-hand accounts of disaster, loss and heroism. One story that has remained with me is of a phone conversation between family members, one of whom had escaped to the roof only to realise that there was no way out. This was to be the last conversation they would have on earth. In this third lament the writer ceases to be a commentator on the suffering of others and describes his own condition. He shares in the grief and pain of the people.

I am the man who has seen affliction
by the rod of his wrath ...
He has made my skin and my flesh grow old
and has broken my bones ...
I remember my affliction and my wandering,
the bitterness and the gall.
I well remember them,
and my soul is downcast within me. (verses 1, 4 and 19–20)

When we move from being commentators on the pain of others and embrace the pain for ourselves, we open the door to empathy and healing. We become more Christlike as we allow ourselves to share the grief and pain of others.

✝ *Spirit of God, enable us to enter into the pain of others.*

Wednesday July 13   Lamentations 3:21–51

GREAT IS YOUR FAITHFULNESS   In the midst of the darkness and despair, the bloodshed, terror and misery, a light begins to shine, hope is born anew.

Yet this I call to mind
and therefore I have hope.   **(verse 21)**

What does the writer call to mind? What could possibly bring hope in such terrible circumstances? He remembers that God is not only Israel's righteous judge, but also her saviour. As the writer reflects on the Lord's relationship with Israel he is reminded that again and again, against all expectations, God has been faithful to his covenant promises.

Because of the LORD**'s great love we are not consumed,**
for his compassions never fail.
They are new every morning;
great is your faithfulness. (verses 22–23)

HG Spafford was a Chicago businessman who lost much of his fortune in the fire which destroyed the city in 1871. But this was nothing compared to the greater loss that was to come. In 1873 his wife and four daughters set sail for Europe. Tragically the luxury liner in which they sailed was rammed by another vessel and sank. 226 lives were lost, including Spafford's four daughters. Yet in the deepest darkness the flame of faith still burned. While sailing to join his grief-stricken wife in Europe, Spafford wrote the lovely hymn 'It is well with my soul' as he passed over the very spot where his daughters had drowned.

When peace like a river attendeth my way,
When sorrows like sea-billows roll,
Whatever my lot, Thou hast taught me to say,
'It is well, it is well with my soul!'

† *In the deepest darkness may we remember your goodness, new*
every morning.

Thursday July 14 **Lamentations 3:52–66**

'DESTROY THEM, O LORD' Grief involves many emotions. One of the strongest and potentially most destructive is anger. In the aftermath of September 11 there were many attacks on mosques, and on Muslims or anyone of perceived Arab background. This was an outpouring of angry grief against those believed to have carried out the terrorist attack. Much of it was irrational and rightly condemned. The writer of Lamentations gives expression to the same kind of grief and anger. To his credit the final judgement, however, is left with the Lord.

O Lord, you have heard their insults,
all their plots against me –
what my enemies whisper and mutter
against me all day long.
Look at them! Sitting or standing,
they mock me in their songs.

Pay them back what they deserve, O LORD**,**
for what their hands have done.

Put a veil over their hearts,
and may your curse be on them!
Pursue them in anger and destroy them
from under the heavens of the LORD.   (verses 61–66)

Jesus, however, has shown us a better way to deal with our enemies. Jesus' way is the radical way of love, not revenge. Not only did he teach us this way, he lived it out, especially in his death on the cross. 'Destroy them, O Lord' is a human prayer of revenge. 'Father, forgive them' is a divine prayer of healing.

† *Help us, O Lord, when we are deeply hurt, to choose the prayer of forgiveness.*

Friday July 15   Lamentations 4

'WHY, O WHY HAS THIS HAPPENED?' The living conditions for those who remain in Jerusalem after the invasion are terrible to behold. The pain of the writer is almost too much to bear as he watches women and children suffer.

Because of thirst the infant's tongue
sticks to the roof of its mouth ...
Those killed by the sword are better off
than those who die of famine ...
With their own hands compassionate women
have cooked their own children.   (parts of verses 4, 9 and 10)

Why has the Lord turned against his people? Why should there be such terrible suffering? The answer given is clear and simple – sin.

The kings of the earth did not believe,
nor did any of the world's people,
that enemies and foes could enter
the gates of Jerusalem.
But it happened because of the sins of her prophets
and the iniquities of her priests,
who shed within her
the blood of the righteous.   (verses 12–13)

This is the writer's conclusion: the root cause of all their suffering is sin. The leadership had failed their people; the prophets and priests had sinned and brought destruction and desolation on Jerusalem and her people. Sin is not some excusable aberration on the part of an individual, a momentary lapse of judgement; sin is a failure to live God's way. In cricket a batsman is run out because he has come up short. It does not matter whether he is short by half the pitch or merely by a centimetre or two. The batsman is out. Sin is coming up short and is so serious in the eyes of God that it results in death. God's remedy for sin is to send his own Son to pay the penalty of sin for the whole world.

✝ *Continue to remind us, O Lord, of the seriousness of our sin and the wonder of your grace in providing Jesus to be our Saviour.*

Saturday July 16   Lamentations 5

RESTORE US, O LORD In this fifth and final lament the writer seeks restoration for the nation. Having recognised the sovereignty of God and his right to judge their sin, he now seeks mercy for the nation.

> **Remember, O LORD, what has happened to us;**
> **look, and see our disgrace.**
> **Our inheritance has been turned over to aliens,**
> **our homes to foreigners.**
> **We have become orphans and fatherless,**
> **our mothers like widows ...**
> **Restore us to yourself, O LORD, that we may return;**
> **renew our days as of old.**   **(verses 1–3 and 21)**

David and Svea Flood went to Africa in 1921 on fire for the Lord. They found the environment hostile and the climate deadly. After the birth of their second child, Svea died and David found the pain too much. He lost faith and lamented that they had only won one child to the Lord. David left Africa a broken man. His baby daughter was left in the care of other missionaries. Years later she sought her father and eventually found him in a rundown apartment with liquor bottles lining the windowsills. She told him of her love for him and of God's care of her. She also told him that the one child he had introduced to the Lord went on to convert his whole village of 600 and become a leader of the church. David Flood was overjoyed and restored to wholeness by the mercy of God. Out of brokenness and pain, desolation and despair, God can bring healing and wholeness.

✝ *Restore us, O Lord, to the wholeness for which you have created us.*

For group discussion and personal thought

Reflect on times of national or personal tragedy:
● What have been your emotional responses to these events?
● How have these events shaped your understanding of God?
● How do you enter into the pain of another person? Do you agree that this can make us more Christlike?
● What does it mean for you to be restored to wholeness?

CELEBRATION 1
Celebrate the festival

Notes by Colin Hurford

based on the New International Version

Colin Hurford, an Anglican priest, has worked in both urban and rural parishes in England. He spent seven years in Sabah, Malaysia, teaching in a secondary school, and some months in Tanzania lecturing at Saint Mark's Theological College, Dar Es Salaam. Married with two sons, he is now retired but feels called to a special ministry of prayer.

In writing this week's notes I am conscious that in many parts of the world there is little to celebrate. In countries where there is war and conflict, and diseases like AIDS, it is often hard to be joyful. Yet I am also aware that in many poor countries there is a joy that overflows despite the problems. In countries where there is sufficient, even plenty, I am sure there should be far more celebration and thanksgiving. But where there are problems, it is true that as we meet to praise God he does lift our spirits, gives us hope and often shows a way through. Let us celebrate the greatness of God as much as we possibly can with joy, laughter and praise.

Text for the week: Revelation 19:6–7

Sunday July 17   **Genesis 21:1–8**

THE GIFT OF LAUGHTER

  'God has brought me laughter.'   **(part of verse 6)**

Mothers will know the anxiety of waiting until a baby is delivered safe and well. Imagine Sarah's anxiety. Even though she had faith in God, she was human and would have doubts and worries, especially at her great age. Then the child is delivered safely and her scornful laughter when she first heard the message of the angels is changed into genuine laughter of great joy. She has a son and the celebrations are wonderful. We should celebrate with her whenever a child is born, because a child is a new creation whom God loves, destined to share eternal life with God. We give thanks too because through Isaac God fulfilled his promise and Jesus, a descendant of Abraham, was born. Think for a moment about laughter, a wonderful gift. Jesus is often thought of as a solemn person. I think that he would have laughed heartily with his friends many times as he worked in Nazareth and travelled with his disciples.

† *Heavenly Father, thank you for the gift of laughter. And thank you for the birth of children everywhere, new lives born to share life with you. Amen*

Monday July 18   **Exodus 23:14–17**

HARVESTS   These three great festivals of the Jewish faith were originally to do with harvest: the barley harvest, the offering of the first fruits, and finally the full harvest festival. Passover, the giving of the law and the feast of tabernacles were also part of each of these three celebrations. The gathering together to celebrate showed that the Jews were a community and depended on each other – as do Christians and all people. Christians celebrate their three great festivals – Christmas, Easter and Pentecost. But we may forget the importance of harvest festivals, sometimes seen as pagan. They remind us of God's goodness and how much we depend on each other. Our food can come from all over the world. So let us celebrate the harvest with joy. At the same time be generous to those who are poor, pray for countries where there is drought and play an active part in trying to see that all have a fair share of the harvests of the world. This may mean supporting fair-trade organisations and being concerned with the problems of changing climates and global warming.

Celebrate the Feast of Ingathering ... when you gather in your crops.   **(part of verse 16)**

– but also have concern for others.

† *Father, we thank you for the harvests of the world. We pray for places where harvests fail. Please give us generous hearts to help those who are hungry. Amen*

Tuesday July 19   **2 Chronicles 30:1–21**

A PASSOVER WITH A DIFFERENCE The Northern kingdom, Israel, has fallen, but the Southern kingdom of Judah is still free. King Hezekiah sent a letter by couriers – they must have been very careful to avoid Syrian occupying forces. Some people, either out of faithfulness to God or to defy the Syrians, made their way to Jerusalem so that the worship would truly represent all Israel. And there was great joy. There were rules for the celebration of the Passover but these were set aside so that the people could unite. Hezekiah prayed for those who could not prepare.

'May the Lord ... pardon everyone who sets his heart on seeking God.' **(parts of verses 18 and 19)**

Are we prepared to break the rules when it seems right? For example, at Christmas, should we invite to receive communion all who want to find God whether they belong to other churches, are children or even have nothing to do with the church? While generally we have to be loyal to the rules of our particular church, there are times when we should be prepared to break those rules out of love for Jesus. Then God gives the joy and the healing.

† *Father, help us to know when to break ceremonial and church rules to obey higher laws of love. Amen*

Wednesday July 20   Nehemiah 12:27–43

THE CITY IS SAFE SO CELEBRATE! There are some cities, including Jerusalem, where even today it is possible to walk on top of the walls. There is room for two, three or four men to walk side by side. So picture the celebrations in Jerusalem when the wall was completed. Imagine the two processions, marching round in full view of all the people, meeting where the temple stood and uniting in a great celebration of praise because the city was complete and safe. The word rejoicing is repeated three times in verse 43.

The sound of rejoicing in Jerusalem could be heard far away. **(part of verse 43)**

It hadn't been easy! There had been many setbacks and delays, much hard and dangerous work and sincere prayer, particularly from Nehemiah, the Governor. But now it is completed. Nehemiah planned carefully so that the ceremony was rich and varied with all kinds of music. Also, perhaps unusually for the Jewish community of the time, he involved the women and children. Let us learn lessons from Nehemiah in planning and preparing our own celebrations.

† *Father, help our celebrations to be full of great joy as we meet to praise you for what has been accomplished through your guidance and strength. Amen*

Thursday July 21   **Psalm 126:1–6**

ONE OF THE MOST BEAUTIFUL PSALMS   If you have a good imagination, try to picture groups of Jewish exiles walking the long road from Babylon to Jerusalem, and imagine the joy and the hopes as they draw near to the city they love. There would be old people who remembered Jerusalem and their young and enthusiastic sons and daughters who had heard many stories about the city. And so they sing, 'We were like men who dreamed...' But the situation when they get home is different: the city in ruins, bad harvests, political opposition, and a huge task ahead. So the joy turns into grim determination followed by sheer hard work – twenty years of it. Eventually difficulties are overcome and they bring home the harvest. Jerusalem is restored, the temple rebuilt, and the worship of God re-established.

> **Those who sow in tears**
> **will reap with songs of joy.**   **(verse 5)**

So it is with us. Being a Christian is a mixture of times of great joy and enthusiasm followed by hard slog as we obey God and try to carry out his purposes. Sometimes we see the result in this life (think of the world-wide Alpha course); sometimes we shall have to wait until we fully enter God's kingdom.

† *Father, thank you for calling us to your service and for the great joy you give. Help us to persevere when times are hard so that we may bring forth a rich harvest. Amen*

Friday July 22   **Ezra 6:13–18**

THE TEMPLE IS FINISHED – REJOICE! The Jews faced many political problems. But when Darius, a pagan, became king and looked at the edict of Cyrus, he ordered the work to go ahead and no one dared to stop it! So God's house was completed. The Jews knew that God did not live in buildings, but completing a special building dedicated to the worship of God was a matter for great rejoicing. So with us, when a church is built there is great celebration.

> **Then the people of Israel – the priests, the Levites and the**
> **rest of the exiles – celebrated the dedication of the house of**
> **God with joy.**   **(verse 16)**

Our churches must never be an end in themselves – we must put God first. But the building can truly be a focal point of worship, of building up the body of Christ and of serving the community. Let us give thanks for our churches and make them places where people can really find God.

† *Heavenly Father, we thank you for our church buildings. May they truly be places of prayer, worship and   meeting with you. Amen*

Saturday July 23   **Revelation 19:6–10**

THE ULTIMATE WEDDING FEAST Imagine a super wedding with crowds of guests, everyone joining in great hymns of praise, a huge feast. There is plenty for all, food and wine (or beer). Now make that picture in your mind greater than you can possibly think of: supreme joy and praise – the wedding feast of the lamb. And picture the bride in the finest white dress (or whatever colour is appropriate in your culture). The gown is made up of the good deeds of countless Christians, including yours! A true marriage is made up of love and the deepest intimacy. And that is how it will be between Jesus and his church – which again includes you! The John who wrote Revelation had this vision at a time of great persecution and hardship for Christians. Despite all the troubles in the world, this feast will come and you will be part of it.

Let us rejoice and be glad
and give him glory!   (part of verse 7)

One other point. John is shown this by an angel – a fellow servant. We human beings are not alone in our struggle. When I say the words of the communion service, 'with angels and archangels...', I picture them somewhere up in the roof of our simple village church joining with us in worship of God the Almighty!

† *Thank you, Lord, for our invitation to your wedding feast. Help us to look forward to it with joy. Amen*

For group discussion and personal thought

● Some churches are rather dull. Some go over the top! Do we have a right balance of celebration and joy in our worship?

CELEBRATION 2
Peculiar parties

Notes by Anthony Loke

based on the Revised Standard Version

Anthony Loke is a lecturer in the Old Testament at Seminari Theoloji Malaysia, the largest inter-denominational seminary in Malaysia. Currently, he is also working part-time on his doctoral studies from the University of Wales in the area of Deutero-Isaiah.

In Malaysia, the word 'Celebration!' is on everyone's lips today when they hold a birthday party or throw a *kenduri* (a Malay word for a large community dinner). People celebrate for different reasons – to give thanks for success, for long life, for an anniversary or birthday, for securing a business deal or for achieving good academic results. In the Bible, we also read of parties or banquets being held on different occasions and for differing reasons. Here are some biblical parties with an uncharacteristic twist.

Text for the week: Luke 17:28–30

Sunday July 24   **Judges 16:23–31**

BRINGING THE HOUSE DOWN

Now the lords of the Philistines gathered to offer a great sacrifice to Dagon their god, and to rejoice; for they said, 'Our god has given Samson our enemy into our hand.'
(verse 23)

The Philistines threw a party in honour of their god Dagon to celebrate the capture of Samson, their greatest enemy. Not content with just feasting and merry-making, they called for Samson to be brought out of the prison to entertain them. This was further humiliation for the already blinded Samson. Unknown to the Philistines, Samson's hair had grown back while he had languished in prison. This meant that his supernatural strength was restored. Samson asked a small boy to lead him to stand between two pillars supporting the house.

With a great push, he toppled the pillars over and brought the house down, killing the three thousand Philistines and their lords. The scriptures record that Samson killed more in his death than in his lifetime. The Philistines came to the party hoping to get a good laugh at Samson but Samson had the last laugh instead. In his last performance as a judge, Samson literally 'brought the house down' but no one was laughing – they were overwhelmed by Samson's bizarre finale.

† *Lord, help me not to laugh over things that may not be pleasant now, lest in the end I shall be laughed at by others. Instead, help me to serve you faithfully to the end.*

Monday July 25   Genesis 43:15–30

A CURIOUS REUNION DINNER

Portions were taken to them from Joseph's table, but Benjamin's portion was five times as much as any of theirs. So they drank and were merry with him. (verse 34)

The Chinese community always holds a reunion dinner on Chinese New Year's Eve. It is a special family dinner where it is customary for every member of the extended family to try to make the journey home to the family house. Thus, if one of them has been constantly absent from home throughout the year, he will return home at this time to be reunited with his family members. The elders of the family are extremely upset if younger members of the family are absent from this meal. The background to today's passage is that Joseph, the eleventh son of Jacob, had earlier been sold as a slave by his brothers and taken to Egypt. With God's help, Joseph not only survived the ordeal but also triumphed and rose to be Prime Minister of Egypt. It was not by chance that a famine struck Egypt and the neighbouring countries, for this brought Joseph's brothers to Egypt to buy grain. Joseph was reunited with his brothers, albeit incognito. They did not recognise him because he was dressed differently. Invited by Joseph to his house for a meal, they went in trepidation and fear of him. With his identity concealed, Joseph was able to enjoy his time with his brothers without their knowledge. They ate, drank and were merry without realising that their gracious host was their long-lost brother. It was only later that Joseph revealed his identity to them. Would they have celebrated in this way if they had known that their host was the brother they had sold as a slave years earlier?

† *Lord, sometimes we celebrate without realising the weight of guilt upon us, but you are always the gracious host who invites us to yourself.*

Tuesday July 26   **Mark 6:21–25**

LOSING YOUR HEAD? LOSING YOUR MIND?

'I want you to give me at once the head of John the Baptist on a platter.'   **(part of verse 25)**

King Herod threw a banquet for his top government officials and the leading citizens of Galilee on the occasion of his birthday. The highlight of the banquet was a solo dance by Herodias' daughter. Herod was obviously pleased with the performance and vowed to give her whatever she wanted. She returned to her mother to ask what sort of gift she should receive. Herodias held a grudge against John the Baptist because he had earlier rebuked her for marrying her brother-in-law, Herod (*verse 19*). So she told her daughter to ask for John's head served on a platter. Herod was caught, because of the vows he had made earlier to give the girl anything she wanted. John lost his head and ended up as the main course in the banquet. The scriptures do not record the reaction of the partygoers, Herod, Herodias or Herodias' daughter, nor do they tell us how the party ended. It must have ended on a very sombre and distasteful note, not exactly what Herod had in mind on his birthday! John the Baptist literally 'lost his head' but Herod must have lost his mind. He had beheaded and silenced the only person who dared to speak the truth about him (*verse 20*). Apparently, losing your head and losing your mind are not very different.

† *Lord, sometimes we make rash vows and others suffer for it. Help us to be careful in what we say lest we regret it later.*

Wednesday July 27   **Luke 14:1–14**

A REVERSAL OF FORTUNE

For every one who exalts himself will be humbled, and he who humbles himself will be exalted.   **(verse 11)**

Jesus was invited to a banquet given by a ruler of the Pharisees but it was a banquet with a difference. It was as if he was being watched by 'Big Brother' (a TV show in the UK where the cameras enable the viewers to see and scrutinise the participants' every move). The Pharisees were trying to catch Jesus making a mistake or a slip of the tongue. Jesus knew that this was not going to happen; instead, he told them a parable. He had seen how the guests were choosing the places of honour at the dinner party for themselves. Even today, it is common to see guests vie for the places of honour at a feast. Apart from being the best seats in the house, they are the places reserved for VIPs. Jesus warns against doing this lest a more prominent person comes along and the host has to ask us to vacate our seat for him. That will cause us to 'lose face', something very embarrassing in an Asian culture. Instead, Jesus suggests that we go first to the lowest place in the house so that when our host comes along and sees us there, he will naturally invite us to take a more important seat. This invitation from the host in the presence of other guests will 'bring face' to us instead. The moral of the story is simple: if we choose the best now, it might not be so for us later. It is better to go for the modest now and be rewarded later with the best.

† *Lord, help me to realise that what I seek for now may not be what I will get later, and that what I lose now I may be rewarded with at the end.*

Thursday July 28   **Numbers 28:16–26**

HOLY DAY OR HOLIDAY?

> **On the first day there shall be a holy convocation: you shall do no laborious work ... And on the seventh day you shall have a holy convocation; you shall do no laborious work.**
> **(verses 18 and 25)**

The Jewish people celebrate the Passover annually. As a community, they recall the deliverance of their ancestors from Egyptian bondage. God desires his people to commemorate this event of their salvation annually lest they forget their humble historical roots. However, it is all too easy to forget in the midst of joyful celebration. 'To forget what?' one may ask. The answer is: God! The Jewish people celebrated their annual commemorations as feasts or festivals. There would be rejoicing, singing, dancing, eating and merry-making. Sometimes these annual feasts would last as long as seven days. However, for the Passover celebration, God commanded that on the first and seventh day there should be a 'holy convocation', a sort of national gathering for worship and prayer. The people were to meet as a nation for worship first before they began their seven days of feasting and they should meet again for worship on the last day, to end their feast. This is the proper way for God's people to celebrate, to begin and end with God in their hearts and minds, lest they turn their 'Holy Day' into a mere 'holiday'.

† *Lord, help us to see that there are proper times to enjoy ourselves but we should not be so carried away with our celebrations that we forget you, the prime reason for our celebrating.*

Friday July 29   **Exodus 32:1–6**

WILD SEX PARTY

And they rose up early on the morrow, and offered burnt offerings and brought peace offerings; and the people sat down to eat and drink, and rose up to play.   (verse 6)

The story of the golden calf is all too familiar to God's people. The people were waiting at the foot of Mount Sinai for Moses to return but he was gone for many days. Not knowing what had happened to him, they asked Aaron, Moses' brother, to create 'gods' for them who would lead the people forward on the next stage of the journey. The golden calf was made out of the people's generous offerings. Did Aaron make a golden calf because he knew that the calf or young bull was often a symbol of virility and strength? Aaron declared the following day to be a feast to honour the Lord. It was a feast with a difference. The people woke up early the next day, as if they didn't want to waste any time in starting their celebration. The RSV says the people 'rose up to play', but there was nothing innocent about their play because the feast soon degenerated into a wild orgy of drinking and sex. They may have initially brought burnt and peace offerings to appease God but God was surely not pleased. Could Aaron have foreseen how the feast would degenerate into an orgy? The time spent waiting for Moses' return brought no honour to the Lord's name. How easy it is for something that is meant to be good to turn into something that brings dishonour and shame.

† *Lord, help me to understand that it is so very easy for something good to turn into something that brings dishonour to your name. Help me always to be vigilant lest I make a mockery of your name.*

EAT, DRINK AND BE MERRY UNTIL...?

They ate, they drank, they married, they were given in marriage, until the day when Noah entered the ark, and the flood came and destroyed them all. (verse 27)

How we wish sometimes that parties would not end, that we could go on and on feasting and celebrating. But we always forget about the day after, when we wake up with a hangover in our heads. When we are feasting, we forget about everything else because we are so caught up in the celebrations. Sometimes we even forget what is happening around us or in our midst. So it was in the time of Noah. The people were so caught up in partying and revelling that they ignored Noah's warnings. The floodwaters came and destroyed all of them except Noah and his family. So it was in the time of Lot. The people in Sodom and Gomorrah were so busy with their partying that they did not realise the magnitude of their sins. Fire and brimstone came down one day and destroyed all of them except Lot and his two daughters (*Genesis 19:24–29*). So it will be in the time of the Son of Man's return to earth. People will likewise be so busy partying and celebrating that they will forget about Jesus' imminent return. They will have embarked on a feast that does not seem to end but it will soon bring a big hangover. When Jesus returns, the noise of the earthly feasting and celebrations will cease and turn into mourning, wailing and a gnashing of teeth. Only those who belong to Jesus will continue with him into heaven, for the eternal heavenly banquet.

† *Lord, help me to be aware that the feastings on earth will end one day and be no more; only those who belong to you will continue to feast at your presence in heaven.*

For group discussion and personal thought

● Have you ever been to a party which ended with a 'twist'?
● What lessons can you learn from this set of stories about these peculiar parties?
● If we know that life is sometimes not what it seems, what can we do about it?

CELEBRATION 3
Dance in celebration

Notes by Philip Wetherell

based on the New English Bible

Philip Wetherell is the Director of Christians Abroad, an ecumenical advice and information agency that helps Christians and others to explore vocations to work in mission and development, and works with other churches around the world to find skilled people and volunteers in health, education and other practical areas of the churches' service to their communities.

Celebration is natural. With families and friends we share our food and drink, we tell stories, we laugh and sing – and dance. The dancing can be formal and controlled, or spontaneous. It is the same in our churches, with the beautiful controlled movements of our ritual and free, spirit-led worship. These different bodily reactions to our thoughts, feelings and events can be seen in biblical stories too. Just as we respond to God very differently, so we are seen by others in very different ways!

Text for the week: Psalm 150:1–2

Sunday July 31   **2 Samuel 6:1–14**

DANCING, ANGER AND DISGUST   The Ark of the Lord, the very presence of God among his people as the Hebrews believed, had been rescued from their enemy. What better reason for God's people to rejoice? Singing, dancing and music from tambourines and whatever else was available – a natural reaction to God who was among them.

David and all Israel danced for joy before the Lord without restraint.   **(verse 5)**

Dressed it seems like a priest, David leads the rejoicing. But then the oxen stumble, Uzzah (perhaps not in the dancing mood?) sees the oxen stumble and saves the ark from falling over, but God strikes him down for touching it. David is angry

– a different natural reaction. Just after the end of this section of the story, Michal, the daughter of Saul, argues with David; it seems that in throwing himself around in dance David has exposed himself. Three different reactions – unrestrained joy, anger, disgust – all from people believing they were right in what they were doing. We don't always satisfy everyone when we try to get it right with God, and the question to ask is: how far can we compromise our feelings and what comes naturally to us in the way we respond to God? How much does God want us to be ourselves – whatever effect that may have on others?

† *Lord, help us to remember that our praise of you can affect how others see us and your church.*

Monday August 1   Psalm 150

LET EVERYTHING THAT HAS BREATH PRAISE THE LORD! The last five psalms in the book of 150 are full of praise, bringing in every kind of person (young and old, from kings to the humble), every climatic event (from fire to snow), and all nature (green things, wild beasts, creeping things and birds). And then Psalm 150: a mighty burst of praise. It is a wonderful ending to a book that has within it every human emotion. How humans react to events and to God in love, anger, questioning, vengeance, sorrow and joy has been examined and placed before God. And there can only be one conclusion:

O praise God in his holy place,
praise him in the vault of heaven, the vault of his power;
praise him for his mighty works,
    praise him for his immeasurable greatness.

                   (part of verse 1 and verse 2)

The next three verses contrast the strong and brash – trumpets, fanfares and tambourines – with the gentle and quieter lute, harp, flute and strings. All will praise the Lord. And dancing is there with the strong and brash; it is the only way that those who can't play an instrument can express themselves. The Psalm ends with the only instrument given a descriptive adjective: 'Praise him with triumphant cymbals' (*verse 5b*). Being with God through the whole range of emotions has only one conclusion: a knowledge that God is all-powerful, he must be praised, and his will must be done.

† *Lord, help us to share with you all that we feel – and to be strong in our praise, however we are feeling.*

Tuesday August 2   **Jeremiah 31:1–14**

GO FORTH AND DANCE

> **I will build you up again, O virgin Israel,**
> **and you shall be rebuilt.**   **(part of verse 4)**

The nation of Israel has fallen, her people driven away or taken into exile. The centre of their faith, the Temple, has been destroyed. Everything that could go wrong has done so. Yet Jeremiah is trying to tell God's people that things will get better again! For a disheartened people, unsure that their God is really there for them, it is a remarkable vision. Here is a loving God who cares for all as a shepherd and a father, who will gather together all his people – the blind and the lame and the women in labour (*verse 8*) as well as the farmers and herdsmen. There will be a place for all in the new kingdom. This new inclusive people will have been comforted (*verse 9*) and led along a smooth path. Could this be a picture of our churches and their pastoral care, welcoming all equally whatever their status? As a result, people will go forth, planting vineyards (*verse 5*), and leading the nations (*verse 7*). This is a picture of our mission, both to plant the word and to give a moral lead in world events. Our mission will have a firm foundation because of the rebuilding, because we are there for all, and because we demonstrate our care and leadership. And then the whole people will rejoice with us:

> **Again you shall adorn yourself with jingles,**
> **and go forth with the merry throng of dancers.**
>
> **(part of verse 4)**

† *Lord, help us to take forward your mission, showing we are there*
for everyone, and demonstrating both care and leadership.

Wednesday August 3   **1 Chronicles 15:25 – 16:3**

DAVID DANCES AGAIN   This passage takes up the story of the Ark that we read three days ago. David goes to collect the Ark from where he left it, and takes it to Jerusalem. The other story from that passage is taken up again too. Michal again sees David dancing, dressed again, it seems, as a priest.

> **As the Ark of the Covenant of the LORD was entering the**
> **city of David, Saul's daughter Michal looked down**
> **through a window and saw King David dancing and**
> **making merry, and despised him in her heart.   (verse 29)**

It is easy to take sides here. Should David show more restraint? Maybe dancing is OK, but is 'making merry'? Are there special responsibilities for priests that are different from those of a king? Or is it simply that Michal is jealous of the man who replaced her father in God's favour? And does our response to this story depend on how we prefer to worship? It is worth reflecting on how outsiders see Christians in our 'home' setting – our churches. Do we impress them by our fervour and shouts of praise, or by quiet devotion? Do we exclude people by what we do, or does that depend on who is watching or even on how they are feeling at the time? Whatever the reason, we certainly need to be pastorally aware that what seems good to us may not seem right to others.

✝ *Lord, help us to remember that there are many ways of worshipping you, and to welcome and encourage everyone who acknowledges you.*

Thursday August 4   Acts 3:1–10

LEAP FOR JOY   In the very early days of the Christian church we learn that Christ's work continues. Peter heals a man crippled from birth, and we are reminded of Jesus' answer to John the Baptist's question in Matthew 11:3–4, when he is asked, 'Are you the one who is to come?' Jesus replies, 'Go and tell John what you hear and see: the blind recover their sight, the lame walk...' Peter demonstrates that those healing powers have come with the gift of God's Spirit to the church. Peter says:

'In the name of Jesus Christ of Nazareth, walk.' Then he grasped him by the right hand and pulled him up; and at once his feet and ankles grew strong; he sprang up, stood on his feet and started to walk. He entered the temple with them, leaping and praising God as he went.
(part of verse 6 and verses 7–8)

The man who can suddenly walk might wonder if that is all he can do. Can I run, can I jump as well? But he saves his testing of this to the time of praise in the Temple; that is where he leaps, and that is where praise is due. Thanksgiving and praise should indeed be our reaction to healing – and for our own doctors too, who are also doing God's work.

✝ *Lord, help us to remember all who do your work, to give thanks where it should be given and praise to you at all times.*

DANCING AT OTHERS' MISFORTUNE? The crossing of the Red Sea is the central event of perhaps the most important part of Israel's history. The Exodus experience has also been central for Christian groups, who have had their own experiences of persecution. Despite what appears as a great act of God in parting the waters and saving his people from the pursuing Egyptians, the story is full of very human doubts and uncertainties. Taken into a strange land, people want the certainties of the past – water and food (*Exodus 15:24* and *16:3*) – and their slavery seems forgotten. And there is what appears to be another human element too: rejoicing over the fate of others. It is natural to rejoice at your own salvation, but is it right to thank God for the misfortune of others?

> **Miriam the prophetess ... took up her tambourine, and all the women followed her, dancing to the sound of tambourines; and Miriam sang them this refrain:**
>
> **'Sing to the Lord, for he has risen up in triumph; the horse and his rider he has hurled into the sea.**
> **(part of verse 20 and verse 21)**

If all the good that happens can be laid at God's feet, then why not all the bad things too? The Egyptian soldiers, not themselves to blame for the decisions of their masters, were to perish. Is God to be thanked for this or any misfortunes that happen to those we disagree with? It is worth remembering that in those times life was as uncertain as it still is today for people living in poverty, with little health care and an unknown future, who offer prayers of thankfulness for survival every morning. To dance and sing is to see God active in your whole life (something we need to learn) – but without gloating at the misfortune of others.

† *Lord, help us to remember that your will is for the good of all.*

A PARTY THAT SHOULDN'T BE? Jesus tells his story of the prodigal son very cleverly. Our sympathies go from one character to another: from the insulted father to the failed younger son starving because of his wasteful ways, then to the hard-working, obedient and dutiful older son. The story is well told. But who are the audience? Two groups, the first tax-gatherers and 'bad characters', and the second Pharisees and doctors of the law, are crowding round (*Luke 15:1*), and this story is for both groups. It is a story of the greatest offence that could be caused in that society. The younger son wants his birthright – now; it is as if he wishes his own father dead. There can be no worse sin. Yet this 'prodigal' son, who has wasted what he should not even have asked for, who admits he no longer has the right to be called a son, is forgiven. The festivities begin.

> 'The older son was out on the farm; and on his way back, as he approached the house, he heard music and dancing. He called one of the servants and asked him what it meant. The servant told him, "Your brother has come home and your father has killed the fatted calf".'
>
> **(verses 25–26 and part of verse 27)**

Jesus takes each group with him. Each – the sinners and the self-righteous – will feel that Jesus is on his side at one point or another. And there is no conclusion. We are left to wonder what family relationships might be in the future. But we know who the party is for.

† *Lord, help us to remember your message of forgiveness.*

For group discussion and personal thought

● How would you or your congregation react to King David, or to Miriam? Would you be as full of self-justification as the older son in Jesus' story of the prodigal?
● Rejoicing is great – but what are the limits? And does what you do in your worship offend or attract people?

MATTHEW 5
Parables of the kingdom

Notes by Iain Roy

based on the Good News Bible

Iain Roy is a retired minister of the Church of Scotland with a background of ministry in an area of urban deprivation and industrial chaplaincy. He is a former moderator and clerk of the Presbytery of Ardrossan, and is regularly engaged in leading worship.

The parables of Jesus may seem simple stories, but only to those who lack discernment. They were addressed to several different audiences: the disciples, the leaders of Israel, the people of Jesus' time. To understand them we have to be aware of not only the original setting in which they were spoken, but also the situations which arose later and made the church cherish and preserve them as a word for their time; and we have to approach them with the awareness that they still have the power to be a word for our time, bringing God's rule and purpose into our lives.

Text for the week: Matthew 13:34–35

Sunday August 7   Matthew 13:24–30

DELAYED JUDGEMENT   It was difficult for the farmer of Jesus' place and time to distinguish the growing weed, darnel, from the emerging healthy wheat in the early stages of its growth. It was good husbandry, therefore, to delay its removal until he could.

> **'Let the wheat and the weeds both grow together until harvest. Then I will tell the harvest workers to pull up the weeds first, tie them in bundles and burn them, and then to gather in the wheat and put it in my barn.'** (verse 30)

The leaders of Israel lacked that kind of patience. They could not understand how Jesus kept company with publicans and sinners, and were swift to condemn them. But Jesus had the patience of God himself, the love that can wait for potential to be realised, and knows also that those for whom we cherish great hopes can disappoint us. Perhaps we too should learn in our relationships to 'wait and see'.

† *Lord, make us slow to condemn and swift to forgive.*

Monday August 8   **Matthew 13:31–32**

SMALL BEGINNINGS   Living, as we do, in an age which is easily impressed by size and success, status and wealth, it is not difficult for us to see how the leaders of Israel might have been unimpressed by the ministry of Jesus and his disciples.

> **'It is the smallest of all seeds, but when it grows up, it is the biggest of all plants. It becomes a tree, so that birds come and make their nests in its branches.'**   **(verse 32)**

If ever a mission seemed doomed to fail, it surely must have been the mission of Christ and his disciples to bring God's love to fruition in the lives of humanity. The men and women of the early church must have felt the same as they struggled to spread the gospel, particularly in the face of persecution. It is certainly a thought that must cross our own minds as we try to communicate God's truth and love in a world which is sometimes hostile, sometimes indifferent to them. But God goes on working, the growth coming sometimes in the most unexpected places and in the hearts of the most unexpected people.

† *Lord God, remind us that you are always working your purposes out, giving growth unseen to our labours. Teach us to persist so that your love may prevail.*

Tuesday August 9   **Matthew 13:33**

TRANSFORMATION   It might be thought at first that the message of this parable contradicts the previous parable with its message of quiet but eventually spectacular growth. But in fact the emphasis is the same – dramatic transformation – but here swift and visible.

> **'The Kingdom of heaven is like this. A woman takes some yeast and mixes it with forty litres of flour until the whole batch of dough rises.'**   **(part of verse 33)**

God's truth and love can bring ferment and disturbance into a life before it is changed for good. Christ was seeking this kind of change not only in his disciples but in the leaders of Israel themselves, confronting their existing deeply-held convictions. We should learn from them to beware if we only find our religion comforting!

† *Lord Jesus, change us and our world, turn us and it upside down, whatever the time it takes, or the drastic change it brings to the way we speak or think or do.*

Wednesday August 10   **Matthew 13:44–46**

DIFFERENT PATHS, SAME LORD   These two parables give every appearance of being identical twins! But they are not.

'The Kingdom of heaven is like this. A man happens to find a treasure hidden in a field ... A man is looking for fine pearls...'   (parts of verses 44 and 45)

In one story the discovery is accidental: in the other it comes after persistent searching. Jesus was aware that there are many ways to come to him. But, however we come, he asks the same searching question about the level of our commitment that these two parables asked of their heroes. They emphasise what men will do for material gain. The question they leave with us is whether we are as committed spiritually.

† *Lord, help us to care about the things which really matter in life. Give us your sense of proportion based on love.*

Thursday August 11   Matthew 13:47–50

ALL KINDS   The scarcity of fish stocks in the waters off the Scottish coast has led to severe restrictions for Scottish fishermen and a loss of jobs in the industry. Net fishing, even today, is often indiscriminate, catching fish of all kinds, and both the mature and the immature.

'The Kingdom of heaven is like this. Some fishermen throw their net out in the lake and catch all kinds of fish.'   (verse 47)

The church too is made up of 'all sorts and conditions of men and women'. That is one of its glories – that its members come from different backgrounds, with different life-histories, with different jobs and different abilities, from different nations, young and old, male and female. Yet Christ has a special place for each of us, especially for those who feel unloved or unwanted.

† *Assure us, O Lord, of the place we have in your love, and, if we feel alone, depressed, unwanted, lift our hearts by your presence with us now.*

Friday August 12   Matthew 13:51–53

SEEK UNDERSTANDING   It is one thing to listen, quite another to understand. The parables are easy to listen to but they are not always as easy to understand as their brevity and familiarity might sometimes suggest to us.

'Do you understand these things? ... Every teacher of the Law who becomes a disciple in the Kingdom of heaven is like the owner of a house who takes new and old things out of his storeroom.'   (parts of verses 51 and 52)

Jesus in his teaching drew on a long tradition of story-telling in the Jewish religion. He was reflecting all the teaching of the Old Testament that both he and his listeners were familiar with. But he was also putting forth original and radical views that challenged, in particular, men like Nicodemus and Joseph of Arimathea. Our Christian faith can never just be received wisdom. What we know must always be balanced by what we have still to learn or re-learn, or discover.

† *Help us, Lord, to respect all that we have learned from others, yet also to learn to think for ourselves with the prompting of your Holy Spirit.*

Saturday August 13   Matthew 13:54–58

A REAL HUMANITY   The attitude of people in Jesus' home village is very understandable in human terms. Familiarity, if it does not always actually breed contempt, certainly creates a tendency to disbelieve that anyone we have known could ever be exceptional in any way.

> **'Where did he get such wisdom?' ... 'What about his miracles? Isn't he the carpenter's son? Isn't Mary his mother?'**   **(parts of verses 54 and 55)**

It is still for Christians today the most difficult truth to take in – that God's love and truth were fully disclosed in a truly human life. The church down through the ages has had to battle with the persistent temptation for Christians to think that Christ's humanity must somehow be different from their own. It is a temptation to resist, an excuse often for us not to attempt to make visible in our own humanity the same love and truth Christ came into the world to reveal. The real difference lies in what he and he alone achieved.

† *Christ Jesus, help us to make real in our day the love your Father has for all humankind. Enlarge our compassion and deepen our insight into our neighbour's need.*

For group discussion and personal thought

● Think of some of the people you know and their journey of faith. Contrast and compare it with your own.
● What do you most value in your faith, and what do you see as the main obstacle to communicating the gospel to others today ?

MATTHEW 6
Signs and wonders

Notes by Ann Hadley

based on the Good News Bible

Ann Hadley spent many years in Africa, first in Zimbabwe and later in Zululand. She is now a priest in the Anglican church and lives in the Diocese of Worcester, England.

This week we look at a wide variety of Bible stories as written in Matthew. We may say that life has changed greatly since Jesus told them and question whether they still have a message for us today. There is a sense in which parables can lead us to discover what God wants us to discover. They are about ordinary human failures and successes, fears and hopes, and about God's power to redeem our lives – things we have in common with all who have lived down the ages. So as you meditate upon the scripture set for each day, picture yourself at the scene; perhaps identify yourself with one of the characters. Then give time to allow Jesus to speak into your situation. What is he requiring of you?

Text for the week: Matthew 21:22

Sunday August 14   **Matthew 14:13–21**

COME AND EAT

> **'All we have here are five loaves and two fish.' ... 'Then bring them here to me,' Jesus said.   (part of verse 17 and verse 18)**

It seems Jesus and his disciples had hopped into a boat and were trying to get away from the crowds for a bit of peace and quiet. That idea was short-lived – you know the feeling, I expect. People had run round the lake and were again clamouring to see him. They had already witnessed the miracles Jesus had done but many more needed help. What, then, are we to make of this story of the loaves and fishes? (Incidentally, the crowd must have been more in the region of 10 000 when women and children were included.) It was sad that the disciples wanted to send the people away. No doubt they were tired. Then Jesus said, 'They don't have to leave' and invited everyone to stay and share in the meal.

Jesus turned what seemed impossible into the possible and that is the key to this story. We never know what possibilities we are releasing when we invite someone to come to church with us, for instance. Or perhaps we feel we do not have much to offer God, but if we use what talents we have, there is no knowing what he will do with us. Sometimes we are fearful in offering what we have in case it is rejected, or we feel it is not good enough. We can exclude people and send them away, or include people and invite them to come and join us. We need to help each other feel that we belong as a child of God.

† *Lord, help us to remember this week that small offerings sincerely given are always great in your hands.*

Monday August 15   Matthew 14:22–33

HELP! I'M SINKING   We often have to face up to situations in life where we feel out of our depth. Swimming is an appropriate example. We happily splash around when our feet can touch ground and we feel safe. But what happens when we venture too far out of our depth? It's very scary and things get difficult; we panic; we start to sink and cry for help. We cry for someone to save us. Observing Peter in this passage, he seems to have been quite an impetuous man. He was out of his depth, scared that he would drown – until he realised Jesus was really there and could rescue him.

> **Peter spoke up. 'Lord, if it is really you, order me to come out on the water to you.' 'Come!' answered Jesus. So Peter got out of the boat and started walking on the water to Jesus. But when he noticed the strong wind, he was afraid and started to sink down in the water. 'Save me, Lord!' he cried. At once Jesus reached out and grabbed hold of him and said, 'How little faith you have! Why did you doubt?'**
> **(verses 28–31)**

Some of us have personal responsibilities at home or at work which from time to time seem too much for us; or the effects of unemployment can make us feel as if we are about to sink beneath the waves. It is as if there is no solid ground under our feet. Feelings of imagined disaster make us irrational, lost and frightened. We tend to think no one else is affected the way we are. The crux of this story, however, is the moment when Peter took his eyes off Jesus and looked at the stormy waves instead. This is a lesson we have to learn over and over again: to look beyond what is bothering us to Christ who gives us the courage not to be afraid.

Tuesday August 16   **Matthew 14:34-4–36**

WHAT DOES IT MEAN TO BELONG?

The people recognised Jesus. So they sent for the sick people in all the surrounding country and brought them to Jesus. They begged him to let those who were ill at least touch the edge of his cloak; and all who touched it were made well.   **(verses 35–36)**

At first glance these two verses may appear to say very little of importance. However, perhaps they can serve as a reminder. All too easily scripture can become so familiar that we pass over sections which could reveal fresh meaning if we allowed a little more time. Here in a few words we have a revealing picture of Jesus. Whenever he appeared anywhere, the crowds gathered for his blessing. There is no mention that Jesus preached or taught at length but he did show people that God cared. Each human being is special in his sight. We are told Jesus healed all who came for help. However, there is a down side. When we read this brief passage it is clear that thousands of people only came to Jesus for what they could get out of him. Once healed, many were not really prepared to commit themselves any further. We may hear of people in our own neighbourhood who believe in God but feel nothing else is necessary. Anyone can say they are a magnificent footballer, but there is no way they can play without the rest of the team! Neither can we be effective Christians without belonging to a worshipping congregation where nurture, faith and love are to be found.

† *Lord, the scripture says, 'There is a time for silence and a time for speech.' Teach me to silence my own heart that I may listen to the gentle movement of the Holy Spirit within me and sense the depths which are of God.*   (From a 16th-century prayer)

Wednesday August 17   **Matthew 15:21–28**

DOGS AND CRUMBS

The woman came and fell at his feet. 'Help me, sir!' she said. Jesus answered, 'It isn't right to take the children's food and throw it to the dogs.' 'That's true, sir,' she answered; 'but even the dogs eat the leftovers that fall from their masters' table.' So Jesus answered her, 'You are a

woman of great faith!'
                    (part of verse 25, verses 26–27 and part of verse 28)

Here we have a very persistent woman but one who is willing to
settle for crumbs – perhaps unusual in the world today where
everyone wants the biggest and best. Her daughter has 'a demon'
and is in a terrible condition. She pleads for Jesus to help but at first
he ignores her. What do we do when Jesus appears not to answer
our requests? It does happen! The temptation is to give up and stop
praying. We may even take our disappointment a step further and
start to ignore the one who seems to be ignoring us! A kind of
retaliation: 'OK, God, I'm not going to bother any more' and our
Christian life begins to fall apart. Not so with this Canaanite
woman. She persisted in her task, recognising that there was
nourishment even in the crumbs under the table. If the dogs (a
derogatory term for the Gentiles) could snatch them, why shouldn't
she benefit too? Crumbs are opportunities. The woman could be
any one of us asking for grace and healing in our own particular
circumstances. We may be wondering why God keeps us waiting
but are we prepared for God to act when we least expect him? Be
ready for opportunities and take them.

† *Lord Jesus Christ, you healed those who suffered in mind as well*
   as body. Look in your compassion on people among us who are
   mentally or physically ill.

Thursday August 18   **Matthew 15:29–39**

REACHING OUT   At first glance it may seem that the feeding of
the 5000 we read about last Sunday and the 4000 today are different
versions of the same incident but that is not so. The time, people
and place are different, as also is the message. On this occasion
there appeared to be many Gentiles present (they see God as the
God of Israel, see verse 31) after Jesus had healed yet more people:

and they [the Gentiles] praised the God of Israel.
                                          (part of verse 31)

Already Jesus is hinting that his love reaches out everyone. Here
is a symbol that the bread of God was not to be confined to one
group of people. All may share it. It carries a message to us and our
churches today. We are all parts of the same Body of Christ. To try
to exclude those who appear not to conform to our ideas leads to a
divisive rather than a united church. It is possible for Christians to
destroy each other from within. How, then, can we effectively stand
together in the name of Christ in these very difficult days?

† *Lord Jesus, gather us once more to yourself and feed us with the Living Bread. Forgive our dissensions, that those who profess the Christian faith may no longer exclude one another but be kind and accepting of all.*

Friday August 19   Matthew 20:28–34

USING OUR OPPORTUNITIES

Jesus stopped and called them, 'What do you want me to do for you?' he asked them. 'Sir', they answered, 'we want you to give us our sight!'   **(verses 32–33)**

These two blind men, seated strategically on the roadside, were about to get the opportunity of a lifetime to escape their world of darkness. Perhaps there are those of us who feel we need a new vision for ourselves, and chances of help wouldn't come amiss! All of us in our hearts probably have regrets of some kind: the way life has turned out, we wish it could have been different. It is possible to go on yearning, too, for something that up to now hasn't happened. Or regretting those things that have occurred and cannot be changed. No doubt these two blind men felt all of this because they had reached the bottom of the human pile, feeling outcasts and suffering loss of self-worth. This gospel story really is Good News for the downhearted. The words 'persistent', 'determination' and 'taking the opportunity' not to let Jesus pass by are all there as positive thinking. So often we are inclined to say, 'Wait till I've done this or finished that', or 'I can't be bothered, nothing will happen anyway'. Watch for your God-given opportunities this week and use them. Ours is a God who is able to perform the possible out of the seemingly impossible.

† *God of surprises, when I think you are not present in my life, you suddenly reveal yourself and nurture me in your everlasting love. You bring hope out of despair and create opportunity out of difficulty. Thank you, Lord.*

Saturday August 20   Matthew 21:14–22

GROWING CONFLICT Once again we find Jesus in a situation of conflict. Many sick people were being healed and children were shouting,

'Praise to David's Son!'   **(part of verse 15)**

However, he was being watched closely by the chief priests and leaders of the day. They were incensed by Jesus' popularity and vowed to get him! Jealousy, anger, fear are three negative emotions that come to the surface when we feel threatened by someone or something. Do we recognise any such emotions affecting us? How are we going to deal with them?

He saw a fig tree by the side of the road and went to it, but found nothing on it except leaves. So he said to the tree, 'You will never again bear fruit!' At once the fig tree dried up. (verse 19)

This parable of the fig tree also takes up the idea of condemnation. Here was a tree with leaves; the leaves were a claim to produce figs; the tree had no figs so its claim was false. Jesus appears to use his power to condemn the tree but to take this story literally presents difficulties. Anyway, it was the wrong time of year for figs! To blast a tree which could not satisfy his hunger seems unfair. However, if we take it as a symbolic action, we can begin to see what Jesus was getting at. The people of Israel, throughout their history, had been looking forward to the promised coming of the Messiah. Eventually, when he did come, people didn't recognise him and even accused him of false claims to be a king. The priests and other authority figures professed faith in God but in practice they were out for Jesus' blood. Therefore they stood condemned. This highlights what has always been a problem for the church. The tree with its leaves seemed to be offering something but did not. How many people today profess the Christian faith without actually practising it? Yet commitment is essential for an effective worshipping community. By our fruits we shall be known.

† *Lord, we pray for all those who lead worship in our churches. Inspire them with your Holy Spirit to produce services which are relevant and attractive, that people may be drawn to belong as well as believe.*

For group discussion and personal thought

● Take the text for the week and consider the negatives and positives of such a statement.
● With which characters in the readings do you most identify? Why?
● How can we encourage those who lead our church worship to make services attractive and inclusive?
● Discuss the concept of believing without belonging, of professing faith without practising it. How does this harm the church?

TEXT MESSAGES TO THE FAITHFUL 1
From the brothers

Notes by Val Ogden

based on the New Revised Standard Version

Val Ogden is a British Methodist minister who previously worked in education, training and commercial radio. She served as a minister of the United Church of Zambia for 6 years and is now on the staff of the United College of the Ascension, Selly Oak, Birmingham, a global community for mission education and encounter.

James and Jude offer short, pithy letters in the biblical canon. In some parts of the Christian tradition they are regarded as being related to Jesus. With this in mind, let us listen to what they have to say to their brothers and sisters struggling to make sense of faith in a hostile world.

Text for the week: James 4:11

Sunday August 21   **James 1:1–6**

DEAR EVERYONE... We are used to letters in the New Testament addressed to particular places and communities: to the Corinthians, Philippians or Thessalonians, for example. James, it seems, has a much wider readership in mind.

> **To the twelve tribes in the Dispersion: Greetings. My brothers and sisters, whenever you face trials of any kind, consider it nothing but joy.**   **(part of verse 1 and verse 2)**

The language of 'dispersion' and the 'twelve tribes' would have been very familiar to Jews finding themselves scattered among Gentile communities outside Palestine. As the people of Israel, they felt a strong, unifying bond as they struggled to keep their faith and identity alive. Here, James adopts this same form of address for dispersed Christians from both Jewish and Gentile backgrounds. The followers of Jesus find themselves scattered far and wide, and face many trials as they try to live out the memory and mission of Jesus. Look at world Christianity today and the evidence of that

187

dispersion is very real. In which part of the world and in what circumstances are you reading this book, I wonder? And what of another IBRA reader in a totally different part of the world? Was James crazy to think he could write a letter that would hold meaning for such a variety of people and places? No, because right away he points to what unites us as people of faith, at a fundamental level: our trials and our joys. One reader's circumstances may seem to be worlds apart from another's, but there's no follower of Jesus on earth who is without a testimony to the trials of faith and the painful yet joyful cost of maintaining faith.

† *Pray for an IBRA reader in another part of the world, naming them if you can, and asking for the companionship of Christ to be theirs in their trials and joys.*

Monday August 22   James 1:16–18

A CONSTANT, CHANGELESS GOD   James speaks the language of astronomy a little here. He refers to God as 'Father of lights' – creator and controller of the planets, stars and heavenly bodies.

Every generous act of giving, with every perfect gift, is from above, coming down from the Father of lights, with whom there is no variation or shadow due to change.

(verse 17)

Interest in the movements of the planets is common to many societies. We have all watched the changing colour and shape of the sun and moon at their rising and setting. An eclipse of the sun, when the world goes temporarily dark, can make us both fascinated and fearful. Some believe that the movements of the planets affect our lives for good or ill. Reading a daily horoscope and acting upon it (or simply worrying about it!) plays a large part in many people's lives. Astronomical thinking has influenced the strong counter-emphasis in the Jewish-Christian tradition on the constancy and changelessness of God. We stare into space as the heavenly bodies shift and change but are reassured that the One who ultimately holds all things together is constant, not variable. And there is no finer expression of this truth than in the hymn 'Great is thy faithfulness' by Thomas Chisholm (1866–1960), who wrote: 'Sun, moon and stars in their courses above, join with all nature in manifold witness to thy great faithfulness, mercy and love.'

† *Great is thy faithfulness, O God my Father,*
  There is no shadow of turning with thee.

Tuesday August 23   **James 2:1–4**

DISTINCTIVE FAITH   The readings for today and tomorrow are so direct and to the point that there hardly seems need for a commentary on them.

> **For if a person with gold rings and in fine clothes comes into your assembly, and if a poor person in dirty clothes also comes in, and if you take notice of the one wearing the fine clothes and say, 'Have a seat here, please,' while to the one who is poor you say, 'Stand there,' or 'Sit at my feet', have you not made distinctions among yourselves?'**   **(verses 2–4a)**

A friend of mine who used to be a sister in a religious order tells the story of when her community was expecting a guest lecturer to come and lead a retreat. He was well-known and had written a number of books, and on the day of his anticipated arrival everyone was excited and busily preparing to welcome him. At about 2.00pm, the kitchen doorbell rang at the back of the Convent, the place where people looking for food or assistance usually came. Annoyed by the interruption, the Mother Superior hurriedly went to answer it and frowned to see a rather scruffy-looking man with windswept hair and wearing an old raincoat. 'Now what do you want?' she said crossly. 'I can give you something to eat quickly, but that's all.' 'Oh, thank you so much,' replied the man. 'And would it be any trouble to show me the room I'll be lecturing in tonight?' Do our churches and communities truly welcome all, without fear or favour?

✝ *God of all people, teach us to serve others with distinction but without discrimination.*

Wednesday August 24   **James 2:14–17**

DEAD FAITH   We can all think of times when our faith seemed to lack something, when it wasn't up to standard, when it seemed weak and inadequate. But would we say that at those points faith had actually died? In these verses, James implies as much.

> **If a brother or sister is naked and lacks daily food, and one of you says to them, 'Go in peace; keep warm and eat your fill', and yet you do not supply their bodily needs, what is the good of that? So faith by itself, if it has no works, is dead.**   **(verses 15–17)**

James locates this teaching very much within the local Christian community. It is a brother or sister with a visible need who receives a blessing, maybe well-intentioned, but no bread to go with it. This for James is an example of dead faith. Words from the believer's mouth have not been translated into action through the believer's hand. Just like a corpse, the limbs of the Body of Christ, once active, have become limp and useless. Quite simply faith is dead, argues James, when there are no obvious signs of activity. When we observe but don't respond, when we sympathise but never leap forward to help, when we pray but fail to involve ourselves in being the answer to prayer. It is a tough lesson. I can cope with thinking about my faith as sometimes slow or sickly and needing revival, but to be accused of demonstrating 'dead' faith? This is shocking, and certainly no witness to the one who burst alive from the tomb on Easter Day.

† *Lord, I know I am not saved by works, but if my works witness to a living faith in you, may that not lead another on the road from death to life?*

Thursday August 25 — James 4:11–12

ONE JUDGE   My aunt in England was talking about a man and woman she knew who had chosen to live together in the same house but not get married. She disapproved strongly. 'I call it living in sin,' she said, 'but no one dares to say that these days.' I can imagine this moral dilemma raising different opinions in different cultures, even among Christians. Does this passage from James give us any help in how to approach such an issue?

There is one lawgiver and judge who is able to save and to destroy. So who, then, are you to judge your neighbour?
(verse 12)

In James's experience, brothers and sisters were speaking evil of each other. Tongues were wagging in judgement (3:5–10) and condemnation seemed to come more easily than compassion. The golden commandment of Leviticus 19:18 ('love your neighbour as yourself') was clearly being ignored. There are many in the world, quite often politicians and journalists, who enjoy it when the Christian church speaks out in judgement and condemnation. They can then in turn judge and condemn the church for being bigoted or out of touch. What useless and ungodly debates these usually turn out to be. It is always part of the church's calling to wrestle with what is morally difficult or confusing, and to do that prayerfully and intelligently. It may well be the church's calling to offer sensitive teaching on marriage and relationships, out of love and goodwill. But is it the church's calling to sit in judgement, when even the Son of God declared his intention was to save the world, not judge it (*John 3:17*)? This passage is a timely one about where true authority lies. One church, one faith, one baptism – one judge.

† *When my lips are tempted to open in reckless condemnation of others, O Lord, may they close again quickly, in awe of your better judgement.*

Friday August 26   **James 5:13–18**

HEALING MINISTRY   It seems that in the early days local Christian communities were largely organised under the care of elders. This is also mentioned in Acts 15 and the books of Timothy and Titus. When ministry to the sick in the community is required, elders have two specific roles, according to James.

> **Are any among you sick? They should call for the elders of the church and have them pray over them, anointing them with oil in the name of the Lord.**   **(verse 14)**

In the churches in Zambia where I served, this instruction from James's letter was taken literally. Elders saw it very much as part of their role to pray for and anoint the sick, and the sick called upon them specifically for this ministry. Returning to the Methodist Church in Britain I rediscovered that lay leaders (pastoral visitors or church stewards – the equivalent of elders) did not generally see healing ministry as their responsibility. In fact, many of them would have been nervous or embarrassed at the thought of praying for or anointing the sick. The picture of healing ministry painted by James's letter challenges us to look again at lay leadership and ministry in our own settings and congregations. Maybe James's scenario is not one that would be appropriate in our own context. There is very rarely a biblical blueprint for ministry in the twenty-first century. But surely we have the sick among us? Surely the ministry of healing is as central to the church's ministry as preaching or pastoral care? So then, we can't escape these key questions for church life. Who is called to pray for and attend to the sick in ministry? And how will they be recognised and equipped?

† *Pray for your local churches' leadership. Pray for new ministries and gifts to be recognised and encouraged.*

Saturday August 27   **Jude 3–6**

FIRMNESS IN FAITH   The letter of Jude is short but, in some ways, not very sweet. It is full of warnings and predictions of doom for those who have left the way of Jesus themselves or led others away from the right path. It is an urgent appeal to those remaining to stand firm.

> **For certain intruders have stolen in among you, people who long ago were designated for this condemnation as ungodly, who pervert the grace of our God into licentiousness and deny our only Master and Lord, Jesus Christ.** (verse 4)

Jude's intruders seem to wield enormous influence over the faithful. The letter suggests that the saints are at great risk from those 'devoid of the Spirit' (*verse 19*), and that the wavering ones must be 'snatched from the fire' (*verse 23*) before it is too late. The sense of urgency on behalf of young believers in Jude is unmistakable and hard to recreate in our day and age. But it does suggest an issue well worth addressing. How easily can we, today's saints, be snatched away from the Christian path, like those seeds in the parable pecked up by hungry birds (*Matthew 13:4*)? When I first went to university to study theology, aged 18, I remember being warned by well-meaning people at my church about the professors, teachers and fellow students who would try to shatter my faith and turn me against Christianity. Well, they didn't! Nor did they try to, actually. True, I was made to look very critically at the Christian faith, examine arguments for and against the existence of God and get to grips with some serious biblical exploration. But Christianity, to my mind, became even more convincing as a foundation for life. And in moments of confusion and head-scratching, there was always the reassurance of prayer and worship. Even when understanding wavered, commitment continued. It may not always be possible to prevent an intruder breaking in and stealing our worldly goods, but no intruder can carry off the deepest truths which are our heavenly possession – unless we choose to let them.

† *Pray that in times of doubt, wavering believers may know the quietness and confidence of Christ's abiding presence.*

For group discussion and personal thought

● What does healing mean to you?
● Who are the 'intruders' who have made it more difficult for you to remain confident in and committed to the Christian faith?

INTERNATIONAL BIBLE READING ASSOCIATION
1020 Bristol Road, Selly Oak, Birmingham, Great Britain B29 6LB

ORDER FORM – for 2006 books

Name: _____

Address: _____

Postcode: _____

Telephone number: _____

*To qualify for 2006 books at these special IBRA readers' prices, this order form must be used (photocopies not accepted). Your order will be dispatched when **all** books are available. Mail order only.*

Code	Title of book	Quantity	Unit price	Total
ZYW63	Words for Today 2006		£7.00	
ZYL61	Light for Our Path 2006		£7.00	
ZYL62	Light for our Path 2006 *large print*		£7.00	
ZYW63c	Words for Today 2006 *on cassette*		£7.00	
ZYL61c	Light for our Path 2006 *on cassette*		£7.00	
ZYF0910	Finding Our Way Together Book 2		£8.00	
ZYF0938	Finding Our Way Together Book 3		£8.00	
ZYF0974	Finding Our Way Together Book 4		£8.00	
ZYF0910-SET	Finding Our Way Together series (3 BOOKS)		£20.00	
ZYD0989	Discovering Christ *Advent & Christmas*		£8.00	
ZYD0994	Discovering Christ *Ascension & Pentecost*		£8.00	
ZYD0999	Discovering Christ *Lent & Easter*		£8.00	
ZYL0781	Living Prayers For Today		£15.50	
ZYM0902	More Living Prayers For Today		£15.50	

❏ I enclose a cheque (payable to IBRA)

❏ Please charge my MASTERCARD / VISA / SWITCH:

Card no: _____

Issue no (Switch): _____

Expiry Date: _____

Signature: _____

Total cost of books	
UK postage included Overseas – add £3.00 airmail per book	
Donation to International Fund	
TOTAL DUE	

Payments in pounds sterling, please.

Please allow 28 days for delivery.

The INTERNATIONAL BIBLE READING ASSOCIATION is a Registered Charity

International Bible Reading Association

Help us to continue our work of providing Bible study notes for use by Christians in the UK and throughout the world. The need is as great as it was when IBRA was founded in 1882 by Charles Waters as part of the work of the Sunday School Union.

Please leave a legacy to the International Bible Reading Association.

An easy-to-use leaflet has been prepared to help you provide a legacy. Please write to us at the address below and we will send you this leaflet – and answer any questions you might have about a legacy or other donations. Please help us to strengthen this and the next generation of Christians.

Thank you very much.

International Bible Reading Association
Dept 298, 1020 Bristol Road
Selly Oak
Birmingham B29 6LB
Great Britain
Tel. 0121 472 4242
Fax 0121 472 7575

Charity Number 211542

TEXT MESSAGES TO THE FAITHFUL 2

From the rock

Notes by Alec Gilmore

based on the Revised English Bible

Alec Gilmore is a Baptist minister with 20 years' experience in pastorates in Northampton and West Worthing, followed by a similar period in Christian publishing, mainly for the benefit of the Third World and Eastern Europe, first as Editor of Lutterworth Press and then as Director of Feed the Minds. He lives in Sussex and is a freelance writer and lecturer. Recent books include *A Dictionary of the English Bible and its Origins* (Continuum), *Aid Matters* and *Preaching as Theatre* (SCM Press).

Some people always feel like wallflowers! Nobody ever notices them or hears them when they speak. They live 'on the wrong side of every counter'. Who does that remind you of? An individual or a group, maybe. They are people who for various reasons need encouragement, hope and occasionally a helping hand. Some are aliens, exiles, hostages, asylum seekers or just plain nonconformists who refuse to toe the party line. It is to people like these that Peter is writing – tiny isolated communities. So what does he say?

Text for the week: 1 Peter 1:3–4

Sunday August 28   1 Peter 1:3–7

A LIVING HOPE   When we are at a low point it is all too easy to focus on those minor irritations we would normally take in our stride and to forget the broader picture. So we become obsessive about an ache or a pain, worrying whether we might have offended a friend, or allow ourselves to get screwed up over something a friend said or did. As communities we feel neglected, see other groups as better than ours and resent the fact that those we would expect to help seem no longer to care. The churches to which Peter was writing, surrounded by Greek culture and never part of the Jewish tradition, felt isolated. Peter tells them to focus on God and what he has done in the resurrection:

he gave us new birth into a living hope, the hope of an inheritance, reserved in heaven for you, which nothing can destroy or spoil or wither. (part of verse 3 and verse 4)

The bigger picture may not solve the niggling problems, but it does provide a healthier perspective. It reminds us of a God who can do remarkable things and springs surprises; that not all is lost and something better is always possible. Then, in a strange way, believing this often opens the door to achieving it. That is the hope that has kept many a hostage alive in the most appalling circumstances.

† *Father, turn my attention to others who have also experienced low points and triumphed.*

Monday August 29　　　　　　　　　　　　　　1 Peter 2:4–10

FEELINGS AND REALITY　The fact that we feel rejected or ignored does not necessarily mean that we are. Try two tests. One, focus on somebody who always makes you feel good. Two, think about the gifts you have even if other people seem not to notice them. Every believer and every community has its own distinctive place in God's plan. Each of us is a living stone, like Jesus,

the living stone which was rejected by men but chosen by God and of great worth to him. You also, as living stones, must be built up into a spiritual temple, and form a holy priesthood. (part of verses 4 and 5)

When it is difficult to keep hope alive for yourself, exercise your 'priesthood' by trying to bring hope to others. Put yourself in their place. Enter into their experience. Address their plight, for often in offering hope to others we find it ourselves. A comedian may handle his own sadness by bringing laughter to his audience. Ministers who feel low may find strength by offering comfort to their flock. Many a mother's pain has been eased as she cared for a distraught child.

† *Gracious God, never let me get so low that I fail to appreciate the needs of others and lose the desire to help.*

Tuesday August 30　　　　　　　　　　　　　　1 Peter 3:18–22

POSITIVE SUFFERING　The preceding verses suggest that there is nothing wrong with a bit of suffering if it is the result of doing something good. Think of it as being like the natural tiredness that comes from climbing a mountain or working excessively hard for somebody else's benefit. Expect a bit of pain in those circumstances and count yourself happy. Remember:

Christ too suffered for our sins once and for all, the just for the unjust, that he might bring us to God; put to death in the body, he was brought to life in the spirit. (verse 18)

Only through suffering was Christ able to enter into a new way of living, richer and fuller than before: in the spirit rather than the body. It is a different way of life, rooted in baptism, and what makes it possible is involvement in a community of like-minded people. For Jesus, it was the companionship of the disciples. For us it is the constant awareness that we are part of that 'vast throng, which no one could count' (*Revelation 7:9*).

† *Father, when I feel most isolated and cut off, help me to get out and immerse myself in the wider community of men and women and try to find some kindred spirits.*

Wednesday August 31   **1 Peter 5:8–11**

SPOT THE ENEMY   On a day when you are really under the weather the important thing may be to identify 'the enemy' and go for him!

Stand up to him, firm in your faith, and remember that your fellow-Christians in this world are going though the same kinds of suffering. (verse 9)

Peter's description of 'the enemy' as 'the devil, like a roaring lion', prowling around looking for someone to devour (*verse 8*), suggests that the real enemy is fear – not what the devil does, has done or might do, but what he threatens and the way in which he threatens it. It isn't only isolated Christians who feel this – all Christians feel it! Isolation often leads us to feel that nobody else has our problems. Suffering in isolation then feeds the notion that nobody else suffers like we do. But when the doctor identifies a complaint and then says, 'This is a very common problem, there are lots of people out there living normal lives with your complaint', the cloud is lifted. You are no longer alone. Outwardly nothing has changed. Fear may still be there but at least the fear of isolation has gone. One 'devil' has been identified and we have earned the right to move on.

† *Loving God, help me always to remember that time with you identifying the enemy is never wasted and may be the first step to victory.*

Thursday September 1   **2 Peter 1:16–18**

AM I RIGHT? Christians fall into two camps: those who worry in case they haven't 'got it right' and those who worry because they are so sure everybody else has got it wrong. Peter is writing to people in the first category. There are doubts and questions everywhere. Some seem to feel they have been 'conned'. They fear that what they have always been told is just not true and their disbelieving friends never fail to remind them of it. The pressure is to drop outlandish ideas, like Christ's return, which were an embarrassment in a modern world of Greek culture, so Peter is anxious to reassure them that it is all genuine and they haven't just made it up. So he writes:

> **He was invested with honour and glory by God the Father, and there came to him from the sublime Presence a voice which said, 'This is my Son ...' We ourselves heard [it] ... we were with him.** (parts of verses 17 and 18)

There is nothing like a personal testimony. It may not be quite the same for them, but with Peter's conviction their fears are allayed and they can face their critics. They know someone who knows!

† *Father, if I have an experience I can share with others to help them, never let me hold back.*

Friday September 2   **2 Peter 3:8–10**

SEEING AND BELIEVING Peter's personal testimony in yesterday's reading was helpful but apparently not enough – the people 'believed' it but they couldn't 'see' it. They needed evidence. Peter's response is a call for patience. Many early Christians had difficulty with the failure of the new faith to deliver. Long on promises, it was short on results. Jesus had implied that some of the things he promised would happen in their life-time – but they hadn't. So church leaders concluded he would come back and complete the job. That worked up to a point. But he still hadn't come back! And that was the problem. So Peter suggests that God has a different time-scale.

> **Here is something ... which you must not forget: in the Lord's sight one day is like a thousand years and a thousand years like one day.** (part of verse 8)

We are called not only to trust but also to humility. God is not slow – he has time, and he can wait. Before we pass judgement or give up, we need to contemplate the bigger picture. Even then we shall never live long enough to see the whole.

† *Loving God, teach me what I need to know. Just enough and no more. Then let me leave the rest to you.*

O LORD, HOW LONG? There is a sense of desperation here. It is about 120 CE. The first generation of Christians has passed away and the second generation of church leaders has not yet emerged. These people are lost. Things are drifting. Why is nothing happening? There must be a reason for the delay, and there is. If God had not been patient and willing to fulfil his purposes over a very long period, some of these Gentile churches, especially the more remote ones, would never have heard of Christ. It would all have been over before the message got there. But what to them has proved a benefit and a blessing is now the reason why they cannot get on to fulfilment as fast as they would like. What they have to remember is that

our Lord's patience is an opportunity for salvation.
(part of verse 15)

Paul also said this, to them and to many others. Sometimes, when we feel under pressure and others seem slow to act, or perhaps even to care, we must give them as much time as it takes, because it is more important that we all get to the finishing post in the end than that some of us get there first.

† *Father, when I am impatient to the point of being irritable and even aggressive, teach me how to wait.*

For group discussion and personal thought

● Recall one or two occasions when you felt a sense of personal isolation and loneliness. Which of the emotions of these early Christians resonates with your own experience and which of Peter's responses would you have found most helpful?

● Focus attention on one group of 'aliens' or 'exiles' in today's society. See if you can work out the similarities and differences between their experience and that of these early Gentile churches. How differently do you think Peter might have written if he had been writing to them?

● Read a story of a hostage (for example, *Taken on Trust* by Terry Waite or *Some Other Rainbow* by John McCarthy and Jill Morrell). Jot down some of their most poignant thoughts and feelings. Work out what it was that enabled them to survive. Now re-read some of this week's verses from 1 and 2 Peter and see how their experience gives flesh to Peter's words and how Peter's words might have helped them in their struggle.

TEXT MESSAGES
TO THE FAITHFUL 3
From the Elder to the Lady

Notes by Peter Russell

based on the New Revised Standard Version

Peter Russell is a retired minister of the British Methodist Church. He has worked in pastoral ministry in England (for some time as a university chaplain), in ministerial training in Nigeria and Zimbabwe (where he got into trouble as convener of the Rhodesia Christian Council's National Affairs Committee) and in mission training in Selly Oak, Birmingham. He has published various articles, newspaper pieces and poems, and has three sons.

Reading the letters in the New Testament is rather like listening to one side of a telephone conversation: we do not know quite what is going on at the other end, but we have hints and can often make good guesses. We know very little about the writer of these letters, but he has a great deal in common with the author of the fourth gospel. He stresses the love of God and the truth that Jesus is the Christ and is truly human, and he talks of false teaching and of people breaking away from the church. We may therefore guess that these were the things troubling the church he is writing to.

Text for the week: 1 John 4:16b

Sunday September 4   1 John 1:7–10

LIVING IN THE LIGHT   Most people have had the experience of being in a place without light – we fall over things, we cannot find anything, and we have problems getting where we want to be. For our author this is a picture of life lived without God: it is hard to find the right direction and we make a mess of things. This is probably personal testimony and, like many people who come to know God, he finds life has changed. He can see where he is going and the messes of the past are cleaned away.

**If we walk in the light ... the blood of Jesus ... cleanses us
from all sin.**   **(parts of verse 7)**

In the gospels we read of many people coming to Jesus in
shame and sorrow for what they have done. He always speaks
to them of God's forgiveness, and this is echoed here. If we
confess our sins and want forgiveness, God, who is faithful and
just, will forgive us. 'Faithful and just' (*verse 9*) – 'faithful' tells
us that God is to be trusted; 'just' in the New Testament
suggests taking away, rather than inflicting, punishment. We
are in the light, and the darkness of the past is taken away.

† *I am a sinner: dear God, forgive me.*

Monday September 5   1 John 2:9–11

LOVE IS ALL THAT IS ASKED OF US   Jesus taught us that the
two greatest commandments are 'Love God' and 'Love your
neighbour'. The love he talked about was the sort of generous
love he showed to people, the love that in the end took him to
the cross. It is hard to love like that, but at least we can
understand something of what it means to love our neighbour
as ourself. But how do we love God? God does not have needs
as people do; have we anything to give to him?

Whoever loves a brother or sister lives in the light.
                                                    (part of verse 10)

Because God loves every human being and cares greatly about
what happens to them, he accepts what we do for people as
gifts to him. He has no needs that we can meet, but his children
do, so that we keep the commandment to love God by keeping
the commandment to love our neighbour. What we cannot give
to him directly, we give through his human family.

† *Thank you, God, for people whose lives touch mine. Make me
loving in my dealings with them.*

Tuesday September 6   1 John 3:13–17

WE HAVE LIFE BECAUSE WE LOVE   The Christians to
whom this letter was written seem to have been suffering from
the hostility of their pagan neighbours. There is always a
danger for groups which are closely knit and meet often that
people will suspect them of various crimes. Early Christians
were accused of lechery and cannibalism, possibly because
people misunderstood the nature of the love they talked about

and the sharing of the Body of Christ in the Eucharist. But, more deeply, they were hated because the way of love they advocated was a challenge to the world. And it still is! Talk of generous love contradicts much of the motivation of modern society, which often refuses to help the brother or sister in need.

We ought to lay down our lives for one another.
(part of verse 16)

Here, as in yesterday's reading, the New Revised Standard Version talks of 'brothers and sisters' where older translations have just 'brothers'. The Greek language had a word for 'sister' but where there were siblings of both sexes, the word for brothers was used. The word for brothers is often used for fellow Christians, and of course love must be part of the church's life, but it also has a wider meaning: in the end all humanity are children of God and our brothers and sisters.

† *Make me a channel of your love.*

Wednesday September 7   1 John 4:16–19

NOTHING BUT LOVE   God is love! What an amazing thing to say about the Creator God, who made the universe, who is in the burning of the countless stars and the power of the tiny atom, the God who sometimes appears in scripture as an angry God. Jesus taught his friends to call God 'Abba', the name used by a child to a loving father. John puts this in a more abstract way: God's heart is the love of which we catch glimpses in loving mothers and fathers, and more than that, God is love. As you get to know more of God you find only new depths of love.

God is love, and those who abide in love abide in God, and God abides in them.   **(part of verse 16)**

When they wanted to talk about the God they had learned to know in Jesus, the early Christians used the rather unusual word *agape*. Then they had to explain its meaning: Saint Paul says, 'God proves his love for us in that while we were still sinners Christ died for us' and 'Love is patient, love is kind ... it does not insist on its own way...' (*Romans 5:8; 1 Corinthians 13:4ff*). Our writer says, 'In this is love, not that we loved God, but that he loved us and sent his Son to be the atoning sacrifice for our sins' (*4:10*). These descriptions of infinitely generous love are descriptions of God, and God's holiness is not different from his love: it is his love at war with all un-love.

† *Help me to abide in your love.*

PEOPLE CAN ALWAYS FIND FORGIVENESS   It is difficult to know what our author means by 'sin that is mortal'. It is something that can be seen, so he must be referring to sinful actions, not inward states of mind. Jesus says that the sin against the Holy Spirit is unforgivable, but we never see Jesus turning away anyone who comes to him grieving for their sins; so mortal sin, unforgivable sin, must be turning your back on God, refusing to acknowledge your sin, denying that you need forgiveness. John may therefore be writing of those he has referred to earlier, who have left the Christian community and no longer 'abide in God'. Others may still share the life of God and receive forgiveness.

We know that we are God's children.   (part of verse 19)

'All wrongdoing is sin, but there is sin that is not mortal' (*verse 17*). One of the amazing things about God is forgiveness, the love that waits for the returning prodigal and accepts him with open arms. God wants to forgive, to bring us to the state in which we can be forgiven, and that, says John, is why Jesus came. People may cut themselves off from forgiveness: God will not cut them off.

† *Loving God, help me to know I am forgiven.*

TRUTH IS IN JESUS   Who is the Elder? Christians in Asia used the word for the generation of Christians who were their link with the Apostles, so it is possible that this letter was written by one of them. The elect lady to whom this letter is addressed, who is loved 'by all who know the truth', is probably not one person, but a church community. The Greek word for church, *ecclesia*, is a feminine word and churches were called 'she'. It seems that this church was in danger from false teachers.

Whoever abides in the teaching has both the Father and the Son.   (part of verse 9)

In the history of the church there have always been false teachers; the problem has been to distinguish them. The answer the Elder gives is that the false teachers do not confess that Jesus Christ has come in the flesh. They do not believe Jesus comes from God, and they do not 'abide in the teaching of Christ' (*verse 9*). That is the acid test: does this person who claims to speak for God speak of the love, the forgiveness and the sacrifice that were the marks of the teaching of Jesus? Do they sound like Jesus? Do they act as Jesus taught us?

† *Teach me to know the truth as it is in Jesus.*

Saturday September 10   3 John 1–4

REJOICING FOR GAIUS   3 John looks like a person-to-person letter; unfortunately Gaius is just a name to us, one of that great band of unknown people who have kept the faith and handed it on – our ancestors in the faith. The writer regards him as one of his 'children', meaning one of the Christian community in which he was a leader, possibly also one converted under his ministry.

> **I have no greater joy than this, to hear that my children are walking in the truth.**   **(verse 4)**

We have seen in the first two letters the writer's concern about false teaching, and here we share his joy that one of his 'children' is faithful to the truth. But 'walking' suggests more than simply believing. Here is a man living in the truth of Christ, living the way of love that the elder had taught him was the true way to follow Christ.

† *Help me to walk in the truth.*

For group discussion and personal thought

● Who do you think are the false teachers in today's church?
● How do we love God?

SYMBOLIC ACTIONS 1
Warnings

Notes by Anne Roberts

based on the New International Version

Anne Roberts trained as a geographer and taught in Uganda for two years. She worked in church teaching and administration for twenty years and is now a teacher in Further Education and a freelance writer. She lives in Bolton in northwest England with her husband Howard and enjoys walking amongst its hills.

There are many symbolic actions or acted parables in the Bible. Many of those in the New Testament (for example, Jesus washing his disciples' feet) appear elsewhere in this year's readings, so most of the ones in this theme are taken from the Old Testament. The symbolic actions are usually carried out by one person, often at great personal cost, in order to convey a message from God to a group of people or an individual. In the first week we look at acted warnings of the consequences of people's current behaviour and intentions. In the second week, we focus on actions which speak of God's forgiveness and loving acceptance.

Text for the week: Isaiah 20:5

Sunday September 11   Isaiah 8:1–4

GOD KNOWS   God has told Isaiah that the hordes of Assyria will soon descend on Judah's enemies, Syria and Israel. So the phrase, 'quick to the plunder; swift to the spoil' is to be displayed publicly and Isaiah's own son given it as a name. King Ahaz wants to ally his kingdom with Assyria, but Isaiah counsels him that God knows what he is doing – and it wouldn't save them anyway. Judgement is imminent.

> I went to the prophetess and she conceived and gave birth to a son. And the LORD said to me, 'Name him Maher-Shalal-Hash-Baz. Before the boy knows how to say, "My Father" or "My Mother", the wealth of Damascus and the plunder of Samaria will be carried off by the king of Assyria.' **(verses 3–4)**

It can be hard to trust God when life itself seems to turn against us. The Bible and Christian history are littered with examples of

God's faithfulness in dire situations, but each of us has to learn individually that he keeps his promises. Looking back on the darkest part of my life I know God knew what he was doing. He understood my panic and despair and ultimately brought me into a better place.

† *Father, forgive us when we do not bring our fears and anxieties to you. Teach us to trust you and witness to your saving help.*

Monday September 12   Isaiah 20:1–6

GOD WILL ACT   God's people were treating life like a lottery. Who shall we back today? Assyria? Egypt? Cush? They would not believe that God's power alone would save them. Egypt and Cush looked like a safe bet, but Isaiah was told to act out before their eyes the shame these nations would suffer.

'Take off the sackcloth from your body and the sandals from your feet ... Just as my servant Isaiah has gone stripped and barefoot ... so the king of Assyria will lead away stripped and barefoot the Egyptian captives and Cushite exiles ... Those who trusted in [them] will be afraid and put to shame.'   **(parts of verses 2, 3, 4 and 5)**

Life isn't a lottery. When God says he has sovereign control over our lives he is not deceiving us. We feel unloved and look for love in the wrong place. We are hard up and tempted to earn money in an unholy way. We want to seek revenge rather than forgive. Trusting in any of these alternatives will lead to disappointment and perhaps even shame. We should listen to God before he has to bring disaster upon us in order to bring us to our senses and teach us to trust in him.

† *Almighty God, whatever this life may bring us, grant that it may never take from us the full faith that you are our Father.*

(George Dawson, 1821–76)

Tuesday September 13   Jeremiah 13:1–11

GOD SPEAKS

'Go and buy a linen belt ... Take the belt you bought and are wearing round your waist, and go now to Perath and hide it there in a crevice in the rocks.' So I went and hid it ... The LORD said to me, 'Go now to Perath and get the belt ...' It was ruined and completely useless.

     (part of verse 1, verse 4, and parts of verses 5 , 6 and 7)

God had bound his people to him intimately. Their lives were to be a demonstration of his goodness to those around, but they preferred to serve other gods, worthless idols. The people were already becoming useless, like the gods they served. The ruined belt declares that when they were exiled to Babylon their betrayal would run on to its completion. We should never suppose that we could not drift away and become spiritually useless as these people had. Even those who have known God intimately can do so. If pride can cause it (*verse 9*), let us stay humble and have a right view of ourselves and of God. If refusing to listen can cause it (*verse 10*), we must always pay attention to God's word. If stubbornness (*verse 10*) can do it, we must keep short accounts with God, mending our ways quickly whenever we find ourselves drifting away from the truth.

† *Almighty and most merciful Father, we have ... strayed from your ways like lost sheep. We have followed too much the ... desires of our own hearts... Have mercy upon us.*   (Book of Common Prayer)

Wednesday September 14   Jeremiah 19:1–13

GOD SMASHES TO PIECES   At first sight there is no comfort in today's reading. The Lord Almighty has had enough! The people are beyond redemption, like the leopard that cannot change its spots (*Jeremiah 13:23*). Openly and deliberately they do those things which God expressly forbids.

The LORD says: 'Go and buy a clay jar from a potter. Take along some of the elders ... and go out to the Valley of Ben Hinnom ... Then break the jar ... and say to them, "This is what the Lord Almighty says: 'I will smash this nation and this city.'"'   **(parts of verses 1, 2, 10 and 11)**

The comfort is that we have a God who means what he says. He cares too much for his world to let it go its way unchecked for ever. He does not lower his standards to make his teaching more palatable. Christians are stewards of God's word in today's world. There is a strong temptation in those parts of the world where church attendance is decreasing to water down God's word to make it more acceptable to modern tastes. If we do this we risk paving the way to judgement for those who find false comfort in what we have to say. Who will be today's Jeremiahs?

† *Help us, Lord, to set the agenda for our lives by what your word says. Draw us back when we stray from its teachings, before we come to judgement.*

Thursday September 15 — Jeremiah 27:1–18

GOD VINDICATES HIMSELF   There are pessimists who predict gloom where others see only hope and there are optimists who are confident a matter will turn out fine when they do not really know what the outcome will be. We may mistakenly suppose that faith demands we see only a positive outcome – even in the short term. 'Of course God wants you strong and well, financially secure, vindicated.' 'Of course God wants his church to have a triumphant testimony.' 'Of course God would never use the ungodly to bring judgement on his people.' Wouldn't he? If we think that, the facts may destroy our faith – or help us to grow up!

> The LORD said to me: 'Make a yoke ... and put it on your neck ... If any nation or kingdom will not serve Nebuchadnezzar ... I will punish that nation ... So do not listen to your prophets, your diviners, your interpreters of dreams ... who tell you, "You will not serve the king of Babylon."'   (parts of verses 2, 8 and 9)

King Zedekiah wanted to know the opinion of everyone who had one! Many years previously Elijah had asked the people, 'How long will you waver between two opinions?' (*1 Kings 18:21*). It is important if we are giving an opinion that we allow it to be tested by the revealed word of God.

† *Lord, may I be quick to listen to you and ready to acknowledge my ignorance, rather than say just what pleases others or brings false comfort.*

Friday September 16 — Ezekiel 4:1–17

GOD IS GOD   Today's parable is a reminder that God does not forget if we do not repent. It also symbolises the horrors that lie along the path of disobedience.

> 'Now, son of man, take a clay tablet, put it in front of you and draw the city of Jerusalem on it. Then lay siege to it ... Then take an iron pan, place it as an iron wall between you and the city and turn your face towards it ... Then lie on your left side ... for 390 days.'   (verse 1 and parts of verses 2, 3, 4 and 5)

God had added up the years of Israel's rebellion. There had been some periods of genuine repentance during those years but, overall, unfaithfulness had marked their national life. God tells Ezekiel to enact his determination to bring them to justice. During the siege human excrement would be the only fuel, nasty enough to any of us but abhorrent to a person who knew God's law about what was unclean. Could this be a warning to us that when God withdraws his protection because of our sin, there are no horrors which cannot affect us, individually or as nations? Some people may too easily read something as judgement when it is not, but we must not let that make us dismiss the concept altogether.

† *May I keep myself within the boundaries where God's love is able to reach me.* (Adapted from Jude 21, *The Living Bible*)

Saturday September 17   Acts 21:10–15

GOD'S WILL BE DONE!

> **[Agabus] took Paul's belt, tied his own hands and feet with it and said, 'The Holy Spirit says, "In this way the Jews of Jerusalem will bind the owner of this belt and hand him over to the Gentiles."' ... When [Paul] would not be dissuaded, we gave up and said, 'The Lord's will be done.'**
> **(verses 11 and 14)**

Paul's friends took this acted parable as a warning. 'Don't go!' they pleaded. Paul took it as a promise! He saw an opportunity to make a very public witness to his faith. In contrast to the people we have read about earlier in the week, Paul will not be diverted from the path of obedience, whatever the cost. Today there are Christians who are free to practise their faith amidst little or no opposition. Other Christians face persecution or even death if they are open about their faith. This week's readings show us, through vivid acted signs, that in whatever circumstances Christians find themselves, there are those who remain faithful at any cost and those who are easily put off and drift away. We should watch ourselves!

† *Lord, strengthen me by your Spirit, so that whether I face apathy or active opposition I shall have what it takes to remain faithful.*

For group discussion and personal thought

● Are we easily deceived into believing that we are keeping God's law, when our lifestyles or some aspect of them are a denial of it?
● I have not mentioned Jesus in this week's notes. Where does our relationship with him come into this matter of pleasing God by keeping his laws?

SYMBOLIC ACTIONS 2
Signs of hope

Notes by Kate Hughes

based on the New Revised Standard Version

Kate worked for the church in Southern Africa for 14 years. When she returned to England in 1990 she became a freelance book editor and a writer and editor of distance learning courses in theology. She has recently moved into an old people's bungalow but doesn't feel elderly and continues to work as an editor and to be active in her local community. She is currently editor of *Light for our Path*.

Last week's readings were concerned with symbolic actions which warned the people of Israel of what would happen if they did not repent and change their ways. This week, the actions bring hope, reassurance and comfort.

Text for the week: Jeremiah 32:14–15

Sunday September 18   **Leviticus 16:20–22**

A FRESH START If only getting rid of our sins was this easy! Symbolically load them onto a goat, drive the goat away, and your sins go with it. Away from you, your family, your neighbours, your town. Out into the wilderness, to disappear for ever. The Jews believed that the scapegoat took their sins out of society, so that a fresh start could be made in living together, in ritual worship, in society. And perhaps this year they could do better.

The goat shall bear on itself all their iniquities to a barren region.   **(part of verse 22)**

But the goat was no more than a symbol. It had no real power to deal with sin, even if it helped the Jews to hope that this year things would be different. The symbol became a reality when God took the initiative to deal with human sin. Perhaps John the Baptist should have called Jesus 'the scapegoat of God' instead of 'the lamb of God' (*John 1:36*), because it is he who truly takes away the sin of the world.

† *Lord, you give us so many opportunities to make a fresh start; help us to go forward in hope, knowing that you have taken away our sin.*

Monday September 19   **Numbers 21:4–9**

GOD THE HEALER As so often, when things didn't go exactly as they hoped they would, the Israelites started grumbling. This time, they became impatient; the journey was too long, there wasn't enough food and water, and what food there was was horrible. What the desert did have, however, was poisonous snakes, and their appearance, and the damage they did, were interpreted by the Israelites as God's punishment for their grumbling. They knew they were in the wrong and deserved some punishment (even if we may feel that the punishment was excessive). The Lord agreed: they had lacked faith in him, they did deserve to be punished, but, as Paul says in 1 Corinthians 10:13, 'God is faithful, and he will not let you be tested beyond your strength, but with the testing he will also provide the way out so that you may be able to endure it.' So the Lord doesn't take away the poisonous snakes, but he provides another snake, which will neutralise their bad effects:

Whenever a serpent bit someone, that person would look at the serpent of bronze and live.   (part of verse 9)

The bronze serpent was a symbol of God's compassion and healing power, an example of his justice, and a hopeful reminder that repentance is met with remedial action. The symbol became reality in Christ, who was lifted up on the cross so that all people might believe in the love, compassion and healing power of God (*John 3:14–15*).

† *Thank you, Lord, that even our sins can, through repentance, become opportunities for deepening our trust in your forgiveness, compassion and healing.*

Tuesday September 20   **Jeremiah 32:1–15**

WE HAVE A FUTURE The future looked grim: Jerusalem was about to be besieged and taken by the Babylonians, the king captured and deported. And what does Jeremiah do? He buys property. Something enduring and secure for afterwards – though it may be many years afterwards: the deeds in the earthenware jar have to survive 'for a long time' (*verse 14*). But Jeremiah is acting out his symbol in accordance with the Lord's directions. Yes, there will be a catastrophe, but afterwards life will go on:

'Houses and fields and vineyards shall again be bought in this land.'   (part of verse 15)

Jeremiah acts out a symbol of death and resurrection: catastrophe followed by restored life, a recurrent pattern in the

Bible. The pattern here looks forward to the ultimate symbol of hope, the death and resurrection of Jesus.

✝ *Lord, help us to believe that catastrophe can be followed by renewed life, to look for your resurrection power when we are faced with the darkness of death.*

Wednesday September 21   Ezekiel 37:15–28

NEVER AGAIN

Never again shall they be two nations, and never again shall they be divided into two kingdoms. They shall never again defile themselves ... with any of their transgressions.
(parts of verses 22 and 23)

Part of Israel's dream of the future was the reunification of the divided kingdom. But the division of the kingdom had been the result of sin: pride and resentment, an unwillingness to compromise (*2 Chronicles 10*). God promises restoration, but before they can again be his people, they need to be saved and cleansed. As we saw in Monday's reading, God takes sin seriously: it cannot just be pushed aside, as if it never happened. But if there is repentance and a willingness to accept the consequences, the sinner can emerge stronger and God will reward the effort. So he is very definite here about the end of the process of restoration: in his words to Ezekiel, he repeatedly says, 'I will' do this and 'I will' do that. This is what God will bring about, and it will wipe out the past. Ezekiel's acted sign here is very simple: two sticks written on and brought together. ·But it is enough to give the people of Israel hope. Later in their history, another simple two pieces of wood joined together and raised up on a hill outside Jerusalem became an even more powerful sign of hope for God's people.

✝ *Lord, help me to look at the wood of the cross and say 'never again' to all that separates me from you.*

Thursday September 22   Hosea 3:1–5

LOVE AS THE LORD LOVES

'Love a woman ... just as the LORD loves the people of Israel.'   **(part of verse 1)**

Today's symbolic action is not simply a matter of driving away a goat or putting sticks together. It is an action which changes

Hosea's life for ever, a serious step with great consequences both for himself and for the woman involved. Yet because of this, it is an immensely powerful symbol. Hosea is not told simply to take a wife; he is also commanded to love her. He is not asked to ignore or excuse her faults; he takes her with his eyes open. His love has a toughness about it: he imposes conditions upon his new wife, in order to bring about improvement and give the marriage some hope of succeeding. All this makes his action a worthy reflection of God's love for his people. God's love is realistic and open-eyed – he does not close his eyes to our faults. He will impose conditions on our relationship with him, in order that we may become better people. He is prepared to pay a price to restore our relationship with him, but his love is not a soft option. If we are prepared to accept God's conditions, then his love will transform us. His own love has no conditions – we do not have to earn or deserve his love. But, like Hosea's wife, we need to learn to love him in return and to discover what real loving entails.

† *Lord, love us into life, love us into loving you in return, with the same steadfastness and commitment that you give us.*

Friday September 23 **Matthew 19:13–15**

CITIZENS OF THE KINGDOM By taking time to lay his hands on children and pray for them, Jesus made an important statement about them; his actions were symbolic.

**[I]t is to such as these that the kingdom of heaven belongs.
(part of verse 14)**

Children have no power in society, therefore they tend to be publicly ignored. They may be loved within their families, but for most of history they have been regarded as contributing nothing to public life. Their place is in the home, except when they leave it to be trained for their adult role in society. Certainly, no first-century rabbi would be expected to take any notice of ordinary children. Yet their parents must have seen something in Jesus' attitude to the young which encouraged them to bring their children to him for prayer and blessing. Perhaps it was his appreciation of the openness of children, as they offered him their unconditional love and shared with him their simple treasures of toys or newly discovered natural objects. Perhaps Jesus enjoyed their very powerlessness; unlike his supposedly adult disciples, children were not constantly fighting for the best place and special favours. Perhaps it was their willingness to learn and discover new things, or their lack of concealment, which attracted him. What his actions said was that you can learn more about what is required from citizens of the kingdom of heaven by imitating children than by emulating the adult leaders of this world. Childlikeness, not childishness, is the hallmark of the kingdom.

† *Lord, help me to develop the openness and joy of a happy child which will equip me to be a citizen of your kingdom.*

Saturday September 24   Acts 9:10–19

Our final sign of hope this week seems to be for the newly-converted Saul alone. Blind and stunned by his experience, he has been led on to Damascus and given hospitality by a man called Judas. For three days he has sat in his new and sudden darkness, neither eating nor drinking (*verse 9*). What was he thinking about? What sense was he making of his experience? The sign seems to be the action of Ananias in laying hands on Saul and giving him the Lord's message:

'The Lord Jesus . . . has sent me so that you may regain your sight and be filled with the Holy Spirit.' **(part of verse 17)**

That was truly a sign of hope for Saul, but the symbolism of Ananias' action began before that. The very fact that he visited Saul at all was a symbolic action – for all Christians, not just for Saul. Saul was the enemy, coming to Damascus specifically to persecute the Christian disciples. Yet God told Ananias to minister to this enemy, to reach out to him in love, to give him the help and support he needed. Ananias' walk from his own home to the house of Judas was a significant symbolic action. It was a sign of hope for reconciliation, for peace, for the acceptance of all human beings created by God. It was an act of faith in God's ability to know what he is doing, even if our human minds cannot always grasp it. A single obedient disciple can change the world for good.

† *Lord, I may not have a spectacular ministry like that of Paul, but use me in your work of redemption, even if you ask no more of me than to walk down a street and reach out to an enemy for your sake.*

For group discussion and personal thought

● Symbolic actions can be small in themselves, but carry significant messages. Have you experienced any similar signs of hope acted out by other people? What was the symbolic action and what did it say to you?

READINGS IN LEVITICUS 1
The Law of the Lord is perfect

Notes by Robert Draycott

based on the New Revised Standard Version

Robert Draycott is a Baptist minister who is currently Chaplain of Eltham College, London. Previously he served as a minister in Northamptonshire and as a missionary in Brazil.

Many Christians who read Leviticus find themselves puzzled and confused by both its assumptions and the details of the sacrificial system described in it. One way to gain access to its enduring message is to compare this experience to that of visiting a foreign country. Many things are different, including the language, yet the people have the same needs – for forgiveness, reconciliation and good relationships with God and other people – as we have. These notes sound clearly to us across the centuries.

Text for the week: Leviticus 10:10–11

Sunday September 25   **Leviticus 2:1–16**

GETTING IT RIGHT   When we set out to visit a friend's house for the first time, we are anxious to 'get things right'. We expect to find that some things are slightly different in someone else's home. This is also true about our contact with God. The book of Leviticus gives clear guidance about how to maintain our relationship with God.

> **When anyone presents a grain offering to the LORD, the offering shall be of choice flour; the worshipper shall pour oil on it, and put frankincense on it, and bring it to Aaron's sons, the priests. After taking from it a handful of the choice flour and oil, with all its frankincense, the priest shall turn this token portion into smoke on the altar, an offering by fire of pleasing odour to the LORD. (verses 1–2)**

Just as we recognise and use symbolic gestures in everyday encounters with our friends, so encountering God involves symbolic actions. We also know that the type of gesture varies from country to country: for example, from the English handshake to the Brazilian hug and back slapping. In other words we need to understand something of the symbolism involved in this passage. The grain offering was presented as a gift to the Lord, just as we also take gifts such as flowers or chocolates to friends. The friend does not 'need' the gift; we need to offer it, as a symbol of our friendship.

† *Lord, show me what gift I may offer to you.*

Monday September 26   Leviticus 4:1–35

OUTSIDE THE CAMP   Yesterday we imagined setting off to visit a friend's house. We arrive and we exchange greetings. Then we would expect our friend to invite us into their home. We would not expect to be kept outside. As Christians, one way of understanding our relationship with God is that we are his guests. We also know that as guests we can make mistakes without meaning to. We then feel guilty. Today's reading is part of a passage which gives instructions about animal sacrifice to remove guilt.

> **The priest shall make atonement for them, and they shall be forgiven. He shall carry the bull outside the camp, and burn it as he burnt the first bull; it is the sin- offering for the assembly.   (part of verse 20 and verse 21)**

As God's guests we must remember that we have been invited inside. When we sin we need to remember that atonement has already been made through the death of Christ on the cross (outside the camp); we have been forgiven. Just as the owner of the house does not expect guests to put the rubbish outside, so we know that God deals with the rubbish of our sin and guilt whilst we remain his welcome guests.

† *Lord, thank you for your goodness and mercy; may I dwell in your house my whole life long.*

Tuesday September 27   Leviticus 5:1–13

A GO-BETWEEN   When visiting a foreign country one person who is a great help to us is an interpreter. Many people have found that a good interpreter does more than just translate the language. They explain things and act as guides to both the country itself and its customs so that the visitor has a much richer experience This is because the interpreter acts as a go-between. In the book of Leviticus the priest has this role.

You shall bring to the LORD ... two pigeons, one for a sin offering and the other for a burnt offering. You shall bring them to the priest ... Thus the priest shall make atonement on your behalf for the sin that you have committed, and you shall be forgiven. (parts of verses 7, 8 and 10)

The role of the priest is very important in Leviticus as he acts on behalf of the worshippers in maintaining their relationship with God. As Christians we are grateful for all that Jesus Christ is as our Great High Priest, but we are also grateful for those Christians who act as go-betweens, encouraging our relationship with God.

† *Thank you, Lord, for all your servants who remind me of your forgiveness; help me to follow their example in my own life.*

Wednesday September 28   Leviticus 6:14–23

BECOMING HOLY One of the things about staying with friends is that we discover some things about them that we want to imitate. 'That's good,' we think, 'we should be like that.' Some things are contagious. Someone once said that Christianity should be caught, not taught. Today's reading points us to holiness, a quality that is best caught from the example of others.

This is the ritual of the grain-offering ... I have given it as their portion of my offerings by fire; it is most holy, like the sin offering and the guilt offering ... anything that touches them shall become holy. (parts of verses 14, 17 and 18)

This passage refers to the role of priests who were to be caught up into holiness. That holiness would then infect those with whom they came into contact. As Christians we are reminded of the Apostle Peter's call to all Christians to be holy (*1 Peter 1:15–16*). Most people take more notice of what we are than of what we say. Let your holiness be catching.

† *Lord, thank you for every person from whom I have caught something of your holiness. Amen*

Thursday September 29   Leviticus 7:11–38

THANKSGIVING

This is the ritual of the sacrifice of the offering of wellbeing that one may offer to the LORD ... your thanksgiving sacrifice of wellbeing. (parts of verses 11 and 13)

Some Christians reading these notes may belong to churches which have many rituals in their services. Such rituals may include a procession that follows the cross, or may involve the use of candles, special clothes or colours. Other Christians may not feel comfortable with what they tend to see as mere outward observances. It is important to see the meaning of rituals, and the way in which life is full of rituals. We are familiar with the pre-match ceremonies before an international sporting fixture. The teams line up for the national anthems, the captains will shake hands and exchange pennants. These are ritual actions indicating respect for the opposition and the ideal of sportsmanship. Those Christians who are tempted to frown upon what they consider empty actions in worship should remember that at the heart of the faith is the sharing of bread and wine – in obedience to our Lord's command. That symbolic action is full of meaning and is a means of grace.

† *Father God, may thanksgiving be a daily ritual in my life,*
overflowing into a life of service and love.

Friday September 30   **Leviticus 8:1–17**

CONSECRATION

Then Moses took the anointing oil and anointed the tabernacle and all that was in it, and consecrated them ... He poured some of the anointing oil on Aaron's head and anointed him to consecrate him.   **(verses 10 and 12)**

This passage talks about a consecrated place and a consecrated person. We need special places like the tabernacle, places where God may be found and where God may find us. The Bible reminds us that this special place may be the temple, as it was, for example, for Isaiah's vision and Samuel's call. We need to go expectantly to our local house of God, wherever that is and whether large or small, elaborate or simple. The Bible also speaks of Jacob's dream as he slept in the open with a stone for his pillow, and of the still small voice that came to Elijah on the mountain. We need to be open to the voice of the Lord wherever we are. In today's passage, Aaron, as the High Priest, was the consecrated person, the one representing God to the people and the people to God. Guided by the writer to the Hebrews, Christians look to Jesus Christ as the one wholly consecrated God, through his death on the cross. 'Since, then, we have a great high priest ... Jesus, the Son of God, let us hold fast to our confession. For we do not have a high priest who is unable to sympathise with our weaknesses ... Let us therefore approach the throne of grace with boldness' (*Hebrews 4:14–16*). Through the consecrated person we find the place of consecration.

† *Find me, Lord, when I am lost, and when found give me a heart which searches for you.*

Saturday October 1   Leviticus 10:8–20

THE COMMON AND THE HOLY We began the week by thinking about what is expected of us when we go to visit friends and are invited to stay. Directly or indirectly, you understand the rules of the house. Today's reading gives us a good example of rules that are still important in the Jewish faith.

> **'You are to distinguish between the holy and the common, and between the unclean and the clean; and you are to teach the people of Israel all the statutes that the LORD has spoken to them through Moses. '**   **(verses 10–11)**

As Christians we remember Peter's vision described in Acts 10:9–16, and say that this distinction between clean and unclean, the common and the holy, is no longer imposed on Christians. What is important for us, however, is to see that we still live by the principle enshrined in these verses. We need places that are holy, set apart for God; we need to be holy ourselves, set apart for God's service. We need to learn to recognise both that which cleanses and that which corrupts in life. The outward expression of some rules may change, but the underlying principles do not. In this case the principle is that of being set apart for God in the life of holiness.

† *Lord, we praise you for all that your chosen people have contributed to the life of the world.*

For group discussion and personal thought

● What rituals do you find helpful both in public worship and in your personal relationship with God?
● Why is it important to have holy places, set apart for God?

READINGS IN LEVITICUS 2
Rules for a holy life

Notes by Philip G O'B Robinson

based on the New Revised Standard Version

Philip Robinson is the Immediate Past President of the Jamaica District of The Methodist Church in the Caribbean and the Americas (MCCA) and the current President of The Jamaica Council of Churches. He is Chairman of the National Religious Media Commission and Methodist Chaplain to the University of the West Indies (Mona Campus) and The University of Technology, both in Jamaica. He is also chaplain to the Excelsior Education Centre, the largest educational institution of the MCCA.

The book of Leviticus focuses on the holiness of God and the corresponding responsibility of his people to live holy lives. The detailed accounts of ancient rituals and practices may raise questions about its relevance for today. However, when the book is examined in light of the broad principles of holiness, sin, atonement and the like, the book is as relevant to the twenty-first century as today's newspaper and provides an ever-important background to understanding the gospel of Christ.

Text for the week: Leviticus 19:1–2

Sunday October 2   **Leviticus 11:1–47**

RULES FOR HEALTH AND HOLINESS

> **This is the law pertaining to land animal and bird and every living creature that moves through the waters and every creature that swarms upon the earth, to make a distinction between the unclean and the clean, and between the living creature that may be eaten and the living creature that may not be eaten.** (verses 46–47)

The reader who is familiar with the New Testament may wonder whether Jesus' statement that it is not what goes into a person that defiles him but what comes from the heart (*Matthew*

15:11, 18) contradicts these instructions to the children of Israel which were meant to help them to be a holy people. They do not, as we shall see. Since holiness suggests not only moral and spiritual cleanness but also physical cleanness and health (where these latter are achievable), the dietary restrictions were meant to achieve just that – the prevention of diseases that could be transmitted by the groups of animals and birds mentioned. In addition, forbidding this kind of association with the named creatures separated Israel from the surrounding nations to whom many of these creatures were of religious significance. It was the total separation of a people unto God, the real essence of holiness.

✝ *Lord, in practice and in precepts help us to be a people separated unto you.*

Monday October 3   **Leviticus 12:1–8**

RITUALS AND SYMBOLS OF HOLINESS

> **When the days of her purification are completed ... she shall bring to the priest at the entrance of the tent of meeting a lamb in its first year for a burnt offering, and a pigeon or a turtle dove for a sin offering ... then she shall be clean from her flow of blood.   (parts of verses 6 and 7)**

In every culture, people depend on symbols and rituals to appreciate and to communicate spiritual realities. There is something sacramental about the process of purification for women after childbirth as required by the Mosaic Law. 'An outward sign of an inward and spiritual grace' is one way in which a sacrament can be defined. The woman's uncleanness is different from that of the creatures mentioned in chapter 11. It is ritual and does not suggest a moral or health deficiency. The seclusion is part of the ritual. It recognises the importance of cleansing and purity if holiness is to be achieved and maintained, hence the offering of a burnt offering and a sin offering to atone for sins committed against a holy God. All of this reminds us that God provides ways for us to be restored to holiness by being 'ransomed, healed, restored [and] forgiven' as one popular hymn goes.

✝ *We thank you, God, for the grace of purification and restoration through which you bring us back to yourself in holiness.*

Tuesday October 4   **Leviticus 13:1–8**

MORE THAN PHYSICALLY WHOLE

When a person has on the skin of his body a swelling or an eruption or a spot, and it turns into a leprous disease on the skin of his body, he shall be brought to Aaron the priest or to one of his sons the priests.   **(verse 2)**

Leprosy described a variety of skin disorders – some highly contagious. The first time I saw a leper was while I was serving in Guyana (South America) as a young minister. I visited the leprosarium at Mahaica and saw people with portions of their body eaten away by the dreaded disease. Under Mosaic Law, the priest would declare one ceremonially clean or unclean. Jesus once responded to a leper's cry for help and did what was unthinkable at the time – touched him (*Mark 1:40–42*). He then instructed him to follow the rules in the law as a testimony of his restoration (*Mark 1:44*). I appreciated the compassion of our Lord as I stood among the lepers in Guyana. I understood their joy at hearing the good news that Jesus, our High Priest, is able to make and declare us more than physically whole, and holy.

† *Lord, you are able to make us whole and holy. If you choose, you can make us clean. May we feel your touch today.*

Wednesday October 5   **Leviticus 14:1–9**

GOD ASSURES AS HE RESTORES

Then he shall wash his clothes, and bathe his body in water, and he shall be clean.   **(part of verse 9)**

It is interesting to note that these detailed rites, as described in the passage, took place after the disease had healed and a clean bill of health had been given. Therefore they were not a means of healing. The process is full of powerful symbols; every object and every act had meaning. The overarching act of grace should not be missed. The disease was healed by God, but the human mind needed some assurance that any infirmities (physical or spiritual) that could defile had been removed and that the victim could renew social interactions as well as his religious duties. The sacrifices and offerings pointed to something done on the leper's behalf. They typified a divine act, exemplified in what the law required, that would restore him to holiness. Then and only then should he do the final act by himself – wash his clothes and bathe his body. The order is clear: healing, purification, then restoration.

† *Thank you, God, for every means by which we come to appreciate what you have done for us.*

Thursday October 6   Leviticus 16:1–19

AT ONE – GOD AND HUMANITY

No one shall be in the tent of meeting ... until he comes out and has made atonement for himself and for his house and for all the assembly of Israel.   **(part of verse 17)**

A person or thing is holy when he or it is set apart in honour of God. The sheer majesty and nature of God set him apart from us and inspire a sense of awe within us, but this does not create a barrier that prevents a harmonious relationship between God and people. It is sin with its corrupting influence that creates that barrier. The law required atonement, that act as a result of which God restored a relationship of harmony between himself and human beings. The priest (*verse 11*), the whole nation (*verse 17*) and the places of worship (*verse 16*) had to be atoned for first, before the people could approach God. They had to be set apart themselves, as holy to the Lord. Jesus has made atonement, once for all, for our sins. Yet nations today need to recover that sense of awe and reverence for God that should make a difference in how we live.

† *Cleanse us, O God, through the atoning blood of Jesus, that we may be reconciled to you.*

Friday October 7   Leviticus 19:1–14

A HOLY NATION

You shall not strip your vineyard bare, or gather the fallen grapes of your vineyard; you shall leave them for the poor and the alien: I am the LORD your God. You shall not steal; you shall not deal falsely; and you shall not lie to one another.   **(verses 10–11)**

Culture is broadly defined as the way of life of a people. The laws of God were meant to affect for good the moral and ethical conduct of the Children of Israel. Holiness was to be reflected in the very culture of the nation. Love for God would be demonstrated in their love for their neighbours. The holiness God requires maintains good social order and is a powerful witness to God's holy character. John Wesley exhorted the Methodists to 'spread scriptural holiness throughout the land' at a time when corruption, drunkenness, gambling and moral decay were rife. This led to a spiritual revival in England and other countries. It is holiness with a purpose (see *1 Peter 2:9*). God is able to bring about in the lives of ordinary, sinful people the kind of change that makes us different in a positive way and causes our lives to affect others for good.

† *Thank you, God, for the privilege of being one of your people; may our witness do honour to your name.*

Saturday October 8   Leviticus 19:15–37

DARE TO BE HOLY

You shall keep all my statutes and all my ordinances, and observe them: I am the LORD.   **(verse 37)**

Whenever people of different cultures mix there is an assimilation of beliefs and practices. The Israelites were often warned not to adopt the lifestyle of the people among whom they lived (see for example *Deuteronomy 12:29–32*). Holiness requires obedience to God's rules and standards in all circumstances of personal and national life. Human nature has not changed. Before we begin to condemn Israel, let us think for a moment. As it was with the Israelites, so it is with many people today. Things of which God disapproves are done in the name of God; values are embraced that are contrary to divine principles; misplaced priorities do not give God pre-eminence in our lives; and many try to justify this kind of unholy living to others and even to themselves. In his law God mercifully provides a road map and important guidelines to holy living, for both the individual and the nation. We must dare to be holy.

† *O God, help us to obey your law so that your kingdom may come and your will be done among us.*

For group discussion and personal thought

● Examine your own culture in the light of God's holiness and your response.
● Have we lost our sense of awe and reverence for God? If so, how may it be restored?
● Based on the week's reflections, make a list of guidelines for holy living for yourself, your community, your country.

READINGS IN MATTHEW 7
Suffering and transfiguration

Notes by Iain Roy

based on the Good News Bible

Suffering is a this-world experience, a reality in human life for someone somewhere every day. The Transfiguration by contrast must have seemed to Peter and James and John an almost out-of-this-world experience. But the real test of any religious experience is how it helps us to cope with the world and our life as it is.

Text for the week: Matthew 16:24

Sunday October 9   **Matthew 16:13–20**

THE ULTIMATE QUESTION   Matthew's gospel is keen to emphasise that Jesus is the Messiah of Jewish expectation. But to that the gospel adds the ultimate question for Christian faith.

> **'What about you?' [Jesus] asked them. 'Who do you say I am?' Simon Peter answered, 'You are the Messiah, the Son of the living God.'**   **(verses 15–16)**

Faith must have a personal dimension. However much we enter into the knowledge of faith through the experience of others, eventually our faith must be first-hand, not second-hand. Though Jesus directed his question to all the disciples, it is Peter alone who answers him. This is what each of us has to do – answer personally the challenge and demand of Christ to follow him, committing both ourselves and our gifts to him.

† *Lord, speak to me that I in turn may speak to others of your love through what I am and try to be.*

Monday October 10   **Matthew 16:21–28**

A LOT TO LEARN   Peter's transformation from saint to sinner is swift and dramatic.

> **'I must go to Jerusalem and suffer...' Peter took him aside and began to rebuke him ... 'That must never happen to**

you!' Jesus turned around and said to Peter, 'Get away
from me, Satan!'** (parts of verses 21–23)

Peter had a lot to learn about discipleship. Don't we all? He had
no idea of the true cost of love, despite sharing with the other
disciples the daily companionship of Jesus. Only the reality of the
cross itself can ever bring that cost home to humanity. It is not that
Jesus is the only one to have suffered in this world. It is rather that
in his suffering all human suffering is seen as God's concern, and
through Christ's suffering God reaches out in love to ours.

† *Lord, never allow us to be insensitive to the suffering of others,
but rather in their suffering help us to see yours, so that we may
commit ourselves to them in love and compassion.*

Tuesday October 11　　　　　　　　　　**Matthew 17:1–8**

ON A HIGH　The task of evangelism is never easy, but the
experience of the church over the centuries has been that it must
always begin where people are.

**Peter spoke up and said to Jesus, 'Lord, how good it is that
we are here! If you wish, I will make three tents here, one
for you, one for Moses, and one for Elijah.'** (verse 4)

It is easy to forget that the first disciples were, like Jesus himself,
Jews. Here we are reminded of that fact as Peter tries to come to
terms with this new spiritual experience through his existing
experience as a Jew. This incident has a resonance with the
giving of the Law to Moses on the mountain. What Peter and
the other disciples receive here is a unique experience of the
presence of God in Christ, but like every spiritual experience, its
testing-place is in daily life itself.

† *Lord, let your presence help us to cope with our every day, and let
your Spirit make each day a unique experience of your love.*

Wednesday October 12　　　　　　　　**Matthew 17:9–13, 22–23**

THE UNIQUE DEATH　The relationship between John the
Baptist and Jesus remains mysterious even after years of biblical
research, but no one can deny that each of the gospels emphasises
the close relationship between their respective ministries.

**'I tell you that Elijah has already come and people did not
recognise him, but treated him just as they pleased. In the
same way they will also ill-treat the Son of Man.'** (verse 12)

The fate of John the Baptist and Jesus was the same, death at the hand of their enemies. But the significance of each death is not the same. Many have suffered an unjust death and still do today in many countries in our world. But faith perceives the death of Jesus as unique, calling us and our world to account, demanding that we commit ourselves to oppose evil of every kind in Jesus' name.

✝ *Lord, make us vigilant for the innocent who suffer in this world today – the poor, the oppressed, the refugee, the asylum-seeker, the unjustly imprisoned, and all denied their true human rights and dignity.*

Thursday October 13   Matthew 19:23–30

NO FAVOURED STATUS   It is a long-standing human folly to ask, even of religion, 'What advantage is there in it for me?'

Then Peter spoke up. 'Look,' he said, 'we have left everything and followed you. What will we have?' (verse 27)

Peter is not alone in thinking that religious faith should confer benefit on the believer, a favoured status. But Jesus condemns this attitude wherever he finds it, both in his disciples and in his enemies. Our faith does not exempt us from the difficulties, the pains or the hurts of this life. Nor does it allow us to claim that we stand in a special relationship to God. Indeed, it has often been the arrogance of such claims which has led to religious bigotry and persecution. We all have to learn that there is only one way to walk with God – humbly.

✝ *In your presence, Lord, let us see others as better than ourselves, and be content that though you see us as we are, yet you still offer us your love and your forgiveness.*

Friday October 14   Matthew 20:17–23

UNPALATABLE TRUTH   There is a distinct impression in this gospel that the disciples were unwilling to take in what they saw as the unpalatable truth of Jesus' suffering, however often it was repeated.

'Listen,' he told them, 'we are going up to Jerusalem, where the Son of Man will be handed over to the chief priests and the teachers of the Law. They will condemn him to death and then hand him over to the Gentiles, who will mock him, whip him, and crucify him.'   (verse 18 and part of verse 19)

Since the gospel was written after the event, this may just be hindsight by the author, letting him see plainly what understandably was hidden from the disciples themselves. Even if that is the case, however, his perception of human unwillingness to take in unpalatable truth is still valid. For we are all reluctant to face up to certain truths in life, especially about ourselves, or about the implications of God's love for our daily living.

† *Give us the courage to face the truth, and the grace to take it into our lives and act upon it.*

Saturday October 15   Matthew 21:33–44

THE RIGHT CHOICE   The parables of Jesus have many functions but one basic function is always to give insight. Here the particular insight is to enable his Jewish hearers (and the Jewish readers of the gospel) to see how God's own people have so often rejected him.

> **Jesus said to them, 'Haven't you ever read what the Scriptures say?**
> **"The stone which the builders rejected as worthless turned out to be the most important of all."'** (part of verse 42)

I acted as labourer recently to an elderly gentleman in our village as he built a drystone wall for me. It was an education to see him choose which stone to use and which to reject. In building our own lives, it is very easy to choose the wrong building blocks. But to choose Christ – his way, his truth, his life – is to begin the building on a sure foundation.

† *Give our lives, Lord Jesus, the sure foundation of your love, and help us to remember the cost to you as well as your generosity to us.*

For group discussion and personal thought

● What do you think you still have to learn in your own personal discipleship ?
● Identify some specific groups of people in the world today whom you see as 'innocent sufferers'. Make them the subject of your group's or your own personal prayer.
● Using this week's readings as your guide, look at the repeated failure of the disciples to take in what Jesus wants to communicate to them. What do you see as blind spots in your own understanding of Jesus' teaching?

READINGS IN MATTHEW 8
Judgement and truth

Notes by Alec Gilmore

based on the New Revised Standard Version

Judgement may be easy, or it may be hard. It may be welcome or distressing, depending on what it is. But think of it more as a moment of truth than as an ultimate event. Notice how Jesus uses a moment of truth to bring us to judgement, sometimes by a question but often by a hard saying which hurts at first, sends us away to think, and then has the capacity to change our life for the better.

Text for the week: Matthew 25:40

Sunday, October 16 (World Food Day) **Matthew 16:1–12**

SIGNS   When we feel wronged, a first reaction is often to look for evidence that we were right. When our spiritual life is under fire we look for a 'sign' that we are on the right lines. Possibly in this case the scribes and Pharisees were setting a trap, but give them the benefit of the doubt; assume it was a genuine enquiry. Jesus says:

> **'When it is evening, you say, "It will be fair weather, for the sky is red." And in the morning, "It will be stormy today, for the sky is red and threatening.' You know how to interpret the appearance of the sky, but you cannot interpret the signs of the times."(part of verse 2 and verse 3)**

Jesus feels that if they cannot recognise the signs which are there already in his ministry, then they are not likely to recognise any other signs he gives them, and he will not 'turn on specials' just so that they will. He will do what he has to do. His hearers will be judged by their judgement.

† *Father, help me to see your hand in what you are doing every day, especially in the miracle of providing abundantly for us all and in your giving us the privilege of organising and sharing, and then standing back and waiting for us to recognise it.*

CELEBRITIES AND TARGETS   With the modern emphasis on idols and celebrities, league tables and targets, no wonder we go looking for 'the greatest' and 'the best'. We need a role model. But who? To answer the question, Jesus sets a child in the midst and says,

> **'Truly I tell you, unless you change and become like children, you will never enter the kingdom of heaven. Whoever becomes humble ... is the greatest ... Whoever welcomes one such ... welcomes me.'**   **(parts of verses 3–5)**

Children in our western society are different from children in the time of Jesus, so it is not possible to know precisely what Jesus had in mind. Humility is not immediately obvious in children as they jostle for recognition in the playground or the family. So what is it about today's children which, with our understanding of the gospel and Christian teaching, seems relevant to the kingdom? Try making your own list. Here are a few starters. A sense of wonder and enquiry. An enthusiasm to learn and grow. A natural response to love and affection. A perceptiveness which says clearly what adults often miss or are afraid to utter.

† *Father, next time I see a child, make me open to him (or her) and through them help me to see the wonder in your eyes.*

RELIGIOUS EXPERIENCE   Here is a man looking for a spiritual experience. He knows it exists. He has seen it in the lives of others. He covets it for himself. He knows there is something better and thinks Jesus may have the answer. After dismissing any notion that he sees himself as someone with 'answers' and failing to satisfy the man with the traditional answer ('Keep the commandments'), Jesus says,

> **'If you wish to be perfect, go, sell your possessions, and give the money to the poor, and you will have treasure in heaven; then come, follow me.'**   **(part of verse 21)**

Whether Jesus knew him and chose his words carefully or was simply making a general observation is not clear, but he obviously hit the nail on the head. It was the one thing this man could not do! In one verse Jesus says two things. One, be generous, to the point of poverty. Don't just give it away and then make more (so that you can give that away too!). Two, learn how to surrender the one thing you treasure most and then brace yourself for a totally different way of life. Follow me!

† *O Jesus, that is tough. I need your help even to wrestle with the idea and I'll need your forgiveness every time I fail to make it.*

Wednesday October 19   **Matthew 20:1–16**

GENEROSITY   We live in an age of increasing litigation. Our desire to ensure fair shares for all too easily becomes getting a fair share for me. So when Jesus suggests equal pay for unequal work it is hardly surprising that he causes a bit of a rumpus. Surely those who have struggled all day deserve better treatment, but the householder will have none of it.

> **'Friend, I am doing you no wrong; did you not agree with me for the usual daily wage? ... Am I not allowed to do what I choose with what belongs to me? Or are you envious because I am generous?'**   **(part of verse 13 and verse 15).**

The parable reflects two different understandings of life and values. One is 'contract'. You get what you agree to – no more, no less. The other is 'trust'. You may not always get what you expect but you are always liable to get more. It offends because we usually see it through the eyes of those who went for 'contract'. Try identifying with those who went for 'trust'. It may still offend but it gives a better understanding of how God works: generous with everybody.

† *Father, thank you for all your generosity, love and forgiveness to me over the years. Help me always to rejoice when I see your generosity overflowing to others.*

Thursday October 20   **Matthew 23:1–12**

OSTENTATION VERSUS HUMILITY   The charge against the scribes and Pharisees is not because of their doctrine but because of their practice. Jesus says:

> **'Do whatever they teach you and follow it; but do not do as they do, for they do not practise what they teach.'** **(verse 3)**

Today's world may be different but the challenge to examine the gap between our beliefs and our actions still stands. The more fervent our teaching, the more likely we are to fall short. The more familiar our actions, the less likely we are to notice how hypocritical they can look to others. The Pharisees apparently created burdens for others to carry and then did nothing to help. How does that compare with offering some of our more questionable doctrines and practices to others, while refusing to take a closer look to see if they really are all necessary and whether we might have got it wrong? The Pharisees were also charged with ostentation – so what does that say to us about the methods we use to promote our cause without ever stopping to consider how our single-mindedness strikes others?

† *Father, help me to see what I do through the eyes of the other person, to be more willing to listen than to speak and to learn rather than to teach.*

Friday October 21   Matthew 24:32–50

WATCHFULNESS   The early Christians expected Christ to return soon, hopefully in their lifetime. It didn't happen. When they began to lose hope, their leaders focused on the need for watchfulness. It might happen at any time. Nobody knew when. Leaves on the fig tree might tell you that summer was coming – but nothing more!

'About that day and hour no one knows, neither the angels of heaven, nor the Son, but only the Father.' (verse 36)

Today, the idea carries little sense of immediacy but the need for watchfulness remains. Not perhaps a watchfulness that springs from a fear that at any moment we may be called to account. That way, if the call never comes, we grow slack and indifferent and begin to turn things to our own advantage. What we need is more a growth in watchfulness that is commensurate with a growth in faith, and a daily reminder that even if he were never to come, we would at least have proved ourselves faithful servants. This is the 'eternal vigilance' that is 'the price of freedom', and that pays attention to the little things that matter and to the people who feel ignored.

† *Lord, help me to focus today on someone or something and reflect on how I might see them differently if you had suddenly appeared.*

Saturday October 22   Matthew 25:31–46

SHEEP AND GOATS   It is crystal clear what Jesus feels about human care and the criteria which separate the sheep from the goats. The sting is in the tail – the element of surprise!

'Then the righteous will answer him, "Lord, when was it that we saw you hungry and gave you food, or thirsty and gave you something to drink ... a stranger and welcomed you, or naked and gave you clothing ... sick or in prison and visited you?"'   (verse 37 and parts of verses 38–39)

The righteous had no idea what they had done. The others had no idea where they had failed. Surprise all round! This is not a reversal of judgement, whereby right is now wrong and wrong is now right. Nothing had changed. See it rather as a wake-up call to believers who never have any doubt about which side they (and others!) will be on when the last call comes. One group had never realised how effective they had been in the service of the kingdom; their best work had been totally unselfconscious. The other group had never realised how restrictive they had been and what a limited view of the kingdom they had.

† *Lord, give me an open mind and never let me forget that what is most unprepossessing may always be a jewel in your crown.*

For group discussion and personal thought

● Recall a moment of truth when you suddenly found yourself pulled up with a jerk, after which life was never the same again. Reflect on what previously you had missed or misunderstood and give thanks for the change.

● Recall a book or a play which ostensibly had nothing to do with faith or religion but which opened your eyes to new truth. Did you see it as a judgement at the time? If yes, with what result? If no, why not?

● If you are part of a group, divide the group into two, sheep and goats, for a role-play. Invite each group to enter into the parable and discuss how they felt when they heard the judgement. After about 15 minutes, invite them to list some of the characteristics associated with their group in contemporary society, possibly naming groups or public figures by way of illustration. After a further 20–30 minutes, bring the two groups together and let them exchange their feelings and ideas. What surprises do you find?

PRISONS AND PRISONERS 1
The faithful imprisoned: Joseph

Notes by Chris Duffett

based on the New International Version

In preparation for writing this week's Bible studies I researched the web to find out how many Christians are in prison. I was shocked to read reports of scores of saints across the globe who have been incarcerated for their faith. While the appalling injustice of the imprisonment of millions of Christians worldwide is a worthy topic for study, this week we shall look at the benefit of prison life for one man. We shall study God's hand at work in the life of Joseph, where the apparent injustice of slavery and prison actually had God's fingerprints all over it. This week is about the way God chose to allow the bad things in Joseph's life for his good, so that his character could be moulded and made to be more like that of Jesus.

Text for the week: Acts 7:9–10

Sunday October 23   **Psalm 105:16–22**

JOSEPH, A MAN LIKE JESUS As we consider the life of Joseph in prison, there are many similarities between his circumstances and those of Jesus. Joseph was sold by his own people into slavery. He was cast into prison but then rose from humiliation to exaltation. Jesus rose victorious from his humiliation, death and the grave. Indeed, the story of Joseph, like that of Jesus, reveals God's immaculate plan for his people:

> **and he sent a man before them –**
> **Joseph, sold as a slave.**   **(verse 17)**

Psalm 105 gives us a clear synopsis of Joseph's life and reveals some poignant lessons for us in our journey as followers of Jesus. Firstly, God is in control. We serve a sovereign God, whose plans are far cleverer than we can perceive. Psalm 33:11 states that the 'plans of the Lord stand firm for ever, the purposes of his heart through all generations'. Secondly, life isn't always easy. Joseph had to endure great hardship before he tasted the power of being Pharaoh's right-hand man.

† *Almighty God, help me to know that you are in control.*
Almighty God, help me to trust in you, and you alone.
Almighty God, help me to see you at work in my life. Amen

Monday October 24   **Genesis 37:3–4, 12–28**

A TERRIBLE THING, ENVY Out of the twelve sons of Israel, Joseph was the favourite. As well as bestowing great privileges and love upon his preferred son, Israel rewarded him with a handsome coat. Joseph was exempt from labouring in the fields, and in such a loving, relaxed environment Joseph had many dreams of how God would exalt him above his brothers. The dreams were not well received.

'Here comes that dreamer!' they said to each other. 'Come now, let's kill him and throw him into one of these cisterns and say that a ferocious animal devoured him. Then we'll see what comes of his dreams.' ... When the Midianite merchants came by, his brothers pulled Joseph up out of the cistern and sold him for twenty shekels of silver to the Ishmaelites, who took him to Egypt.   (verses 19, 20 and 28)

The brothers' envy was so aroused that their plan was to kill him. Imagine if they had murdered him. The whole of history would be very different: the rescuing of Israel's family from starvation, the twelve tribes of Israel, the Exodus from Egypt. All this would not have happened! In the midst of raw emotion and what looked like a very delicate situation, in which Joseph nearly died, God was in full control. God has our lives in his hands. Job 14:5 states that, 'Man's days are determined; you have decreed the number of his months.' Psalm 139 declares that God has ordained all the days for each one of us. Let us learn from Joseph that we serve a sovereign God who is one hundred per cent in control of our lives, and he alone knows when we will be called home to be with him in heaven.

† *Jesus, you alone know how many days I have to live here on earth, and you are preparing a place for me in heaven for me to be with you. Help me to live with heaven in mind, and help me to know each day that I live on earth that I can see your kingdom come and your will be done. Amen*

DO YOU KNOW GOD'S FAVOUR? In every circumstance Joseph served God wholeheartedly and knew his favour. When tempted with an offer of sex, Joseph chose to follow God's way. Perhaps Joseph was able to say no to the persistent offer because of his close relationship with God; temptation wasn't an issue because he knew that God's love for him was 'better than life itself' (*Psalm 63:3*). When you are confident of the love and care that your heavenly Father has for you, then you can act with integrity in every circumstance, like Joseph.

> **Now Joseph was well-built and handsome, and after a while his master's wife took notice of Joseph and said, 'Come to bed with me!' But he refused. 'With me in charge,' he told her, 'my master does not concern himself with anything in the house; everything he owns he has entrusted to my care.'   (part of verse 6 and verses 7–8)**

Do you know God's favour and love for you? Jesus was a man who knew the favour of his Father. 'And Jesus grew in wisdom and stature, and in favour with God and men' (*Luke 2:52*). All Christians have preferential treatment and are treated by God as if we were a favourite child, such is his love for each one of us. Spend time today meditating on the favour that God has poured on you as his child.

✝ *How great is the love that the Father has lavished upon me, that I should be called a child of God! Help me to know that that is what I am. Amen*

ANYWHERE, ANYTHING, ANY TIME How would you be feeling if you had just been betrayed by your siblings, thrown down a pit, sold into slavery and hurled into prison? I know that I would probably be full of self-pity and doubt that God had any purpose for me. Not so for Joseph...

> **Pharaoh was angry with his two officials, the chief cupbearer and the chief baker, and put them in custody in the house of the captain of the guard, in the same prison where Joseph was confined ... [Joseph] saw that they were dejected. So he asked Pharaoh's officials ... 'Why are your faces so sad today?' 'We both had dreams,' they answered, 'but there is no one to interpret them.' Then Joseph said to**

them, 'Do not interpretations belong to God? Tell me your dreams.' (verses 2–3, parts of verses 6–7, and verse 8)

Even in a dungeon Joseph was willing to be used by God. He cared for his fellow prisoners and looked to help them, rather than seeking his own comfort. As he began to care for the needs of others, he was given boldness to state that God had the answer to their dreams. As an evangelist I have seen time and time again that a simple gesture of help can turn into an opportunity for proclaiming the good news of Jesus. However, being able to share the wonders of God with people comes with a price: availability. Being willing to serve and care for others at any time and anywhere means laying aside our lives and putting others before our own interests.

† *I lay my life before you.*
I give my time to you.
I give my hopes to you.
I want to live for you.
I want to show your love.
I want to be used by you. Amen

Thursday October 27   **Genesis 41:1–45**

TAKING THE LONG VIEW Trusting that God has our best interests at heart can be a difficult exercise. Joseph, after his spectacular performance of interpreting the cupbearer's dream, must have imagined that his release from prison was imminent. However, he had to wait a further 24 months until he saw daylight again:

When two full years had passed, Pharaoh had a dream ... In the morning his mind was troubled, so he sent for all the magicians and wise men of Egypt. Pharaoh told them his dreams, but no one could interpret them for him ... So Pharaoh sent for Joseph, and he was quickly brought from the dungeon. When he had shaved and changed his clothes, he came before Pharaoh. (part of verse 1, and verses 8 and 14)

Two years may not seem a long time. However, having visited numerous young men in prison who have had a matter of months to spend inside, I know that each day can seem like a week. Two years without freedom, stuck in a dungeon, must have seemed like a lifetime. Nevertheless, Joseph seemed to have a really strong trust that God was in control. Without demanding justice or seeking revenge, Joseph launched himself into the service of Pharaoh and prophetically discerned his dreams. His reward came to him in abundance, all because he was able to take the long view and know that God is worthy to be trusted!

✝ *I want to trust you for all that I do*
I want to trust you for all that I am going through
I want to trust you when life is difficult
I want to trust you when life is good
Help me now to trust in you. Amen

Friday October 28   Genesis 45:3–28

PURPOSE IN THE PAIN After years of service to Pharaoh with all its challenges, following on years of prison life, Joseph was able to declare the purpose of all the pain:

> **And now, do not be distressed and do not be angry with yourselves for selling me here, because it was to save lives that God sent me ahead of you ... it was not you who sent me here, but God. He made me father to Pharaoh, lord of his entire household and ruler of all Egypt. (verse 5 and part of verse 8)**

Joseph was able to proclaim God's purpose to his brothers, because he could see the fruit of such misery: God used him to save lives. The opening sentences in 2 Corinthians reveal that God comforts us in our despair so that we in turn can comfort those who are going through similar circumstances. Paul goes on to write, 'our light and momentary troubles are achieving for us an eternal glory that far outweighs them all' (*2 Corinthians 4:17*). Troubles are sometimes allowed by God so that we can become more like him. The eighteenth-century spiritual leader Madam Guyon is quoted as saying, 'It is the fire of suffering that brings forth the gold of godliness.'

✝ *You have a perfect plan for my life. Thank you!*
You have a purpose for me. Praise you!
You desire to prosper me. Thank you!
You are my shepherd who looks after me. Hallelujah!

Saturday October 29   Acts 7:9–16

IF GOD IS FOR YOU, WHO CAN BE AGAINST YOU? At the beginning of this week, Psalm 105 gave us a first-rate synopsis of what happened in Joseph's life; likewise Stephen's great speech to the Sanhedrin gives us a perfect summary. Stephen simply states:

God was with him and rescued him from all his troubles.
(part of verses 9 and 10)

What does it mean, that God is with you? Just as God was with Joseph, he is also with you; he looks after you just as he cared for Joseph. Many biblical texts tell us what God's presence with us means, and the troubles from which he can rescue us: he protects us from the wicked tongues of others (*Job 5:21*); he answers us in distress (*Psalm 20:1*); he is our hiding place and surrounds us with songs of deliverance (*Psalm 32:7*); he brings us to unity (*John 17:11*); he protects us from 'the evil one' (*2 Thessalonians 3:3*). When troubles come, we can confidently watch out for God's rescue. Like Joseph in his prison, we may have to wait patiently for a long time, but God is faithful. He is with us in the darkness and is preparing a way out for us, as he did with Joseph.

✝ *Thank you, Lord Jesus, for the way you shepherd me.*
Thank you, Holy Spirit, for the way you cover me with your fire.
Thank you, Father, for the way you draw me close in your arms,
sheltering me from the storm. Amen

For group discussion and personal thought

- How can you actively trust God more in your life? Think of one thing that you could do to show God that you trust him.
- In what ways do you show others that despite difficult times you still believe that God is in control of your life?
- This week, try and comfort someone you know who may be going through difficult times.
- Do you know anyone in prison? If you can, make contact with them this week and let them know that you are thinking of and praying for them.

PRISONS AND PRISONERS 2
The faithful imprisoned: others

Notes by Philip Wetherell

based on the New English Bible

These readings show how faithful people have lost their freedom through refusing to renounce their faith. Common threads in the stories are: the effect of this faithfulness on the leaders and ordinary people who witness it; and the example this gives us in our very varied work in mission today.

Text for the week: Daniel 6:16

Sunday October 30   **Daniel 6:1–24**

DANIEL – PRISONER OF CONSCIENCE   Sometimes even those who make laws come to realise that this is not always the same as doing justice. King Darius agrees to a law that will unite his kingdom – no one shall worship any other god or man. His faithful and most trusted servant Daniel is put in a position where he has no option but to defy the law – just as his jealous colleagues know will happen. He prays three times a day to his God. He is imprisoned; it is expected that he will die. Yet even the king acknowledges the power of his prayer:

> **The king gave orders and Daniel was brought and thrown into the lions' pit; but he said to Daniel, 'Your own God, whom you serve continually, will save you.'** **(verse 16)**

The king spends the night fasting; Daniel spends it with angels who shut the mouths of the lions, and in the morning this prisoner of conscience is still alive. Where people are persecuted for their faith today, it does not always happen like that. Faithful Christians still suffer and sometimes die. King Darius may have ordered that all should worship Daniel's god, but today we recognise that personal freedom is more important. Faithfulness is real witness, prisoners of conscience inspire us and release us from our own captivity, even if they cannot save themselves.

† *Pray that in any test of faithfulness today, big or small, God will be served.*

Monday October 31 Isaiah 53:7–12

THE POWER OF TRUE SERVICE OF GOD From yesterday's Daniel, a powerful man in an earthly kingdom, we come to the servant – who also suffers unjustly. We are reminded of the situation of many of the poor in today's world: stuck, unable to save themselves, prisoners in their own situation, victims of the sins of the powerful and greedy.

> **Without protection, without justice, he was taken away ...**
> **He was assigned a grave with the wicked,**
> **a burial-place among the refuse of mankind,**
> **though he had done no violence.   (parts of verses 8 and 9)**

Isaiah's servant is suffering because of the sins of others – and we are guided to think of Jesus, a 'tortured servant ... who had made himself a sacrifice for sin' (*verse 10*). A remarkable transformation happened through Jesus and can happen today too. Through his suffering new life comes for others. In one sense that happens for the rich today – who benefit physically and economically through the suffering of the poor. They have the 'good life' from others' captivity. But Jesus releases us all – the poor to show the wealthy true values and the wealthy to repent and share the real riches of God's kingdom.

† *Pray today that the powerful and rich will learn to serve God more faithfully.*

Tuesday November 1 Jeremiah 37

COURAGE AND COWARDICE Jerusalem has been under siege, but the surrounding army has temporarily left. Jeremiah tries to leave too, is falsely accused of going over to the other side – and is thrown into prison. Just like Herod (with John the Baptist) and Pontius Pilate (with Jesus), King Zedekiah does not have the courage to set an innocent man free. This gives his officers the impetus to humiliate Jeremiah, as happens today when the winners in battles and wars and everyday political confrontations find delight in exposing and humiliating their captives and the 'losers'.

They flogged him and imprisoned him ... for Jeremiah had been put into a vaulted pit beneath the house, and here he remained for a long time. (part of verse 15 and verse 16)

For his own purposes, and afraid of the power of this prophet, King Zedekiah tries to ease the conditions under which Jeremiah is kept, and even meets him in secret. Jeremiah's honesty and prophetic truth is still recognised, but fear of his officers prevents Zedekiah from doing what he knows he should. Often spurred on by leaders looking at their own political gain, or afraid of public opinion or unpopularity, we still brutalise prisoners today.

† *Pray today for those who work for prison reform.*

Wednesday November 2   Matthew 4:12–17; 11:2–6

JESUS IS MOVED BY THE PLIGHT OF PRISONERS I once had to preach in a prison on John the Baptist – whom Jesus described as the greatest person ever born of a woman (*Luke 7:28*). And here he is in prison. The first earthly voice to proclaim the kingdom of God is silenced. But

When he heard that John had been arrested, Jesus withdrew to Galilee. (verse 12)

It seems Jesus was deeply affected by this great man's imprisonment, as he was and is by any unjust suffering and by the situation of so many prisoners today, who are often life's casualties, low achievers and themselves the victims of the failures of their society. But Jesus acted on his feelings. This was the spur to his preaching of repentance, because, as John had intimated, 'The kingdom of Heaven is upon you' (*verse 17*) and the kingdom brings release for all of us. Let injustice be our spur to prayer and action.

† *Pray today for all who offer a ministry to prisoners, wherever they are.*

Thursday November 3   Acts 5:12–26

DISTURBING CHRISTIANS This is the first of two stories in which an angel of the Lord intervenes on behalf of imprisoned early Christians. Today's reading suggests jealousy as a motive for imprisonment, tomorrow's a concern for public stability. The believers were held in high regard: 'People in general spoke highly of them' (*verse 13*) but, more worrying for the authorities, 'numbers of men and women were added to their ranks' (*verse 13*). It did not matter to the authorities that their popularity was due to the active help they gave to people:

In the end the sick were actually carried out into the streets and laid there on beds and stretchers, so that even the shadow of Peter might fall on one or another as he passed by. (verse 15)

There are still many places in the world where Christians or other people of faith are treated in this way by those in authority, places where public preaching and, particularly, any suggestion of growth or popularity is disturbing and seen as threatening. Christians are still imprisoned for holding to their belief that they must 'obey God rather than men' (*verse 29*). In each place, Christians must decide how to deal with authorities who see Christianity as part of western dominance or undermining local culture. However, what created jealousy in this biblical story – the work of healing – can now show authorities that Christians have a concern for the whole community. It is this service to all, rather than preaching, that releases the closed minds of opponents and leads to a truer freedom for all.

✝ *Pray for all who work in difficult circumstances, under threat or danger, to show God's love through service to their community.*

Friday November 4   **Acts 12:1–19**

PRAYER WORKS The first apostle to be martyred, James, has been beheaded (a method which implies a political charge). Christians were obviously now seen as dangerous to the status quo and to the peace and unity of the nation that the Roman authorities allowed the Jewish King Herod Agrippa to rule – provided that he kept the peace. When the public seemed to approve, Herod also imprisoned Peter:

He put him in prison under a military guard, four squads of four men each, meaning to produce him in public after Passover. So Peter was kept in prison under constant watch, while the church kept praying fervently for him to God. (verses 4–5)

The night before he was to be produced, Peter was released from prison by an angel, who arrived in a blaze of light. Peter's chains fell off and he was led past unseeing or impotent guards; gates opened of their own accord and Peter was free – though it seems that those who had prayed did not believe it: 'You are crazy', they told Rhoda, who opened the door to him. 'It must be his guardian angel' (*verse 15*). God wanted Peter to lead his church and when God wants what we want, prayer is answered. Brutality continued, however, and Peter's guards were interrogated and executed.

† *Pray today for all who work in prisons, that they may respect those in their care and be respected for their fairness, and that all may recognise the goodness that is in everyone.*

Saturday November 5   Acts 21:27–36

FALSE ACCUSERS Paul was well known in Ephesus and it was visitors from there who planted the idea in Jerusalem that he had polluted the holy Temple by taking a Gentile into the Inner Court – an offence punishable by death. The supposed offence caused a riot, and Roman soldiers stationed there for precisely this kind of event were quickly on the scene. They prevented further beating of Paul but arrested him. In the confusion they ended up as his protectors as much as his captors.

> **As [the commandant] could not get at the truth because of the hubbub, he ordered him to be taken into the barracks. When Paul reached the steps, he had to be carried by the soldiers because of the violence of the mob. For the whole crowd were at their heels yelling, 'Kill him!'**
> **(part of verse 34 and verses 35–36)**

At the end of these two weeks of looking at prisons and prisoners, it is worth ending with a thought for those whose task is to keep law and order, to maintain the balance between security and humanity in our prisons, and between individual freedom and the sometimes different wishes of the majority. We have seen biblical evidence of much abuse and evil, and many parallels between the scenarios of biblical times and today, and we need to work and pray for fairness for any accused of any offence, for those committed to prison and for those whose difficult task it is to tread those thin lines between excess and control. Paul would approve.

† *Pray for all whose task it is to make and enforce laws, that justice and humanity may be their aims.*

For group discussion and personal thought

● What can you do, through prayer and practical help, to support both prisoners and those who work in prisons?

PRISONS AND PRISONERS 3
The prisoner's cry

Notes by Jember Teferra

based on the New International Version

Jember Teferra is from Ethiopia. She has been working with the urban poor in the worst slums in Addis Ababa for the past 23 years, the result of an early childhood call to work with the poorest of the poor. With her team of helpers she promotes a holistic ministry known as the Integrated Holistic Approach, a philosophy which will now be further promoted at the newly set-up Institute for Urban Workers. This institute will primarily target Christian churches, to encourage them to be more involved in a holistic urban ministry and to focus particularly on poverty alleviation and social justice issues.

The theme for this week is very personal to me because, as I have written in my devotional book, *The Prisoner's Lantern* (published by Keston College in 1988):

> For half a decade I was a political prisoner. But I spent all of those years with convicts and learned a lot of their fears, doubts and ways of life. I was a political prisoner with many others in the same position. I also know what I and my colleagues felt.
>
> When visitors came to see us I also saw supposedly 'free' people who appeared to be prisoners of their own bars. It was then I inevitably asked myself why I felt much freer than those people too.
>
> If you know the Lord there is something – the joy, the peace, the confidence and the faith – that no one takes away from you. This I learned in person. Inner freedom and peace come only from knowing the Lord. Suffering batters us and breaks us, but no one can remove the inner firmness which is only present in those who know and walk with the Lord.

Text for the week: Psalm 142:7

CRY OUT TO GOD FOR DELIVERANCE ... but don't expect to
dictate to God how he should deliver you. David composed this
psalm when he had fled from Saul into a cave in the desert.
Imprisonment begins with your arrest. For some reason, I
found it hard to accept my arrest. My husband, who was a
government official under Emperor Haile Selassie of Ethiopia,
had been imprisoned with many other officials 2 years before
me. It was bad enough struggling on alone with four children
under 8 years old – but then I was arrested as well! Even as a
Christian, I had difficulty in believing at that moment that God
would allow my arrest and ultimate imprisonment. At first,
when my immediate shock and anger at my arrest were over, I
called out to God.

> He sends from heaven and saves me,
> rebuking those who hotly pursue me ...
>> Be exalted, O God, above the heavens;
> let your glory be over all the earth.
>
> **(part of verse 3 and verse 5)**

I expected a dramatic action from God! I wanted my arresting
officer to be punished there and then (rather like Samson in the
book of Judges, who eventually killed and died with his
enemies); I could not accept that God's ways are always
different from mine. A cry for deliverance may not be
responded to in the way we think it should. God may allow
suffering for a purpose.

† *Thank you, O Lord, that we have the gift of faith to call upon you
for deliverance, but help us to accept that you may not deliver in
the way we expect, but may be able to use our suffering for your
purposes.*

DELIVERANCE IN GOD'S OWN CONTEXT

> When my spirit grows faint within me,
> it is you who know my way.
> In the path where I walk
> men have hidden a snare for me ...
> Set me free from my prison,
> that I may praise your name.   **(verse 3 and part of verse 7)**

For 48 hours following my arrest I was in mental bondage
within my physical bonds. I was actually angry with God for

letting me down and allowing my imprisonment. I was so upset that I did not cry, pray or share my anger with my fellow prisoners. On the third day of my imprisonment I spoke to one of the guards. 'I feel it is a mistake that I am arrested. In our culture, which involves family care, how can a mother and a father be imprisoned at the same time, leaving 4 children under 8 years old behind? Please take me to the Prison Administrator – I have to explain.' Before I finished talking she laughed at me and mocked me. 'Mistake?' she ridiculed me. 'Lady, there is no mistake. You are here because you deserve to be. If you are surprised about your imprisonment, lady, you may even be executed!' I think God made her speak like that – in order to break down my resistance to him. I went away to the back yard and wept long and hard until God stopped me to listen. There and then I surrendered and was released out of my double bondage; there and then, too, I prayed, 'Oh God, what do you want me to do here? There must be a purpose because, as a loving Father, you do not allow suffering for no good reason.' To cut a long story short, God delivered me from my bondage to anger and disobedience, primarily by using me to serve the sick in mind and body, the tortured, the damaged and the depressed, to counsel, teach, nurse and evangelise, and to train others to do the same.

† *Our loving heavenly Father, deliver us from disobedience; if we choose to follow you, give us faith to trust you in all circumstances – even imprisonment behind bars.*

Tuesday November 8   Isaiah 24:17–23

'FOR EVER HE WILL BE A LAMB UPON THE THRONE'
How difficult it is to go on believing that God almighty is still on the throne when injustice seems to be the order of the day. Whether under Marxism or any oppressive rule, our faith can be badly hit. During my imprisonment there were two terrible years when the 'Red Terror' claimed the lives of thousands of radical Marxists, mostly young girls and boys and some men and women also. It also included some of us who had supposedly been arrested as the 'oppressing' ex-ruling class; we were also political victims of the 'Red Terror', so we lived knowing that at any time we could be called to be executed! I had great admiration for all those non-Christians who believed in their political ideals and saw their role as saviours of the Ethiopian people from 'revisionist' Marxism. I had many hours of discussion with them and shared my beliefs with them:

Terror and pit and snare await you,
O people of the earth ...
  the LORD Almighty will reign.

(verse 17 and part of verse 23)

I learned and my faith grew to rest in peace and be still while the endless shooting roared day and night, as victims of the Red Terror were hunted both beyond the high walls of our prison and among the prisoners themselves. Today, sadly, I see in Ethiopia what Isaiah said would happen to the powers-that-be:

They will be herded together
like prisoners bound in a dungeon;
they will be shut up in prison.   **(part of verse 22)**

May they learn from their present imprisonment even as we did from ours.

✝ *Help us, Lord, to remember that you are always on your throne, managing the world, even if we cannot always see it. We still pray for peace and justice – your kingdom come.*

Wednesday November 9   Psalm 28

THE LORD OVER-RULES EVIL We prayed day and night even when demonic forces tried to stop us. Twice during my imprisonment I was accused of continuing my 'oppressive' behaviour by imposing regular devotions morning and evening. The second time, all those in the women's compound were called into the presence of the Prison Administrator. My accusers among the women tried to remind the administrator that Ethiopia at that time was ruled by Marxists, and almost accused him of allowing me to impose my values on the other women. This was a mistake, because he became angry and reminded the prisoners of all the help I gave them without payment; when he asked for those who opposed daily devotions to raise their hands, only 5 out of the 450 prisoners did so. The Administrator then said, 'Sister Jember, I permit you to conduct your devotions at breakfast, lunch and dinner time if you wish. You have the permission of the majority of your prison mates!'

The LORD is my strength and my shield;
  my heart trusts in him, and I am helped.(part of verse 7)

As a result, many Marxist young people who opposed the regime found the Lord in prison. They asked me to conduct prayers from their mattress space or stand near them to pray when they had court cases, exams, or suchlike.

† *Even in prison, Lord, you do wonders, answer prayers, heal and perform miracles ... thank you for that too.*

Thursday November 10   Psalm 130

GOD NEVER FAILS, HE IS ALSO GOD OF THE IMPOSSIBLE

> **O Israel, put your hope in the LORD,**
> **for with the LORD is unfailing love**
> **and with him is full redemption.**   **(verse 7)**

Victims of the 'Red Terror' continued to be called from the prison to execution at least 3 or 4 days a week. We prayed every day for this endless killing to stop. And then for some unknown miraculous reason it stopped – God answered our prayers. But during those terrible days God used me to save some women in a very unexpected way when they gave birth to babies during their time of imprisonment. So God enabled a few women to escape who would have been executed during the 'Red Terror'; one of them is now an official in the present government!

† *Thank you for doing the impossible, Lord: thank you for sparing so many lives by stopping the 'Red Terror' completely.*

Friday November 11   Psalm 88

GOD THE SYMPATHISER   In the early days of my imprisonment my mother was also imprisoned for 3 months and then released. My spiritual life suffered a setback when I was hit by bereavement – I was told that my sister, who supported me and my children and was part of the family team helping us in prison, had died from a serious illness. Why did I have to suffer this as well as imprisonment?

> **You have put me in the lowest pit,**
> **in the darkest depths.**
> **Your wrath lies heavily upon me;**
> **you have overwhelmed me with all your waves ...**
> **You have taken my companions and loved ones from me;**
> **the darkness is my closest friend.**   **(verses 6–7 and 18)**

I stopped leading the devotions – I was angry again! Perhaps being a prisoner leads you to go up and down spiritually and emotionally like a yo-yo, more than those who are outside the prison; but I let down so many of the young Christians. When I was persuaded to lead an evening devotion eight days after my sister's death, I just stood and wept and asked God, 'Why do you do this to me, Lord?' I knew he understood and had also wept for his friend Lazarus. Time healed my grief and anger, praise God.

✝ *Heavenly Father, imprisonment makes difficulties and suffering much more unacceptable. We pray that all those in bondage both physically and spiritually may look up to you for healing, release, spiritual renewal and an increase of faith.*

Saturday November 12   Psalm 70

GOD DOES DELIVER

> **But may all who seek you**
>   **rejoice and be glad in you;**
> **may those who love your salvation always say,**
>   **'Let God be exalted!'**   **(verse 4)**

Five years after my arrest and imprisonment, 3 months after my sister's death, the good Lord got me released. One of the women prison guards had said to my prison mates, 'If Jember is released, you all have a good chance of going out free – we thought she would be imprisoned for life!' (Why?) Only five of us out of some twenty remaining women political prisoners in my category came out at that time. There was not even any occasion for release such as a public holiday (which was sometimes used in this way). So God in his mercy heard our cry and delivered me. My children, my mother and my brother who directly took care of us, including other members of the family and friends on both sides, rejoiced. My husband miraculously followed me two years later – praise the Lord. Praise God too for the many ways in which he used me during my five years of imprisonment, rather as he used Joseph. To this day I relive that experience and have never taken his goodness to us for granted.

✝ *Thank you for freedom, Lord: both freedom from physical bondage and from other bondages which are just as bad; only you can give us a holistic freedom.*

For group discussion and personal thought

● This theme has focused on prison and prisoners. In what ways does physical imprisonment differ from other kinds, where people are imprisoned by 'their own bars'?
● Do you find it difficult to accept God's purpose and plans? How can you learn to co-operate better with him?
● Who else, besides Joseph, has God used behind bars?

PRISON AND PRISONERS 4
Setting the captives free

Notes by Kate Hughes

based on the New Revised Standard Version

Long my imprisoned spirit lay
fast bound in sin and nature's night; ...
my chains fell off, my heart was free;
I rose, went forth, and followed thee.

I always sing these words of Charles Wesley with real pleasure, because I know the wonderful feeling of walking from a small, dark cell into light and freedom – not a literal cell, but the imprisonment which is life without knowing and loving God. Freeing captives of all kinds was an important part of the Messiah's work, both in the Old Testament and in the fulfilment of this role by Jesus in the New Testament; we shall be exploring both aspects in this week's readings.

Text for the week: Luke 4:18–19

Sunday November 13   **Psalm 107:10–16**

GOD TO THE RESCUE What puts us into the spiritual dark cell is rebellion against God. If we deliberately try to live without reference to God (and the word is 'rebelled' – a deliberate act, not ignorance) and spurn (deliberately push away) his guidance, we lock ourselves away from him. We put ourselves into a prison and throw away the key, so that we can no longer hear God's voice or see his creation. And this prison is no joke: it is a place of darkness, gloom, misery, constraint (irons), hard labour, exhaustion and distress.

> **Then they cried to the LORD in their trouble,**
> **and he saved them from their distress;**
> **he brought them out of darkness and gloom,**
> **and broke their bonds asunder.**   **(verses 13–14)**

But if we truly want to get out of prison, and are prepared to accept God's terms for liberation (for a start, stopping rebelling and starting to listen to him), then God will break into our prison, shattering the doors and cutting off our leg irons, flooding our darkness with his light.

✝ *Thank you, Lord, that you will break into our prison and lead us out to light and freedom.*

Monday November 14   Psalm 146

SETTING THE PRISONERS FREE   This psalm of praise emphasises the practical goodness of God. Unlike human rulers, who are unreliable and will eventually die anyway, God is the creator who is truly in control of his world. He brings justice to the oppressed, feeds the hungry, gives sight to the blind, rescues the depressed, keeps a special eye on foreigners, widows and orphans and deals with the wicked – and he frees the prisoners.

> **Happy are those whose help is the God of Jacob, whose hope is in the LORD their God.**   **(verse 5)**

In this psalm, the prisoners were not in spiritual or mental cells of their own making. They were real prisoners: captured in war, sold or taken into slavery, imprisoned for debt, or unjustly sentenced. No society is entirely just; there are always those who can only be given justice by God, and the coming of God's justice to prisoners would be part of the reign of the Messiah.

✝ *O Lord our God, we pray for all prisoners, especially those who are unjustly imprisoned; hear their cry and help them.*

Tuesday November 15   Zechariah 9:11–17

PRISONERS OF HOPE   Much of the turbulence in Israel's history was the result of the country's geographical position. Palestine was a small country, a strip of coastal plain and low hills standing between Egypt in the south and Assyria and Babylon in the north. As a result, it was constantly invaded by its powerful neighbours, to ensure that it did not side with the opposition or stop their armies marching through. Like all oppressed peoples, the Israelites dreamt of better times in the future, when God would send his servant to defeat their enemies, bring peace, restore their sovereignty and make them even more prosperous than before. The centuries-old covenant between God and the people of Israel was their reminder that he would liberate them. He would not forget his people, or leave them oppressed by their enemies.

Return to your stronghold, O prisoners of hope;
today I declare that I will restore to you double.   (verse 12)

They might be prisoners, but they were prisoners with the hope of liberation.

† *Thank you, Lord, that however dark our circumstances, we can always look forward with hope to your liberation, because Jesus is the 'yes' declared on all your promises.*

Wednesday November 16   **Isaiah 52:1–10**

THE LORD COMES TO ZION The city is besieged. Food has run short, many of the men have been killed defending the walls, the people are afraid, disease has started to spread. Suddenly, one of the men on the city wall, keeping a cautious eye on the movements of the enemy, notices a small cloud of dust on the horizon. Gradually, the cloud gets bigger. Then the sun glints on armour and weapons, and he can hear the faint sound of hoofbeats. Finally, spread along the horizon is a vast army galloping towards the city. Rescue has arrived! The enemy takes one look at the vast horde and starts running away. The citizens cluster round their windows and clamber onto the walls, laughing and hugging each other. The city gates are opened, and the warriors sweep in. There is a chaos of shouting, greetings, laughter and tears, relief and gratitude. Someone starts a hymn of praise and instantly the whole city is filled with joyful singing –

for the LORD has comforted his people,
he has redeemed Jerusalem.   **(part of verse 9)**

He has redeemed us, too.

† *O Lord, may I never take salvation for granted, but always be filled with wonder and praise that you have rescued me simply because you love me.*

Thursday November 17   **Isaiah 61:1–7**

COMING HOME This part of the book of Isaiah was probably written either while the Israelites were in exile in Babylon, or soon after their return to Jerusalem. They had been forcibly removed and effectively imprisoned in Babylon, taken there against their will. Over the centuries, other peoples have been forcibly removed, or have fled from their homes as refugees. Refugees too are effectively imprisoned: forced to live in camps, perhaps fed and housed in tents by relief agencies but deprived of work and education and cut off from family and home. But all they need is the freedom to return to their own country and their own place, and then, however complete the devastation, the indomitable human spirit will set about rebuilding.

> **They shall build up the ancient ruins,**
> **they shall raise up the former devastations;**
> **they shall repair the ruined cities,**
> **the devastations of many generations.** (verse 4)

The returners may be defeated by a new drought or a new war, but people will always try to rebuild their lives if they are given the freedom to do so. Many people, thankfully, are not refugees or exiles; but if we have suffered devastation in our personal lives and are imprisoned by the past, we too need God to set us free and bring us home so that we can begin to escape from the past and rebuild our lives.

✝ *Father of all, we give you thanks and praise, that when we were still far off you met us in your Son and brought us home.*
(From the Church of England's *Common Worship*)

Friday November 18   Luke 4:14–21

THE MANIFESTO OF SALVATION The prophets of the Old Testament looked forward to a time when God would intervene to rescue Israel from the oppression of its more powerful neighbours, from injustice, from rebellion, from disobedience. Here, in the synagogue at his home town of Nazareth, Jesus uses the passage of Isaiah which we read yesterday to announce that that time has now arrived. Verses 18 and 19 of today's reading (a direct quotation of *Isaiah 61:1–2a*) have been called the 'Manifesto of Salvation' because here Jesus sets out his programme. This is what he has come to do; the 'year of the Lord's favour' (*verse 19*) has now arrived.

> **'Today this scripture has been fulfilled in your hearing.'**
> **(part of verse 21)**

Among the works of Jesus the Messiah will be proclaiming release to captives (*verse 18*): Luke illustrates this by including in his gospel stories of people being freed from sin, guilt, physical illness, possession by demonic forces, and discrimination. And this scripture continues to be fulfilled in our sight, as we see the Holy Spirit carrying out the same programme in our lives.

† *Lord, help us to see the Spirit at work in our lives and to know that we too have heard good news and been released from captivity, given sight and set free.*

Saturday November 19   Romans 7:21–25

THANKS BE TO GOD! 'Stone walls do not a prison make, nor iron bars a cage', wrote an English poet 350 years ago. We can be in a physical prison, but still know spiritual and mental freedom, as John Bunyan, the author of *The Pilgrim's Progress*, did when he spent 12 years in jail. Conversely, we can be physically free but spiritually and mentally imprisoned by sin. The common thread running through all this week's readings has been that human beings cannot get themselves out of prison. The bars on the windows are too hard, the door too tightly locked. Only an attack from outside can release us. Our Old Testament writers saw this rescuer as a future Messiah. We know that it is the present God. Our rescue comes about through Jesus Christ, because he – who was fully human as well as fully part of God – showed us that human beings do not have to sin. It is possible to be totally obedient to God, because the man Jesus did it. And if he did it, we can also do it, because we have exactly the same power to help us as he had: the Holy Spirit of God. This is the ultimate freedom, the greatest of all releases from captivity.

Thanks be to God through Jesus Christ our Lord!
(part of verse 25)

† *Thanks be to God that we are set free from the captivity of sin and death.*

For group discussion and personal thought

● From what have you been set free?
● What still imprisons you? What do you think God may already be doing to set you on the path to freedom?

PRISONS AND PRISONERS 5
Prisoner for the Lord

Notes by Corneliu Constantineanu

based on the New International Version

Corneliu Constantineanu is a Romanian Pentecostal who grew up under the communist regime and experienced the predicament of a system without God. After an engineering degree, he devoted his life to the study of theology, pursuing a holistic integration of Christian faith with the social and political realities of everyday life. Presently, while completing his PhD, he teaches New Testament at the Evangelical Theological Seminary, Osijek, Croatia and serves as the Dean of Graduate Studies. He is married to Ioana and has two daughters, Anamaria and Carmen.

The words 'prison' and 'prisoner' evoke an instant reaction of unease, discomfort, pain, apprehension etc., especially if we have in mind people who are treated unjustly, who are ready to go to prison for the truth in defiant challenge of the unjust powers-that-be. What motivates such people? What powerful vision drives their life? These and similar questions will guide us in this week's reflections, as we explore Paul's descriptions of being a 'prisoner for the Lord' and 'in chains' for the gospel.

Text for the week: Matthew 25:36

Sunday November 20   **2 Corinthians 10:4b-5**

CAPTIVE TO OBEY CHRIST It is rare to find a more definite statement of a single-minded attitude to life than that of Paul:

> **We demolish arguments and every pretension that sets itself up against the knowledge of God, and we take captive every thought to make it obedient to Christ.**
>
> **(verse 5)**

The true 'knowledge of God' was expressed earlier in the truth that Jesus Christ is Lord over all reality (*2 Corinthians 4:4–6*). As Lord of all, Christ is the centre of Paul's existence. In today's world, just like that of Paul, there are many competing ideas, systems of thought, ideologies which pretend to offer the ultimate 'salvation' of humankind and attempt to present themselves as the ultimate reality. In fact, they are false pretenders who set themselves up against the knowledge of God, against the true and ultimate reality: Christ, the Lord. There is no higher personal or socio-political authority to which one should give total allegiance but to the true Lord of all, Jesus Christ, whose purpose is no other but to make it possible for all of us to live again as true human beings: in perfect harmony with God, with the creation, with others and with ourselves.

† *Dear Father, help us to discern every idea or argument that is against your will for humankind and enable us to give our total allegiance to you, the true Lord of the universe.*

Monday November 21   **Ephesians 3:1–7**

A PRISONER FOR CHRIST JESUS   This passage illustrates perfectly one of the reasons for which Paul was ready to be imprisoned. In a world which valued people primarily on the basis of their ethnic origin and social status, Paul had the courage to proclaim a gospel which overcomes all distinctions and declares that all human beings are equally valuable before God. Jews, Greeks, Romans or barbarians, rich or poor, they have all become

heirs together with Israel, members together of one body, and sharers together in the promise in Christ Jesus.
(part of verse 6)

The radical nature of this great 'mystery' of reconciliation of all people brought Paul to prison. But to be 'the prisoner of Christ Jesus for the sake of [the] Gentiles' (*verse 1*) was a great privilege for Paul because he knew that the gospel was the truth, the ultimate reality, the good will and purposes of God. Despite being a prisoner, or precisely because of it, Paul is an even more powerful witness for that truth. To be sure, there is always a price to be paid for the courage and integrity of standing for truth. But equally true is the fact that there is always the hope that the truth will be ultimately triumphant.

† *Lord, open our eyes to see the truth that is in you and give us strength always to proclaim it, knowing that we may have to suffer the consequences.*

THE AUTHORITY OF A PRISONER FOR THE LORD At a first glance, it is somewhat puzzling that Paul launches this beautiful appeal to the believers in Ephesus, from his position of surrender:

> **As a prisoner for the Lord, then, I urge you to live a life worthy of the calling you have received.**   **(verse 1)**

Paul lives out a life worthy of the gospel in his total submission and obedience to Christ – which leads him to imprisonment. And he expects the same kind of commitment from his readers in Ephesus: humility and gentleness, patience and love, peace and unity (*verses 2–3*). But it is because Paul speaks as a prisoner, as the one who pays the price for his commitment, that his appeal is the more powerful, credible and convincing. In today's postmodern, pluralistic context, where there are so many competing claims to truth and life, it will only be as Christians embody the gospel in concrete manifestations of love, truth, justice and reconciliation that they will have anything to offer to this world in desperate need of redemption.

† *Our God and Father of all, we thank you that in our world's difficult situations you give us the comfort and the assurance that you are indeed 'over all and through all and in all' (verse 6).*

A CONTINUOUS CONCERN FOR 'THE OTHER' Paul's letter to Philemon, the shortest and most personal of his letters, was written while Paul was a prisoner in a Roman prison, to a wealthy, free Christian in Colossae, on behalf of a runaway slave, Onesimus. Reading through it one gets a very strong feeling that Paul does not speak with resignation, as if his imprisonment has taken everything from him and he has no more reason to live. On the contrary, the external limitation on his life could not alter Paul's fervent zeal for the gospel and his 'pouring out' his life for others. He writes:

> **I always thank my God as I remember you in my prayers ... I pray that you may be active in sharing your faith ... [As] a prisoner of Christ Jesus – I appeal to you for my son Onesimus, who became my son while I was in chains.**
> **(verse 4, parts of verses 6 and 9, and verse 10)**

What a beautiful illustration this is – of a profound Christian character that has been radically transformed by his encounter with Christ. Indeed, it is only as Paul knows and experiences Christ as the ultimate reality and the Lord of history that, despite his chains, he is constantly concerned for 'the other' and labours for others.

† *Dear Lord Jesus, save us from our obsession with ourselves and help us to find the true meaning of life as we give ourselves for others.*

Thursday November 24   **2 Timothy 1:8–18**

THE GOSPEL OF SUFFERING AND GRACE Paul does not give us the precise reasons for his being in prison. What we find in his letters is rather his unambiguous conviction that he is suffering for Christ and for the gospel. He writes to young Timothy:

> **So do not be ashamed to testify about our Lord, or ashamed of me his prisoner. But join with me in suffering for the gospel, by the power of God ... And of this gospel I was appointed a herald and an apostle and a teacher. That is why I am suffering as I am.**   **(verses 8 and 11, and part of verse 12)**

We learn two important things from today's text: the gospel of life is intrinsically bound up with suffering; and in the midst of suffering we can witness to the empowering and comforting presence of God's grace. The gospel calls everyone to a 'holy life' (*verse 9*) – a life lived by the story of Christ's love and self-giving for the other, which leads inescapably to the cross. But because it is a life lived in truth, it makes us experience the power of true freedom, joy, and hope.

† *Our gracious Father, may you comfort us as we live out your gospel of life, so that we may be able to strengthen, support and encourage all those who live in and by the truth.*

Friday November 25   **Matthew 27:15–26**

HANDING OVER THE INNOCENT   For virtually every person present at the events of this narration, the suffering and crucifixion of Jesus represented a complete defeat of the innocent by the powers that be; a totally helpless and desperate scenario. There is no doubt that many people, especially those closely associated with Jesus, must have asked themselves how it was possible for something so grotesque and unfair to happen to somebody who lived all his life for others: for the needy, the helpless, the sick, the marginalised, the abandoned, the hopeless. One cannot help but ask:

> **'Why? What crime has he committed?' ... But they shouted all the louder, 'Crucify him!' ... [Then] he had Jesus flogged, and handed him over to be crucified.**
>
> **(parts of verses 23 and 26)**

And indeed, for just a very short time the powers that be thought they had had the last word, that their pretension could not be challenged. However, that was not the end of the story: Jesus has risen and has been vindicated by God! The way of the cross leads ultimately to victory and to life. The final triumph of God is secured. The innocent handed over is victorious, albeit through the cross. There is hope for the victim; there is hope for the suffering innocent.

† *Lord Jesus, strengthen those innocent victims who suffer injustice and oppression and be their deliverer and comforter.*

Saturday November 26   **Matthew 25:31–36**

THE PROMISE OF SOLIDARITY We could have not found a more appropriate way to end this week's reflections than this wonderful promise and assurance of final vindication for all those who shared in the sufferings of the victims of this world:

> **'Come, you who are blessed by my Father; take your inheritance, the kingdom prepared for you since the creation of the world. For I was hungry and you gave me something to eat, I was thirsty and you gave me something to drink, I was a stranger and you invited me in, I needed clothes and you clothed me, I was sick and you looked after me, I was in prison and you came to visit me.'**
>
> **(part of verse 34 and verses 35–36)**

Those who hear the cries of the hungry and thirsty, the sick and strangers and those in prison, those who share in solidarity with the innocent, will be finally vindicated by God and share in his life. It is God who has the final word in history. The suffering, the pain, the crying, the imprisonments are not in vain. Our God reigns! Our God comes!

† *Gracious Father, as we anticipate your final triumph and reign over all creation, help us to be signs of hope and joy in the midst of this suffering world, pointing towards your new creation.*

For group discussion and personal thought

- What are some of the challenges facing those who proclaim a gospel of life and freedom, of radical grace and forgiveness?
- How can Christians express their solidarity with the worldwide suffering of the innocent and marginalised?
- What does it mean for Christ to be Lord in the particular context in which I live my everyday life?

COMINGS AND GOINGS 1
Israelites on the move

Notes by Anthea Dove

based on the New Revised Standard Version

Anthea Dove is a great-grandmother, a retired teacher, retreat-giver and writer. She is a Roman Catholic with a strong commitment to justice and peace and to ecumenism. Anthea has lived in India and France and several parts of England, but has now settled with her husband in a cottage near the sea on the north-east coast of England.

During the next 4 weeks we celebrate the season of Advent, which is itself a journey towards the Incarnation of our Lord. It is a time of expectancy and hope as we move forward to the coming of the child Jesus, and also a time to reflect on his Second Coming and what that might mean for us. In many countries where people are caught up with spending and consuming, the four weeks leading up to Christmas can be frantically busy. This is sad, because Advent is an ideal time for prayerful meditation on the son of God.

Text for the week: Genesis 4:9

Sunday November 27   **Genesis 4:8–16**

MY BROTHER'S KEEPER Cain shows a fundamental lack of understanding when he says to God,

'Am I my brother's keeper?'   (part of verse 9)

This is one of the most important questions that we need, as Christians, to ask ourselves, and to keep on asking ourselves throughout our lives. It might well be a theme for us this Advent, as we prepare to meet the Christ-child. Most of us would gladly help our own brother or sister if they were in trouble, but we sometimes forget the 'outsiders', the drunks and beggars on our streets, the oppressed and hungry and tortured, living far away in another country or on our own doorstep, the countless refugees who wander from land to land with no place to call home, as Cain had to do after he destroyed his brother. All these are our sisters and brothers, because like us they are children of

God. To be my brother's keeper is to befriend him. Obviously we can't become a personal friend of everyone we meet, still less of all those we see on our television screens or read about in our newspapers. But there are various ways in which we can befriend those beyond our immediate circle, especially if they are in need: by taking an interest in their lives, praying for them, writing to them or supporting them with practical help.

† *Dear Lord, help me to remember that every child of yours is my brother or sister.*

Monday November 28   Genesis 6:11–22

A VIOLENT WORLD

Now the earth was corrupt in God's sight, and the earth was filled with violence.   **(verse 11)**

The story of Noah is thousands of years old, yet these words might well have been written today. There is a dreadful amount of corruption in our world and a frightening amount of violence. Here we are in Advent, looking forward to the birth of the Prince of Peace, and our world needs peace as never before. There are so many wars, some of which never make the headlines outside the country where they are being waged, and a large proportion of the victims are innocent civilians. Organisations like Amnesty International struggle to root out torture, and the Medical Foundation strives to help the victims of torture. Rich countries make arms and sell them to unstable countries. And it is always the very poor who suffer most. The root cause of both corruption and violence is the lust for power and the greed for the money which brings power. And all of us, however humble and insignificant, share guilt in some measure for the way the world is, unless we are willing to speak out for peace and justice. We might wonder, would there be a place in Noah's ark for us?

† *Dear Lord, forgive us for our apathy and despair. Give us the generosity and courage to stand up for those who suffer as a result of violence and corruption.*

Tuesday November 29   Genesis 12:1–9

ASYLUM SEEKERS

The LORD said to Abram, 'Go from your country and your kindred and your father's house to the land that I will show you.'   **(verse 1)**

In obeying God, Abram was taking a great leap of faith. In those days it was no small thing to leave the home of your fathers and there was great danger in travelling into the unknown. Nowadays millions of people are not asked but forced to leave the land of their birth, fleeing from persecution, torture and death. They have to make long and arduous journeys, hoping to find rescue and welcome at the end, but too often they are drowned at sea or suffocated in the back of wagons, and many of those who eventually arrive at their destination are treated like criminals, without sympathy. Throughout scripture, we are exhorted to welcome the stranger. But sadly, refugees and people seeking asylum are in many places treated as outcasts, despised, bullied and misunderstood. Abram had a choice and he made the brave decision to do God's will. Asylum seekers have only stark choices: to die or to live, to be imprisoned or to escape, to give their children up to death or carry them to safety.

† *Lord, give me imagination, so that I may begin to understand the reality of what it is like to be an asylum seeker.*

Wednesday November 30   Genesis 18:1–10a

RECOGNISING GOD   This passage presents us with a charming picture of Abraham, now an old man a hundred years old, running around like a demented housewife preparing a meal for the three strangers who have suddenly appeared outside his home.

When he saw them, he ran from the tent entrance to meet them, and bowed down to the ground.   **(part of verse 2)**

Scholars believe that at first Abraham thought the three were fellow human beings and only gradually realised that he was in the presence of messengers from God himself, or angels. The old man welcomed these men, who were breaking their journey near his tent, and treated them with courtesy and respect, even though he did not at first recognise that they were of God. It is good if we can also recognise God in one another, for the Spirit of the loving God dwells within each one of us, however hidden and disguised. George Fox, the founder of the Society of Friends, urged his followers to 'walk cheerfully over the world, answering that of God in everyone'. Sometimes it is very hard to see Christ in those we meet, but we have to remember that they may find it equally difficult to see him in us!

† *Dear Lord, make us ready to seek and find you in everyone we meet.*

Thursday December 1   **Genesis 22:1–19**

LOVED CHILDREN The well-known story of Abraham and
Isaac with its dramatic ending is one which prompts all sorts of
questions. How on earth could Abraham bring himself to
sacrifice his son? What were they both feeling on that three-day
journey? Surely Isaac must have screamed and struggled when
Abraham bound him and laid him on the altar?

> **'Take your son, your only son Isaac, whom you love.'**
> **(part of verse 2)**

Today is World AIDS Day, when we are asked to think
especially of the victims of this terrible disease. We think also of
those who work to alleviate the suffering of people with the
illness, and particularly of those parts of Africa where whole
families and in some cases whole villages are wiped out as a
result of this scourge. In this passage we have read of 'your only
son Isaac, whom you love' and we may wonder how many
parents have had to watch their beloved children die of AIDS,
how many children have had to watch their parents die. Feeling
sad is clearly not enough. We can wear a red ribbon to
encourage AIDS awareness. We can support educational
programmes which help to prevent the disease, and the
research of scientists who are working to cure or to eradicate it.

† *Lord, deepen our compassion for children who suffer in any way: from*
abuse, illness, disability, bereavement, hunger, or lack of love.

Friday December 2   **Exodus 12:29–41**

REFUGEES There is a very vivid picture in this chapter of
Exodus. There are about six hundred thousand men with all
their families and a crowd of hangers-on. They are all hurrying
purposefully away from the land where they have lived for four
hundred and thirty years and they didn't even have time to
bake a decent loaf of bread before they left!

> **They baked unleavened cakes of the dough that they had**
> **brought out of Egypt; it was not leavened, because they**
> **were driven out of Egypt and could not wait, nor had they**
> **prepared any provisions for themselves.   (verse 39)**

It isn't too difficult to imagine this scene, because during the
past few years we have seen on our television screens troupes
of weary men and women and children, struggling along the
roads to escape from Rwanda or former Yugoslavia. Like the
Israelites, they were carrying what they could of their

possessions; they had to leave suddenly because there was no time to prepare. But there is a big difference between the Israelites and the present-day marchers. The Israelites were led from Egypt by Moses, who was led by God himself, and they had a sure destination. But there is very little likelihood of a land of milk and honey awaiting those who flee from war. They are homeless, penniless and often quite without hope. Their faces tell the story of their terrible journeys.

† *Dear Lord, before you died you gave us the gift of your peace. Help us to become channels of your peace, working for harmony and trust.*

Saturday December 3   Joshua 3:14–17

INCLUSIVITY Here we have a description of a rather short journey, the crossing of the Israelites over the Jordan river, following the ark of the covenant of the Lord.

While all Israel were crossing over on dry ground, the priests who bore the ark of the covenant of the LORD stood on dry ground in the middle of the Jordan, until the entire nation finished crossing over the Jordan.   **(verse 17)**

The 'entire nation' means everybody. Today is marked as the International Day of Disability. Jesus did not exclude anyone, indeed he spent much of the three years of his active ministry attending to the disabled: the blind, the deaf, the lame, the paralysed and lepers. As his followers, we are called not only never to exclude the disabled, but to fight for their rights. So often they are barred from banks, shops, theatres and even churches; they are made to feel inferior and unworthy and they are not given a chance to develop their talents.

† *Dear Lord, I pray for all who are disabled, physically, mentally or emotionally. I ask that they may know that they are loved by you and that they may find fulfilment in their lives.*

For group discussion and personal thought

● Who is your brother?
● What can you, personally, do about the huge problems in our world?

COMINGS AND GOINGS 2
To and fro between heaven and earth

Notes by Anthea Dove

based on the New Revised Standard Version

Now we begin the second week of Advent. Our first reading is a consoling one, looking forward to the coming of God just as we look forward today to the coming of Jesus at Christmas. In every reading this week there is a journey, and these journeys are as diverse and dramatic as Elijah's riding to heaven by chariot, Jonah's tossing in a fierce gale at sea, and the Queen of Sheba's travelling with 'her very great retinue' to visit King Solomon.

Text for the week: Isaiah 35:9

Sunday December 4   **Isaiah 40:1–11**

GOD'S UNCONDITIONAL LOVE   This passage is full of consolation and hope for the people of God. It describes the effects of God's coming. It promises that God will come in glory, he will forgive the sins of his children, he will come with might to rule. Then suddenly the imagery of Isaiah changes and we see our God in a different light:

> **He will feed his flock like a shepherd;**
> **he will gather the lambs in his arms,**
> **and carry them in his bosom,**
> **and gently lead the mother sheep.**   **(verse 11)**

Because of our experience of life, in some cases because of the way we have been taught, many of us find it difficult to believe in the tender unconditional love our God has for each one of us. Julian of Norwich, the fourteenth-century mystic, described this intimate love of God for us thus: 'He is our clothing, who for love wraps us up, holds us close; he entirely encloses us for tender love, so that he may never leave us, since he is the source of all good things for us.' Such amazing love brings with it a challenge: as God loves me so much, how can I not love in return, not only him but all my fellow women and men?

† *Dear God, my Father, save me from doubting your love for me.*

Monday December 5   **1 Kings 10:1–10, 13**

DISCERNMENT   The fame of King Solomon had spread far over the known world, and the great Queen of Sheba decided to travel a long journey to see him for herself. After meeting him she concluded that the rumours of his greatness were well-founded. So she said to the king:

> **Happy are your wives! Happy are these your servants, who continually attend you and hear your wisdom!**   **(verse 8)**

Solomon had many gifts: God had given him riches and honour. But early in his reign he had spoken with God in a dream. God said, 'Ask what I should give you' and Solomon replied, 'And now, O LORD my God, you have made your servant king in place of my father David, although I am only a little child; I do not know how to go out or come in' (*1 Kings 3*). Then he asked God for an understanding mind able to discern between good and evil. Although this was a dream, Solomon did in reality become renowned for his wisdom. Sometimes we have a slightly distorted idea of what wisdom is. We may think that old age brings wisdom, but this is not necessarily so because we don't all learn from experience. Nor are intelligent people invariably wise. True wisdom is the ability to judge what is right, and this comes from living close to God, from deep thought and deep prayer. The Queen of Sheba's long journey proved worthwhile.

† *Lord, give me a spirit of discernment.*

Tuesday December 6   **1 Kings 19:4–16**

DESPAIR   Elijah the prophet was afraid for his life; he fled from Jezebel who had threatened to have him killed.

> **But he himself went a day's journey into the wilderness, and came and sat down under a solitary broom tree. He asked that he might die: 'It is enough; now, O LORD, take away my life, for I am no better than my ancestors.'**
>
>   **(verse 4)**

The Jerusalem Bible translation of this passage has Elijah saying, 'I have had enough'. This is a phrase in common currency today; we use it when we are tired and want to sit down, or when we feel we have been treated unjustly by our employer. But more seriously, the feeling that we have 'had enough' is the reason why some people take their own lives. They think they simply cannot cope any more and they see no hope at all on the horizon. It used to be thought that suicide was a terrible unforgivable sin, and sometimes still we hear comments like 'How could he be so selfish as to leave his poor wife and children?' We have come to realise that a person wretched enough to take her own life needs the utmost compassion and we can be certain that our God looks on them with love.

† *Lord, keep me ever sensitive to the feelings of others.*

Wednesday December 7   2 Kings 2:1–12

FAITHFULNESS Elijah is on a strange journey; he knows he is near the end of his life. So does Elisha, who steadfastly refuses to leave him, but neither of them speaks of what is going to happen.

Elijah said to Elisha, 'Stay here; for the LORD has sent me as far as Bethel.' But Elisha said, 'As the LORD lives, and as you yourself live, I will not leave you.' (part of verse 2)

Elisha's promise not to leave Elijah, spoken three times, has echoes in other parts of the Bible. It reminds us of Ruth's faithfulness to Naomi (*Ruth 1:16*). And Elisha's promise also reminds us how Jesus, after his resurrection, asked Peter three times, 'Simon, son of John, do you love me?' (*John 21:15–17*). Elisha, Ruth and Peter were all faithful, but this kind of strong loyalty to those who love us is a reflection of God's own faithfulness. We read in Lamentations 3:22, 'The steadfast love of the LORD never ceases, his mercies never come to an end; they are new every morning; great is your faithfulness.'

† *Dear Lord, thank you for your faithfulness. I know that I can journey with you and trust you always. Keep me always faithful to you and to those to whom I am bound in friendship and in love.*

Thursday December 8   Nehemiah 2:1–8, 11

RESTORATION

'If it pleases the king, and if your servant has found favour with you, I ask that you send me to Judah, to the city of my ancestors' graves, so that I may rebuild it.' (part of verse 5)

Nehemiah prayed to God before he made this request of King Artaxerxes. The king, who clearly respected Nehemiah although he was his servant, willingly gave his permission. So Nehemiah set off on his journey and reached Jerusalem, which he was determined to restore to its former glory. Whenever places are destroyed by war or natural disaster, people of courage, determination, imagination and, most of all, love of their own place find the resources to rebuild their towns and cities. We may think of cities devastated by bombing in the Second World War, and more recently of the twin towers of New York. But it is not only buildings which need restoration. Even greater endeavours are needed where there has been strife between peoples. That is why the Truth and Reconciliation project in South Africa brought healing after the ending of apartheid, and why, sometimes, when the victims and perpetrators of a crime meet each other, forgiveness and peace of mind can result. Time and again people of goodwill have tried to bring about peace between Catholics and Protestants in Northern Ireland; time and again others have struggled to reconcile the Israelis and Palestinians.

† *I pray for all those who suffer because of the failure to resolve conflict and for all those who persevere in their efforts for reconciliation and rebuilding, however long the journey may be.*

Friday December 9 Jonah 1:1–17

SELF-SACRIFICE There is something comic and also endearing about Jonah, but his short book is a serious story about repentance and God's forgiving love.

He said to them, 'Pick me up and throw me into the sea; then the sea will quiet down for you; for I know it is because of me that this great storm has come upon you.'
(verse 12)

So Jonah, the unwilling prophet, takes responsibility for the storm and makes a supreme act of reparation. His bravery is astonishing. In a far different context and for a quite different reason, the Roman Catholic priest Maximilian Kolbe gave his life to save a married man in a supremely courageous and selfless act. It happened during the Second World War in the concentration camp at Auschwitz. The man was one of a number ordered to line up for execution on that particular day, and when Maximilian heard him weeping piteously for his wife and children, he simply stepped into his place and walked to his death. The ultimate self-sacrifice, of course, was that of Jesus when he endured so much suffering and gave his life for us on the cross.

† *Dear Lord, though I may never be called to perform an act of great self-sacrifice, help me to be courageous in facing whatever difficulties come my way on my journey through life.*

Saturday December 10   **Isaiah 35:8–10**

HUMAN RIGHTS

And the ransomed of the LORD** shall return,
and come to Zion with singing;
everlasting joy shall be upon their heads;
they shall obtain joy and gladness,
and sorrow and sighing shall flee away.**   **(verse 10)**

Isaiah had a beautiful vision of God's kingdom. There the redeemed, the ransomed of the Lord, will walk upon the highway. They are the ones who are saved from their sins. It seems fitting, as today is Human Rights Day, to think of those who hope to be saved from their suffering, namely the prisoners of conscience and victims of torture who in so many countries are unjustly locked away. Sometimes, through the work of Amnesty International and the writing of letters of protest from its members, such prisoners are set free. Then it is their turn to obtain joy and gladness; then their sorrow flees away. It is a great privilege to meet someone who has suffered in prison because of their beliefs, and is willing to tell their story. Sadly, we are nowhere near to overcoming the worldwide problem of human rights abuse, but there is no need for despair. The work of human rights organisations does produce results, and many people have been released from prison through the faithful persistent writing of letters.

† *Lord, I pray for all prisoners of conscience, for all who are punished because they are brave enough to stand up against unjust authority, and for all victims of torture.*

For group discussion and personal thought

● Which of this week's topics interested you most, and why?
● How do you go about discerning good from evil in a given situation?

COMINGS AND GOINGS 3
Sent out by God

Notes by Anthea Dove

based on the New Revised Standard Version

On our journey towards the Incarnation at Christmas, today we begin the third week of Advent. Every day we will read about different people who were sent by God to take the good news far and wide. Their journeys were full of difficulty, challenge or danger. The seventy-two sent by Jesus himself returned full of joy; all the others worked for the Lord with great courage and enthusiasm.

Text for the week: Acts 9:5

Sunday December 11   **Luke 10:1–9**

THE KINGDOM OF GOD   Today is the third Sunday of Advent. In some churches this is known as Gaudete Sunday, *gaudete* being the Latin for rejoice, and the first words of the service are taken from Saint Paul's letter to the Philippians: 'Rejoice in the Lord always; again I will say, Rejoice' (*Philippians 4:4*). So it is fitting that our reading for today is about the seventy whom Jesus sent out to preach and teach and heal the sick, because they returned from their daunting mission full of joy. Like love and peacefulness, joy is one of the marks by which Christians should be known. The disciples were given many instructions for their journey, of which the most striking is perhaps the last:

> **'Cure the sick who are there, and say to them, "The kingdom of God has come near to you."'**   **(verse 9)**

To be healed from their illness or disability must have brought great happiness to the sick, but perhaps they would be filled with an even greater joy if they could believe that God's kingdom was very near. Every year hundreds of people are taken to Lourdes, hoping to be healed from their illness or their disability. Very few experience miraculous cures, but a large number return home renewed by an inner joy. Later in Luke's gospel he tells how Jesus said, in answer to a question from the

Pharisees, 'The kingdom of God is among you' (*17:21*). If we could only live our lives recognising this truth, then we would indeed be a joyful people.

✝ *Dear Father in heaven, we pray that your kingdom will come.*

Monday December 12   Acts 8:1b-8

PREJUDICE   We know that when the Holy Spirit descended upon the apostles at Pentecost they were all emboldened and went out among the people fired with enthusiasm and filled with courage. There is not much mention of Philip in the gospels, but a good deal of this chapter of Acts recounts his deeds.

Philip went down to the city of Samaria and proclaimed the Messiah to them. **(verse 5)**

To go and try to convert the Samaritan people was a brave choice. Historically, Jews and Samaritans were enemies. When Jesus spoke with the Samaritan woman, she asked, 'How is it that you, a Jew, ask a drink of me, a woman of Samaria?' (*John 4:9*). Jesus broke new ground and made it clear that the good news was not exclusively for Jews, and Philip must have decided to further this reconciling work. There is a curious tradition which persists to this day of people being at loggerheads with those who live in the next county, or town, or region. Usually it is entirely irrational but it is none the less very real. When I lived in Gloucestershire, I was amazed how vehemently so many of the locals disliked the Welsh, across the border only a few miles away. And now that I live in a fishing port it is no surprise that the inhabitants of the next port down the coast are the enemy! So Philip took on a great challenge when he undertook to convert the people of Samaria.

✝ *Lord, save us from pettiness and prejudice.*

Tuesday December 13   Acts 8:26–40

GUIDANCE TOWARDS GOD   After Philip's success in Samaria, he undertook another journey in obedience to God. He listened to the Holy Spirit and so was guided to approach the Ethiopian eunuch. We can imagine how surprised Philip was to find a rather exotic stranger of another race reading the prophet Isaiah. When he asked the eunuch if he understood what he was reading,

He replied, 'How can I, unless someone guides me?' And he invited Philip to get in and sit beside him. (verse 31)

It is surely touching that this wealthy and highly intelligent man was so eager and humble in his desire to learn the scriptures. Many people, all over the world, are seeking a meaning in life, searching for God. In the western world especially, where people have become indifferent to religion and caught up in the pursuit of material success, they find their lives are empty and long for fulfilment. That is why there is such a challenge for those of us who have the gift of faith to try to bring the message of Christ in all its richness to our brothers and sisters who are broken and lost, even if it means going out to them as Philip did. Perhaps we can do this most effectively by the sort of lives we lead.

✝ *Dear Lord, help us by the way we live to be a source of your good news to those whose lives we touch.*

Wednesday December 14 Acts 9:1–9

WHO IS THE LORD? The conversion of Saul is one of the most dramatic events in the New Testament. It is wonderful how he changed so suddenly from being an ardent persecutor of Christians to a passionate disciple of Jesus. Not many people experience a conversion like Saul's. If we are blessed with the gift of faith, it will slowly and gradually deepen and strengthen, as long as our minds and hearts are open to the Lord.

He asked, 'Who are you, Lord?' The reply came, 'I am Jesus, whom you are persecuting.' (verse 5)

It is not easy to answer the question 'Who is the Lord?' because the answer may depend on our experience of life, our education, or our response to God – where we have got on our own journey. Some time ago I met an old man who was ill and unhappy. I asked him if he believed in God. His face lit up when he said, 'Oh yes'. But then he added, 'I know he's up there with his big stick waiting for me to do something wrong.' This man had faith, but his idea of God was very far from the all-forgiving, tender father that our God truly is.

✝ *Dear Lord, help us to grow ever closer to you, so that our understanding of you may be clearer and our own response to your love more effective.*

LIGHT FOR THE GENTILES The earliest followers of Jesus all seem to have been circumcised Jews, and the believers in Jerusalem were at first very critical of Peter when he began to baptise Gentiles. But gradually other disciples began to preach the good news to the uncircumcised and to baptise them:

> **among them were some men of Cyprus and Cyrene who, on coming to Antioch, spoke to the Hellenists also, proclaiming the Lord Jesus.**   **(verse 20)**

So the words of Simeon, which he spoke in the temple at Jerusalem when the infant Jesus was presented there by his parents, came true. Simeon saw that the child would be 'a light for revelation to the Gentiles' (*Luke 2:32*). Sometimes we can be too obsessed with our own particular brand of Christianity, our own tradition. This makes us a narrow and closed body, rather than one which is open to the Holy Spirit, ready to journey out from our secure base and share our gifts and to learn from the treasures of others. Before he died Jesus prayed, 'that they may all be one' (*John 17:21*). It is true that there are still doctrinal differences which prevent us from being completely united, but that is no reason why we shouldn't work for the kingdom of God together whenever we can, enjoying the diversity of our various traditions.

✝ *Dear Lord, help all Christians to grow in love for one another.*

ENTHUSIASM It is almost certain that the Acts of the Apostles were written by the same person who wrote Luke's gospel, and that he travelled with Saint Paul on most if not all of his missionary travels. Luke writes the Acts in the third person, telling us that 'he' or 'they' did this or that, but from time to time he slips into the first person, as here:

> **When he had seen the vision, we immediately tried to cross over to Macedonia, being convinced that God had called us to proclaim the good news to them.**   **(verse 10)**

It is as though Luke is so carried away by the memory of what happened that he forgets he is acting simply as a narrator. Two things strike us about this short passage. First there is the eagerness and urgency of the disciples, bent on God's work (the Jerusalem Bible translates this verse as 'we lost no time in crossing over'). And secondly there is the utter dependence on and faith in the guidance of the Holy Spirit. These men, and the women who joined them, were true enthusiasts, for enthusiastic means Spirit-filled. When we read how the early Christians shared everything, we feel ashamed at our lack of generosity, and when we read how passionate the first disciples were in their missionary work, we feel inadequate and lukewarm by comparison.

† *Lord, increase our willingness to share and make us fervent in our desire to spread your good news.*

Saturday December 17   Acts 28:11–15

THE IMPORTANCE OF FRIENDSHIP The book of Acts ends sadly, with Paul in prison in Rome trying to convince the Jews about Jesus but failing in many instances. He therefore turned his attention to the Gentiles, and for two years welcomed everyone who came to hear him preach. In today's passage, he arrives at last in Rome.

The believers from there, when they heard of us, came as far as the Forum of Appius and Three Taverns to meet us. On seeing them, Paul thanked God and took courage.

(verse 15)

We think of Paul as an incredibly strong and brave man, very close to God. Therefore it is not at all surprising that when he saw that his friends and supporters had come to meet him, his first reaction was to thank God. What is more unexpected is the phrase 'he took courage'. Somehow these words make Paul seem more human. Perhaps he was very tired and frail; perhaps he was dreading prison and his trial. But for once he needed to take courage. On top of his huge faith and trust in God, Paul relied on the many friends who loved him and whom he loved in return. In letters to his friends he is often 'bossy', but he is also deeply affectionate. His friends in Rome showed their friendship by journeying out to meet him, giving him their time and effort as well as their love.

† *Lord, let me never underestimate the value of friendship.*

For group discussion and personal thought

● Try to describe how you experience God.
● Can you think of times in your life when you have been sent out by God?

COMINGS AND GOINGS 4
The coming of God

Notes by Anthea Dove

based on the New Revised Standard Version

During this last week of Advent we are going to read of more journeys. It is a season when it would be especially good to spend time focusing on the wonderful day about to dawn when we celebrate the birth of our Saviour. But in worldly terms it is an exceptionally busy time and it needs a lot of discipline to find a space for stillness and meditation. Perhaps we could make a special effort this week to find this discipline as our gift to the Christ-child.

Text for the week: Philippians 2:7

Sunday December 18 Luke 1:39–45, 56

RELATIONSHIPS Mary's journey to visit Elizabeth cannot have been easy because two thousand years ago in Palestine travel on foot or by donkey was difficult and hazardous. But when Elizabeth welcomed Mary, the journey and her tiredness would have been forgotten in the tender warmth between the two women. And in that moment something happened which must have astonished and delighted them both.

When Elizabeth heard Mary's greeting, the child leaped in her womb. And Elizabeth was filled with the Holy Spirit.
(verse 41)

The visit of Mary to Elizabeth is not one which is often highlighted in presentations of the nativity and it doesn't have a prominent place among the incidents surrounding the birth of Jesus. Yet for Mary and Elizabeth this was an occasion of the highest significance, and the two women, one old and one young, living far apart, had a relationship that was precious to them both. Relationships should not be bound by rigid rules; they can blossom between people of every sort, no matter the differences in age, race, intelligence or sexual orientation. Our lives are greatly enriched when we relate in friendship with people very different from ourselves and are prepared to make the effort to nourish our relationships.

Monday December 19   Luke 2:1–7

OUTCAST Many of us will have heard these familiar words hundreds of times, at Christmas services all over the world. Yet even though we may know the words by heart, I think only a very few will ever tire of the story. Even before Jesus is born, he is identified with the outcasts of the world.

And she gave birth to her firstborn son and wrapped him in bands of cloth, and laid him in a manger, because there was no place for them in the inn.   **(verse 7)**

It is not just that Jesus cared about the marginalised in his society; he came into the world as one of them. To be marginalised means to be put on one side. That is hurtful enough, but some people are described as 'off the page', meaning that they are of absolutely no account. To God, however, everyone counts, everyone is loved and valued by him, no matter how unworthy or sinful a person may feel himself to be. It is not for us to despise anyone; rather it is for us to help and befriend those whom others despise.

✝ *Lord, help me to recognise you in the poor and the marginalised, the refugees and asylum seekers, the homeless and those in prison, the disabled and the unsuccessful, the hungry and the oppressed, the depressed and the lonely. Help me to reach out to them in whatever way I can.*

Tuesday December 20   Luke 2:8–18

REFLECTION Today we continue with the well-loved Christmas story. We read of the shepherds as they hurried on their journey through the night to Bethlehem. They were ordinary, simple folk; indeed at that time in Palestine shepherds were generally despised, considered to be on the bottom rung of society. When they heard the message of the angels they were at first stunned and frightened; as they journeyed they must have been puzzled and anxious, but no doubt they were overcome with awe and delight when they came into the stable and saw the child Jesus. They lost no time in telling everyone about it, and if it had happened today they would have been a gift to the news reporters, the 'paparazzi'.

[A]nd all who heard it were amazed at what the shepherds told them. (verse 18)

As they went back to their sheep, the shepherds must have been excited and elated, but we may wonder what they thought and felt afterwards when they reflected on the events of that night. Perhaps, like Mary, they treasured all these things and pondered them in their hearts, because nothing like this had ever happened before, nor was it ever likely to happen again. However they behaved outwardly, they must surely have been changed for ever.

✝ *Dear Lord, help me to reflect often and with thoughtfulness on the wonderful gifts and experiences you have given me all through my life.*

Wednesday December 21   Matthew 2:1–12

HUMILITY Today we move from the coming of the shepherds to the coming of the magi, the wise men whose journey was possibly the longest of all those we are considering during these weeks of Advent. We know little about them, but they provide a sharp contrast to the shepherds, for as well as being wise and learned, they were important and wealthy people.

On entering the house, they saw the child with Mary his mother; and they knelt down and paid him homage. Then, opening their treasure chests, they offered him gifts of gold, frankincense and myrrh. (verse 11)

Although they came bringing chests of treasure, as soon as the wise men came into the place where the baby Jesus was, they knelt down and paid him homage. Men of status and learning, so full of expectancy, they might well have turned away disappointed and disillusioned at the sight of the child lying in a manger. But they fell to their knees and worshipped him, because for all their dignity and importance, they were truly humble. We do not always act with humility, and we sometimes fail to recognise that others may have hidden gifts which we cannot appreciate. Everyone, gifted or not, deserves our respect.

✝ *Dear Lord, help me to treat all those I meet with humility and respect, remembering that in God's eyes all people are deserving of love.*

Thursday December 22   Matthew 2:13–15

FLIGHT It is not difficult to imagine the panic and terror in the hearts of Mary and Joseph when they received the angel's message and hurried to prepare for a long and arduous journey with their young baby.

Then Joseph got up, took the child and his mother by night, and went to Egypt. (verse 14)

There are some countries in the world where it is extremely unlikely that a family would have to flee by night from danger or death. Yet there are other countries where such happenings are hardly unusual. Where there is civil war or a brutal government, many innocent people are forced to run away from their homes and families. They have to leave their own country to escape across borders and in some cases make their way to distant lands where they cannot understand the language. Such people have terrible stories to tell of torture, rape and murder. Those who live in safe countries, leading lives that are comfortable and unthreatened, have the opportunity to provide a haven for such people, to make them welcome, to listen to their stories and give help wherever it is possible. Sadly this opportunity is not always taken, and instead of welcome and kindness, strangers are treated with hostility and even cruelty.

† *God our loving Father, be with those who live in fear, with those who must flee from their families and homeland, and with those who find themselves lost and lonely in a foreign land.*

Friday December 23   Luke 2:41–51

MARY This was a dreadful journey, or rather journeys, for Joseph and Mary as they travelled up and down the road to and from Jerusalem, frantically searching for their son.

Then he went down with them and came to Nazareth, and was obedient to them. His mother treasured all these things in her heart. (verse 51)

Mary's reaction to this incident, in which she must have been nearly out of her mind with worry, is very similar to her response to the surprising events which took place around the birth of Jesus. Luke told us then: 'Mary treasured all these words and pondered them in her heart' (*2:19*). When a mother or father looks back on the lives of their children, even the times of mischief and naughtiness become a memory to smile about and enjoy. We would do well to imitate Mary's attitude to life: to reflect prayerfully on the things that have happened to us, to look on them with enjoyment or, where this is not possible, with acceptance. This way of thinking leads us to the deep thankfulness which is God's due.

† *Lord, be with me as I remember the events in my life through the years. Help me to accept even the saddest bereavements and losses, and to rejoice again in all the things that have brought me joy. Give me a thankful heart.*

Saturday December 24   Philippians 2:5–8

EMPTINESS Today is Christmas Eve, a day full of expectation for children hoping for gifts from Santa Claus, perhaps, and for all of us who call ourselves Christian, a day of anticipation of the coming into the world of our Saviour. This passage and the three verses that follow are among the most beautiful and moving in the whole of scripture. It is, in the beginning, a different description of the incarnation:

> **[he] emptied himself,**
> **taking the form of a slave,**
> **being born in human likeness.**   **(verse 7)**

Just before he wrote these lines to the people of Philippi, Paul urged them to let the same mind be in them as was in Christ Jesus. This is the mind that is willing to empty itself of all selfishness, to make God the centre and focus of our lives. We know how hard this is, how when we try to be selfless all sorts of desires keep creeping in. Probably only a very few saints have achieved such perfection, but this is no reason for us to stop trying. There is another kind of emptiness, when we stand before God in prayer, still, silent, alone, free of distractions and empty, waiting for him to fill us with his love.

† *Lord, I stand empty before you. Tomorrow you are coming, for me, and for the whole world. Let me come to you, waiting and empty, longing for you to fill me with your peace, your joy and your love.*

For group discussion and personal thought

● What does it mean to be humble?
● What happens when you pray without words?
● Just as the idea of Christmas without extravagant presents and a huge amount of luxury food is alien to some people, so the idea of 'emptiness' can be alien too. What are your thoughts about this?

COMINGS AND GOINGS 5
The journeys of Jesus

Notes by Anthea Dove

based on the Jerusalem Bible

After Christmas day, when our minds are focused on the Incarnation of God's Son, the readings this week take us swiftly through the life of Jesus, looking at some of his significant journeys. Then on the last day of the week, which is New Year's Eve, we meditate on the most important journey we will ever take, the journey into the after-life.

Text for the week: John 1:9

Sunday December 25   **John 1:1–14**

THE LIGHT OF THE WORLD Today is Christmas Day, a day of great celebration all over the Christian world. It is set apart so that we can remember the birth of the Son of God, the one who made the mysterious journey to become man and dwell among us so that he could redeem us through his own suffering. Saint John compares this human being, who was also divine, to a light that shines, dispelling darkness.

The Word was the true light that enlightens all men.
(part of verse 9)

Light is a symbol of everything that is good, whereas darkness symbolises evil. Isaiah, foretelling the birth of Jesus, says, 'The people that walked in darkness have seen a great light' (*Isaiah 9:2*). Simeon prophesies that Jesus will be a light to enlighten the Gentiles (*Luke 2:32*). And Jesus himself, who said, 'I am the light of the world' (*John 8:12*), also said to his disciples, and so to us, his followers: 'You are the light of the world' (*Matthew 5:14*). This presents us with a great challenge which we meet again in Saint Paul's letter to the Philippians when he urges them to be 'children of God without blemish in the midst of a crooked and perverse generation, in which you shine like stars in the world' (*Philippians 2:15,* NRSV). How can you and I respond to the amazing journey of the Son of God and shine like stars?

† *Lord Jesus, on this your birthday, show me how I may be a light for my fellow men and women.*

Monday December 26   Luke 9:28–36

JESUS JOURNEYS TO THE MOUNTAIN TOP   Peter, James and John were filled with awe when they saw Jesus transfigured with Elijah and Moses, and they seem to have been even more overawed, and frightened as well, when the cloud covered them.

> **And a voice came from the cloud saying, 'This is my Son, the Chosen One. Listen to him.'**   **(verse 35)**

This message from God was for the three apostles, but it was surely also for all of us who are disciples of Jesus. How well do we listen to God? What is the best way of listening to him? Surely it is by reading or hearing his word in scripture, by studying the gospels over and over again, reading them slowly and prayerfully so that we come closer and closer to knowing Jesus and to understanding his message. As Saint Richard of Chichester prayed: 'May I know thee more clearly, love thee more dearly and follow thee more nearly.' Another way of listening to God is in our prayer time. If we can find a space and time so that we can still our minds and simply be in the presence of God without saying any words, if we can mentally 'go up the mountain to pray', we may hear his 'still, small voice' or feel ourselves drawn in the way he wants us to go.

† *Dear Lord, you are the one who listens. Help me to find ways of listening to you.*

Tuesday December 27   Mark 10:32–34

JESUS JOURNEYS TOWARDS JERUSALEM   As they followed Jesus towards Jerusalem, the disciples seem to have been confused and fearful,

> **they were in a daze, and those who followed were apprehensive. Once more taking the Twelve aside he began to tell them what was going to happen to him.**
> **(part of verse 32)**

It seems as though the disciples had difficulty at times in understanding Jesus. This is the third time that he tried to explain to the twelve what was ahead of him, but even after his terrible prophecy came true and he was crucified, they seem to have been in a state of fear and despair, completely forgetting his promise of the resurrection. But if the disciples were bewildered, their feelings were as nothing compared to what Jesus was going through as he led them on that journey. As a human being he must have been very afraid. He was innocent, facing a certain and cruel death. On Death Row in the United States, many men and women who are guilty, and a good number who are innocent but have been inadequately tried, have to wait in prison for months, often years, knowing that they are to be executed.

† *Loving Father, we pray for all who are condemned to death, particularly those who must wait for years in miserable confinement for their sentence to be carried out. Change the hearts of those who believe in this vengeful and inhuman system.*

Wednesday December 28   Mark 11:1–11

JESUS JOURNEYS INTO JERUSALEM Towards the end of the year 2003, the leader of the opposition party in Britain, Iain Duncan-Smith, made a speech to his party conference. The people listening to him rose to their feet and gave him rapturous applause, prolonging their standing ovation in an unprecedented show of support. Only a few weeks later the same members of his party gave him a vote of no confidence and he was ousted as leader. Millions watched him face his triumph and then his humiliation on television.

And those who went in front and those who followed were all shouting, 'Hosanna! Blessings on him who comes in the name of the Lord!'   **(verse 9)**

And as we know, less than a week later, many of the same people were shouting, 'Crucify him! Crucify him!' It is very easy to be swayed by a mob, and so to become part of it, carried along by the passion of its leaders. In Britain, when it became known that a little boy called Jamie Bulger had been murdered by two 10-year-old boys, an angry mob, mistaking the identity of one of the boys, went to his house and terrified an innocent family with their brutal bullying. But sometimes, of course, the crowd may be protesting in a worthy cause.

† *Lord, help me to think before I act, and to try to discern your will.*